Israel and Palestine
Out of the Ashes

"Marc Ellis is a brilliant writer, a deeply thoughtful and courageous mind, an intellectual who has broken the death-hold of mindless tradition and unreflective cliche to produce a superb account of post-Holocaust understanding, with particular reference to the Palestinian people and the moral obligation of Israelis and diaspora Jews. He is a man to be listened to with respect and admiration." Edward Said

"[Ellis provides] a vital contribution to solving one of the few remaining intractable problems of our time." Archbishop Desmond Tutu

"Marc Ellis stands in a deeply honoured and disturbing Jewish tradition of prophetic thought and action. ... This is a profoundly religious book and we ignore it at our peril." John Gladwin, Bishop of Guildford and Chair of Christian Aid

"Marc Ellis has demonstrated great courage, integrity, and insight in the very important work he has been doing for years. It has been an inspiration for all of us." Noam Chomsky

"Marc Ellis has done a service to people of all faiths with this book. It is written with passion and a deep yearning for peace in the land of his ancestors. I hope it will be very widely read by those who seek a clearer understanding of the tragic events which have unfolded in Israel/Palestine." The Very Revd Nicholas Frayling, Dean of Chichester

"A breath of fresh air, in a heavily polluted debate, by a self-respecting American-Jewish theologian." Afif Safieh

Israel and Palestine Out of the Ashes

The Search for Jewish Identity in the Twenty-first Century

Marc H. Ellis

LONDON • STERLING, VIRGINIA

First published 2002 by Pluto Press
345 Archway Road, London N6 5AA
and 22883 Quicksilver Drive,
Sterling, VA 20166–2012, USA

www.plutobooks.com

British Library Cataloguing in Publication Data
A catalogue record for this book is available from the British Library

ISBN 0 7453 1957 2 hardback
ISBN 0 7453 1956 4 paperback

Library of Congress Cataloging in Publication Data
A catalogue record for this book is available

10 9 8 7 6 5 4 3 2 1

Designed and produced for Pluto Press by
Chase Publishing Services, Fortescue, Sidmouth EX10 9QG
Typeset from disk by Stanford DTP Services, Towcester
Printed in the European Union by Antony Rowe, Chippenham, England

Contents

To Ann
Who accompanied me into exile

Preface

Despite past changes that will continue to occur over the next years, the map of Israel/Palestine will remain essentially as it is today. Rather than challenging this statement, the inevitability of a Palestinian state reinforces it. For the control of Israel/Palestine by Israel, its control over the geographic area that stretches from Tel Aviv to the Jordan River, will continue. Israel has not only conquered this area and will control it through direct supervision and surrogates, but the land without significant Palestinian population will be occupied, settled and developed by Israel.

Except for a vocal minority of Jews within and outside of Israel, the Jewish community will accept this conquest without criticism. Safely empowered in Israel and the U.S., the Jewish community will continue to stake its historical, political, cultural and religious claims as a major ethical force in world history. In spite of its small numbers – 14 million Jews in a world of more than 6 billion people – Jews will claim for Judaism its standing as a major world religion. Jewish history and ethics will be taught to Jews and others as a model for behavior and religiosity – as the birthing community of monotheism and ethics – to be emulated by others around the world. The Holocaust will continue to be raised as the unique event and epitome of suffering: incomparable, without rival, and to be communicated only by the heirs of the Holocaust.

Because of these contributions and suffering, a certain and profound innocence will be claimed within suffering and empowerment. Though Jewish empowerment in Israel has become increasingly controversial over the years, the fact of that empowerment will override the criticism, thus protecting and projecting the Holocaust as the main identification of Jews, Judaism and the Jewish world.

It is ironic that the safe harbor of Jewish life, the claim to uniqueness and innocence and thus special privileges, has been and increasingly will be an event of such horrific suffering that, despite the repetitive images and public memorials, the mind remains unable to accept its horror. This safe harbor, however, is one of assimilation to the state and power, to dislocation and atrocity, and therefore to every lesson that the Holocaust is supposed to warn against. When the very people who embody this warning use the lessons of the Holocaust against another people, the event itself is trivialized.

I believe that the entire history of the Jewish people is being trivialized in the conquest of Palestine that is now essentially complete. As Jews we are now in a post-Holocaust, post-Israel era; paradoxically, both events remain alive in memory and use. This position of living *after*, even as the force of Holocaust and Israel continue, underscores the duality of difficulty and possibility for Jewish life in the twenty-first century.

What are we to do with this history and this present? How do we claim a Jewishness that is faithful to the past and the present? How are we to witness to the values and struggles of Jewish history at a time where more is being claimed about our contributions and our importance than ever before in our history, at the same time when everything is being lost and squandered in the mad race to be among the nation-states?

In these pages I attempt to structure a narrative argument that might lead to a future worth bequeathing to our children. In the end, as is true for all of us, I leave this actual task to my children as a witness to a face of Judaism and Jewish life that, as I write, is disappearing.

In offering this work to a public audience I am conscious that the tone is at times uneven. Some of the book is written in the first person, using personal experience to enter a difficult question. Some of the book is analytical, using maps and public policy to uncover myths and illustrate issues. Other parts of the book are philosophical and religious, applying and interpreting ideas and biblical themes to the contemporary world, especially to the questions of Jewish identity after the Holocaust and Israel. Most of this book has been written as recent events have unfolded. Some previously published material has been refashioned for inclusion here.

The announcement of this unevenness is cautionary and telling. Contemporary issues of Jewish identity are rarely simple or addressed through either the personal, the realm of ideas or politics alone. Rather a complex synthesis of experience and thought is essential to work through these issues, and even then resolution is only momentary.

There is a complexity about being Jewish in the world that is fascinating, at times discouraging, often energizing. For the sense that others have about Jews, and the internal sensibility concerning

Jewishness carried by Jews, leave little time for quiescence. As has been true throughout history, being Jewish is a full-time job with tremendous internal and external consequences. This was true when we were poor and oppressed; it is true today when we experience affluence, acceptance and power.

I am grateful for all those who have accompanied me and who have given me the strength to think through a Jewish future different than the present. I dedicate this book to Ann, my wife, for the love and the steadfastness she has shown me over the years. I also owe a special thank you to Matthew Larsen for technical and editorial assistance on this book.

What the future will bring only time will tell. I remain, with others, a witness to a Judaism and Jewish life that testifies to the possibility of an ethical path in the world. While I do not underestimate the difficulty involved of invoking such a vision, I focus on the importance of such a witness. For me, negotiating this difficult task is the essence of what it means to be Jewish. It is my fidelity.

Introduction: A Bully in Christchurch

A short while ago I flew into Christchurch from Sydney, Australia, the last stop on a worldwide speaking tour I called 'Quest for Justice'. I had been lecturing on the Israel/Palestine issue in light of the recent Al-Aqsa intifada, first in the United Kingdom, Germany and India, then on to Australia and New Zealand, seeking to raise consciousness on the Israeli violation of the human and national rights of Palestinians.

As a Jew born in the U.S. and steeped, like other Jews of my post-Holocaust generation, in an ethic of fair play and justice, I have been distressed by the continuing and escalating belligerence of Israel. The use of Israeli helicopter gunships against defenceless Palestinian cities, towns, villages and refugee camps angered me. I could not remain silent.

Indeed, I have begun to see that these very machines whose sole purpose is one of destruction and death have come to define contemporary Jewish life. In my mind's eye, I have a vision of replacing the Torah scrolls in the Ark of the Covenant, that focus Jews on God, justice and peace, with a helicopter gunship that speaks of power and might without ethics or morality. What we do, we worship.

Thus the speaking tour. In the course of two months I addressed dozens of audiences on this subject and can recall only a few instances of audience members attempting to disrupt my presentations. In fact, the overwhelming sense that I came away with from this tour is that people around the world are deeply concerned about the behavior of the Israeli government. They also have deep fears about what is happening to the Palestinians.

During this tour, I addressed several Jewish organizations, including a meeting of Liberal rabbis in the United Kingdom, a Jewish organization in Melbourne and a Jewish Studies class at New South Wales University in Sydney. I also met with a number of Jews in the countries I visited, including Israeli Jews, and the concern is shared: Have we as Jews become an oppressor nation? Have the lessons of the Holocaust, which we teach religiously to everyone in the world, been lost to us? Is the threat and use of power and might – by helicopter gunships hovering over Palestinian skies by day and firing their rockets by night – the legacy we want to bequeath to our children?

Speaking tours like these are long and arduous, with much travel and little sleep. Yet they are also rewarding. As a Jew I witness discussions of depth and emotion with other Jews, with non-Jews who have a love for the Holy Land, and of course, with Palestinians whose lives and families are involved, most often in negative ways, with the Israeli–Palestinian conflict.

Though the rewards are many, the jarring notes are what I remember most, the verbal and non-verbal confrontations, most often with Jews, who remind me that the Israeli–Palestinian conflict is central to Jewish history and to the Jewish future.

At the University of Canterbury in Christchurch I had one such encounter. On the first day of the visit, I was asked to attend a class with a visiting Jewish Israeli scholar and political activist, Yossi Olmert. After the lecture we had lunch. That evening I was scheduled to appear with him on a panel addressing the Israeli–Palestinian conflict.

It turns out that Dr. Olmert is the brother of the mayor of Jerusalem, Ehud Olmert; both are nationalists and to the right of the Israeli political spectrum in the mode of Menachem Begin, Benjamin Netanyahu and Ariel Sharon. The Israeli embassy in New Zealand had brought Olmert to New Zealand as part of his more extensive tour of Asia and the Pacific. These tours attempt to counter the negative publicity that has surfaced during Israel's military campaign to quell the Al-Aqsa intifada.

Olmert began his morning lecture on the Israeli–Arab conflict with reference to the wider Middle East region. He correctly pointed out the need for knowledge of the broader context that impacted the relatively small area of Israel/Palestine. What is interesting about this wider context, at least as Olmert analysed it, are the problems in Israel's 'neighborhood'. According to Olmert, the main factors in the Middle East are overpopulation, underdevelopment, lack of democracy and Islamic fundamentalism, a potent mixture that reinforces a cycle of violence illustrated by the Iraq–Iran War in the 1980s, Iraq's invasion of Kuwait in the early 1990s and a spiraling arms race which continues to make the Middle East the most heavily armed region in the world.

Olmert lamented these facts, pointing out the debilitating wastefulness of violence and war, but what surprised me was the superficiality of his analysis. The entire Middle East was summed up in generalities, almost without a sense of differentiation and particular contexts. Overriding the details, and even the generalities, was a sense of failure on the part of the Arab nations, almost a sense of destiny in their tendencies toward instability, dictatorship and terrorism.

As the class continued on, the Israeli–Palestinian focus was addressed. As a nationalist and self-proclaimed right-winger, Olmert claims the land of Israel to include not only Jerusalem but the West Bank as well, a region he refers to as Judea and Samaria. The Greater Land of Israel is indeed Olmert's claim, as the biblical promise and the early claims of Israel and the land are seen to be in force. That Palestinians have always lived in these areas is for Olmert an inconvenient factor perhaps derailing, at least for now, the complete fulfillment of this claim. In no way does it provide Palestinians with a claim rivaling the one he makes for Jews.

As for Jerusalem, the city whose destruction Jews continue to lament and to whose return they prayed for more than two thousand years of diaspora, the Jewish claim is non-negotiable. Palestinians have rights to pray at the mosques in Jerusalem; their rights end there. As for the assassinations of Palestinians, a freely-admitted policy of the Sharon government carried out through the diverse means of detonated cell phones and helicopter gunships, Olmert was firm in describing these acts as reprisals for terrorist attacks on Israeli civilians. They are not only justified, they should continue and perhaps even be accelerated.

What is remarkable about Olmert is not his ideas. He combines the superficial analysis of the Arab world and simplification of Jewish rights to the land of Israel/Palestine that have become commonplace in nationalist right-wing circles in Israel over the last decades. Though Olmert was careful to distance himself from the assassination of Yitzhak Rabin, an event he described as shameful, I felt his analysis was quite close to Yigal Amir, Rabin's assassin. Amir speaks of Arabs and Palestinians in ways not too dissimilar to Olmert's own rhetoric.

Indeed, as the class continued with a lively question-and-answer period, Olmert became more and more animated and sweeping in his generalizations. Arabs and Muslims were defined in increasingly negative terms and outsiders to the Middle East, including New Zealanders and Americans – not exempting Jews who live outside Israel – were taunted for daring to suggest to Israel ethical and moral alternatives to their present behavior. These 'outsiders' always criticized Israel but did not live in their 'neighborhood' and did not pay the price in blood and tears. Israel and the Palestinians should go it alone, and the suggestion that Israel is within an international system of nation-states with laws and obligations, and dependent on the United States for financial and military support, was dismissed with disdain.

This disdain struck me as essential to Olmert's world-view. As the evening panel discussion drew near, I feared this would result in an uneven discussion in which the very principle of the centrality of justice and ethics to Judaism and Jewish life would be characterized as utopian and derided as silly. Or as a recipe for disaster for Israel and Jews who lived within her borders.

After all, isn't every violation of order and decency in the Middle East a violation by Arabs who, if they had the power, would drive the Jews into the sea? Isn't that the aim of every Arab on the street and every Arab government from now until the end of time? Aren't moral arguments made on behalf of the Palestinians actually hypocritical, veiled attacks that carry the ominous prospects of another Holocaust? Am I, with others who criticize the Jewish state, contributing to a gathering storm of violence and retribution that might result in a catastrophe for Jews approaching or even surpassing the mass death of Jews in the twentieth century?

As it turned out, my fears for the integrity of the panel discussion were unfortunately realized. Olmert dominated the discussion as if it were a solo lecture. Not only did he speak far longer than his allotted time, he resisted any attempt to stop him. As his orations grew longer, his vehemence increased.

Olmert seemed obsessed with the era before the 1967 Israeli–Arab War when Jordan occupied east Jerusalem, and the Wailing Wall, the last remaining remnant of the ancient Jewish Temple, was littered with trash and urinated on by animals. Today, of course, Jews dominate this part of Jerusalem and guarantee the freedom of Muslims to worship. But to the question of what freedom is accorded Muslim worshipers when Jerusalem is inaccessible to Palestinians who live outside the city and when the Palestinian population of the Old City is systematically depleted, Olmert, whose brother implements these policies of restricted access and demographic change, simply reiterated in a more insistent voice the charges of Arab desecration of Jewish holy sites.

With the evening ended, I returned to the home where I was staying. I reflected on the discussion and felt almost as if I had been physically violated. Was I smarting because of his debating skills, indeed his street-fighting ways, so typical of vocal and animated Israelis? Had I lost the war of words and now, upon my retreat, been forced to lick my open wounds?

In the morning I had another sense of the previous evening. Rather than by debating skills or truth telling, Olmert had dominated me and the audience with bully tactics. This understanding of Olmert as a bully, remembering that bullies, absent their entourage or, in the case of Israel, an overwhelming arms advantage, are essentially cowards, forced me to a deeper level of sadness with regard to Israel and its future. All Israelis are not bullies to be sure, but why was he brought on this speaking tour by the Israeli embassy? Why was an official from the embassy present and why did she seem so pleased with his words?

In his summation, Olmert again characterized Jewish and non-Jewish dissent from outside Israel as destructive and counterproductive and referred to my criticism in a derogatory way. Among his criticisms one phrase stands out to me: 'He doesn't even speak our language.'

This struck me as an especially hurtful comment, at least initially, but upon reflection Olmert is more correct than he even proposed. As a youngster I learned liturgical Hebrew and can read and write Hebrew in that style. For most of Jewish history Hebrew has been precisely that, a liturgical language of beauty and depth. With the formation of the state of Israel, Hebrew became a modern spoken language with many variations and adaptations. As with most Jews who live outside of Israel, I do not speak that language. According to Olmert, this makes my commitment to Judaism and Jewish life questionable. Real Jews, apparently, live in Israel and argue for the positions he does.

I had the sense that Olmert would have treated a progressive Israeli panelist the same way that he treated me. That very day the progressive Jewish Israeli peace group, Gush Shalom, asked the international community to send a peace force to monitor the situation in the occupied territories and to protect Palestinians from Israeli aggression. Are they less Jewish than Olmert? Are they Jews who, though speaking modern Hebrew, also don't speak 'our' language?[1]

I wonder if the defining character of Olmert's language is Hebrew or its bullying nature. Is this the innovative aspect of modern

Hebrew in its transposition from the liturgical sphere to the nation-state, that it is used less as a praise of God's presence than as an instrument to project state power? Can this humble language be now summed up in a militarism that sanctions the use of helicopter gunships as a way of teaching lessons to a defenceless people?

Indeed, I do not speak Olmert's language and do not wish to. I wonder if Olmert, being secular and leaving behind the ethical and justice-oriented commandments of Judaism and adopting the ways of the nations, represents the arrival of Hebrew-speaking Gentiles. Am I part of a remnant of non-Hebrew-speaking Jews, a community that seeks an interdependent empowerment of Jews and Palestinians, thus recognizing our own rights and the rights of others? Is 'our' language spoken with such vehemence – the language of power and might – that it marks a return to the Jewish ghetto mentality, now armed with nuclear missiles, a nuclearized ghetto, if you will? Does this other language typify a renewed engagement with the world in which Jews, when powerful and despite the Holocaust, can also commit crimes against others?[2]

My encounter with Olmert was just a month before the September 11th attacks on New York City and Washington, D.C. For many these attacks simply reinforced his position, that there is a link between Arabs and terrorism, a connection Israel knows well. For some the lessons that Olmert seeks to impart are now 'our' lessons. Others believe that we now need to adopt the language of violence and retribution as the only language 'we' and 'they' understand.

I view this encounter with the 'bully in Christchurch' as a window into the Jewish world *as it has evolved over the last decades*. With the evolution and expansion of state power in Israel and the accelerated empowerment and achievement of elite influence in the United States, Jewish life around the world has been mobilized and militarized.

This trajectory, however, has often been misunderstood, characterized in fundamentalist religious terms and blamed on right-wing religious Jews in settlement movements around Jerusalem and the West Bank. Though they are not without blame – they certainly make worse the already difficult situation – Jewish fundamentalists are latecomers to Israel and the Jewish world.

Olmert is a fellow traveler to Jewish religious fundamentalists, but likewise a latecomer. In fact, Israel and its continuing expansion are impossible to understand outside the liberal-European-secular Jewish narrative that promoted its creation and its consolidation as a nation-state.

This narrative combines a European context – a Jewish minority at the end of the nineteenth century and early twentieth century that clearly saw the difficulties, if not impossibility, of Jewish life flourishing in modern Europe – with an evolving post-Holocaust consciousness that, especially in the U.S. after the 1967 Arab–Israeli War, commemorates the Holocaust and understands Israel as compensation for suffering and a guarantor of Jewish survival. If we label the European Jewish context 'Zionism' and the American Jewish context 'Holocaust/Israel', we capture the central movements for the establishment and maintenance of Israel.

Clearly both Zionism and Holocaust/Israel identification in their origins and continuity are complex and diverse. Historically, there have been Zionisms, from state Zionism to homeland Zionism and variations in between. Holocaust/Israel identification was weak in the 1950s and 1960s but strong during the late 1960s and 1970s. Today Zionism has been overshadowed by Holocaust/Israel identification, as advanced by American Jewish economic and political elites.

The important point here is that in both Europe and the U.S. the main engines of Zionism and Holocaust/Israel identification have been decidedly secular, although in a particularly Jewish way. Here secularity can include devotion to the Jewish people, a reading of the bible as an ongoing historical narrative, and a sense of historical destiny that includes nationality and peoplehood.

At the same time, the development of Zionism and Holocaust/Israel identification should be seen within an evolving liberal, sometimes socialist and often times non- or anti-religious sensibility. The founders of Israel were decidedly secular and progressive in the European framework. They were driven by an ethic they identified as Jewish in the broadest sense: they saw themselves as internationalists in the humanist cause. Those who pioneered the Holocaust/Israel narrative in the U.S. were Jewish in sensibility and religious only in the broadest sense of the term. They, too, were liberal, espousing civil rights and a society open to all.

The appeal to the larger Jewish community after the Holocaust was precisely because Orthodox Judaism made little sense to the Jewish community in the U.S., both because of the effects of modernity and the religious questions posed by the severity of the Holocaust. While those who reflected on the Holocaust could not agree on the presence of God during and after the Holocaust, they could agree that the central religious tasks of Jews after the Holocaust were remembering the Holocaust and building the state of Israel. In 1968, Emil Fackenheim, the Canadian philosopher, wrote of this commitment as the 614th commandment, adding to or perhaps supplanting the 613 commandments of traditional Jewish religious life.[3]

It is important to understand how the success of state Zionism and the intensification of the Holocaust/Israel narrative in the U.S. laid the groundwork for a secondary, though increasingly important, religiously extreme settler movement, in tandem with a secular extreme nationalism, after the 1967 war. It was not until this period, on the heels of the capture and annexation of east Jerusalem and occupation and settlement of the West Bank, that what we now call Jewish fundamentalism came to fruition.

Jerusalem has obvious significance to both religious and secular Jews but, in the years following Israel's victory, the religious significance was emphasized. Like Jerusalem, the West Bank, known to religious Jews as Judea and Samaria, contained religious sites from ancient times. Complementing the Western Wall of the ancient Temple in Jerusalem, the West Bank territories included the tombs of Abraham, Sarah and Rachel and other sites of religious and historical importance for Jews who aspired to reclaim and perhaps rebuild Jewish life in the promised land.

But the religious movements around Jerusalem, Judea and Samaria were rendered moot with a victory in war and the subsequent planned settlements in these areas. In the crucial time period after the 1967 war, the decision was made within the Israeli government to annex and expand Jerusalem, fortify it with settlements and expand further into the territories for political, economic and military reasons. Since religious fundamentalists have at no time dominated the Israeli government, the annexation of Jerusalem and the settlement of the West Bank should be seen as a calculated state expansion into areas where stakes could be claimed as the spoils of war and where no power could confront that expansion.

American foreign policy was also involved here, as it is today. Though official policies of the the U.S. government have never recognized the Israeli annexation of Jerusalem or the West Bank settlements as legal – nor are they recognized by international law – American foreign aid and security assistance has been essential to these policies.

Here again religiosity is hardly a dominant factor. Rather, the U.S. foreign policy considerations, sometimes spoken of in moral tones, appear to dominate. Domestic pressure from American Jewish groups, Jewish elected officials, Jewish political activists and foreign policy advisers has been instrumental in the pursuit of these unofficial policies.

Jewish spokespeople in the U.S. have been mainstream Jews, decidedly moderate and liberal, and in the main, political Democrats. Those that are religious are, again, moral in tone and liberal in sensibility. It is important to note that the main public figures who have garnered support for Israel in the United States have framed Jewish and non-Jewish support for Israel in Holocaust sensibility and moral language. There are few Jews of major consequence in the public narrative of support for Israel in the U.S. who frame their support in anything resembling Orthodox, right-wing nationalist, or settler language.

Clearly the major spokesperson over the years for Holocaust/Israel consciousness in the United States is Elie Wiesel. Wiesel has been powerful both within the Jewish community and outside of it, having to his credit the Presidential Medal of Freedom, the U.S. Congressional Gold Medal, the Nobel Peace Prize, and a major hand in the development of the United States Holocaust Memorial Museum. He is a friend of presidents as diverse as Ronald Reagan and Bill Clinton, appears often on national television as a commentator on moral and ethical issues, and is seen in prestigious national events like the State of the Union address. Wiesel is religious in a particularly Jewish and liberal ecumenical way that has a broad appeal to Jews who want to claim a post-Holocaust Jewish identity and to non-Jews who want to repent of the sin of anti-Semitism that European Christianity promulgated with such fervor over much of its history.[4]

In Wiesel's written works and public presentations there is no mention of biblical claims to the land of Judea and Samaria – or even the land that comprises the 1967 borders of Israel – nor is there discussion of settlements and settlers or religious shrines and attachments. Jerusalem is spoken about in an abstract, mystical way, as is the 1967 war, where for Wiesel the Israeli soldiers carried Jewish history and innocence into a battle that was forced upon them by the Arab world.

Shorn of the details of occupation and settlement, in Wiesel's narrative Israel becomes a homeland for persecuted European Jews and Holocaust survivors. Jews are innocent in suffering *and* empowerment. Israel is a moral crusade that all of humanity is called upon to affirm and support. In Wiesel's Israel, politics and the army are almost invisible, as are the Palestinians. The U.S. supports Israel because, like Israelis, Americans are innocent and good. Even Christians, now reformed of their anti-Semitism, practice their essential innocence and goodness by holding up Israel as a response to the Holocaust.

In many ways, Wiesel's argument for Israel is one without maps or politics. In the U.S. this is true as well. In a public and national way, there has never been a sustained and rational discussion about Israel in America. This is, of course, most particularly and egregiously true within the Jewish community as well. The arguments about Israel that include Palestinians are between pro-Israel and pro-Palestinian supporters, or at least this is how the debate is defined. The reality of the expanded state of Israel, a state that now extends its reach between Tel Aviv and the Jordan River – with over three million Palestinians in between – is unknown to most Americans and Jews as well.

It is difficult to know how to address this impasse. In the pages that follow I try to uncover some hidden dimensions of the questions facing Jews, Judaism and Jewish history. In Chapter 1, I trace the role of memory in Jewish thought and religion and how that memory has highlighted *and* hidden aspects of Jewish life historically and in the present. Jewish historians of memory, such as Yosef Yerushalmi and David Roskies, are brought to the fore, as are theologians and commentators such as Emil Fackenheim, Cynthia Ozick and Irena Klepfisz.

In the main, these Jewish intellectuals embrace the Holocaust as defining contemporary Jewish life but point, sometimes with certainty and sometimes inadvertently, to a future beyond the Holocaust. Roskies' 'liturgy of destruction', for example, can be confined to the Jewish people, so that Jewish suffering is privileged and future Jewish suffering must be guarded against at all costs. But it can also open Jews to the world of suffering, including and especially the suffering of the Palestinian people, as part of Jewish history, thus calling for an end to Palestinian suffering as a key to the Jewish future.

Similarly, Emil Fackenheim's '*tikkun* of ordinary decency', which he defines as the small acts of generosity that a few non-Jews risked toward Jews in the Nazi era, represented then and represents today the possibility of an ontological and historical healing of the rupture of the Holocaust. But this can move in two different directions. For Fackenheim, the most obvious movement of this *tikkun* – healing or mending in the present – is toward an unequivocal support of Jewish empowerment in Israel, but another latent movement is the further extension of ordinary decency toward Palestinians.

The oppression of the Palestinians represents a further rupture in the universe and in history that also needs mending. In this sense, Jewish outreach toward Palestinians in the twenty-first century may be equivalent to non-Jews reaching out to Jews in the Nazi era. This raises a further fundamental question as to whether Jewish empowerment at the expense of another people represents a healing for the Jewish people or whether Jews can only be healed of the trauma of the Holocaust when Palestinians are healed of their own trauma of displacement and humiliation.

Chapter 2 moves from memory and theology to the map of Israel/Palestine as it is today and how it will be, no doubt with minor adjustments, for the foreseeable future. Memory, identity and formation theology, even ideology, often seek to transcend the realities of the world. In that transcendence all is possible, even the positing of innocence where innocence has become culpability. The map of Israel/Palestine with Israeli control stretching from Tel Aviv to the Jordan River is rarely discussed in Jewish circles. Nor is the planned, systematic, government-sponsored, bureaucratically implemented settlement policy spoken of.

In the main, Jews discuss Israel as if a nation-state is not in place or as if Israel is unlike any other state in its desire for control and expansion. Yet one of the features of contemporary Jewish life is our involvement with nation-states at the highest levels, most obvious in Israel but also aggressively and successfully in the U.S. I suggest here that involvement in the upper echelons of the nation-state as an empowered and favoured community means a major intellectual, political and cultural reorientation of Jewish life.

On these levels, and in the religious arena as well, Jewish leadership enters into an ecumenical and political deal with the non-Jewish establishment in the West and within the international nation-state community through Israel. I call this a Constantinian deal, where Jewish hope, memory, intellect, wealth and religion are mobilized for empowerment, much as the early Christians were mobilized in the Constantinian synthesis of church and state in the fourth century.

Thus we are witnessing today the emergence of Constantinian Judaism in service to the state and power, and in this regard, Jews today are undergoing the most thorough assimilation in Jewish history. While this assimilation seems now almost inevitable, the map of Israel/Palestine is a reminder of the cost of that assimilation, the loss of the Jewish ethical base and hence the loss, too, of the covenantal affirmation carried by Jews and Judaism thus far throughout history.

Here the conquest of Jerusalem becomes a litmus test and a warning to the cost of Jewish power *and* the possibility of choosing a different path. For if Jerusalem is seen as the 'broken middle' of Israel/Palestine – to be fully shared among Jews and Palestinians – and if citizenship rather than religion or ethnic identity is the path of a shared life and responsibility, then Jerusalem can indeed become a beacon of hope for Jews and Palestinians in the twenty-first century.

A shared Jerusalem and the movement toward citizenship in Israel/Palestine is the path away from a Constantinianism in politics and religion that threatens the very heart and soul of Jewish history. It is here that another map comes into consciousness, that we as Jews come after the Holocaust *and* Israel, and that the way forward is to recognize that our innocence in suffering does not translate into innocence in empowerment.

In Chapter 3, I explore the prophetic tradition within Judaism. This tradition has had many twists and turns over the millennia, yet remains the most distinctive Jewish contribution to the world. It is the prophetic that grounds critiques of power and innocence and even provides the foundations of the monotheistic faith traditions. At the same time, these traditions that announce the prophetic also attempt to constrain and seal the prophetic in ritual. Judaism, Christianity and Islam are in turn prophetic in their respective critiques of unjust power and assimilationists when legitimating power that dislocates and destroys.

As has often been the case, the prophetic voice in the contemporary world is in conflict with the traditions that claim the ancient prophets themselves. Hence, those who seek and embody the prophetic call in our time are often in exile. This is especially true for Jews who argue for justice in Israel/Palestine. Since the covenant is at the heart of the prophetic, and since both can never be contained within any system of thought or religiosity, especially systems that mask injustice and culpability with a sense of innocence and entitlement, both the prophetic and the covenant are constantly on the move, traveling among the oppressed and those actively seeking justice.

In the twenty-first century, a community across geographic, cultural and religious backgrounds is forming around the prophetic and pursues the covenant into a broader tradition of faith and struggle. Within this broader tradition a coalition of exiles and refugees comes into a new community of resistance and struggle. As this community evolves, so does the meaning of the prophetic and the covenant.

This evolving community and meaning challenge the memory of suffering, the liturgy of destruction, and the *tikkun* of ordinary decency to attend to the world as it is today, to take the same risks and embody the same possibilities for the suffering rather than shield the once-oppressed and now all-powerful. Can this evolving prophetic community address Jewish culpability the way the ancient prophets did? Will those within this tradition risk exile to speak the truth as the ancient prophets did? Can this tradition be successful in the face of state power?

Within Jewish life there has been a tradition of dissent regarding Zionism, including among Zionists themselves. Much of this tradition is forgotten or deliberately buried. Few Jews know that Judah Magnes, the first president of Hebrew University, Martin Buber, the great biblical scholar and theologian, and Hannah Arendt, the philosopher of the mind and the human condition, were all binationalists, opposed to a Jewish state in Palestine. They argued instead for a cooperative federation of Jews and Arabs.

The responses to these questions are surprisingly relevant. They are, of course, controversial. And they will be answered in the next fifty years. Chapter 4 frames the question in this way: are the boundaries of the Jewish state as they are today, are the boundaries of Jewish life in its Constantinian phase, to be the boundaries of Jewish destiny? I ask if all of Jewish history has come to this, that a small, creative, struggling, often suffering community assimilates to power and the state to survive the vicissitudes of history. I ask also if the prophetic voice and the covenant are now to function only to cloak power and convince the culpable of their innocence.

In this context I try to trace the future of Judaism and the Jewish community in Israel/Palestine and the U.S. if the present course of assimilation remains uninterrupted. In the Epilogue I also suggest an alternative future that exists on the horizon for a minority of Jews who choose exile rather than complicity.

For that is our hope, always there to be chosen, another way of being Jewish and human in a world of empire. That those who gave birth to the ethics of community should now deny that ethics to another people – and thus ultimately to relinquish that privileged claim – is part of the ironic nature of the human journey. What we do with this origin and this irony is defining of our own fidelity, as weak and insignificant as it often seems. In victory and in defeat it is what we bequeath to the next generation who will themselves continue to struggle with the prophetic and the covenant.

1 Jewish Memory in the Post-Holocaust Era

There are few concepts so intimately linked in Jewish life as memory, tradition and the covenant. Contemporary Jewish scholars have spent much of their energy thinking through this connection in the post-Holocaust era.

Yet those who have reflected on the Holocaust and its meaning find memory, tradition and the covenant problematic. How do we remember after the Holocaust? In whose name do we remember? Is there a continuity of tradition before and after the Holocaust? Or does the Holocaust fragment memory and tradition? If memory and tradition are in dispute, what can be said about the covenant? Is the covenant itself in fragments? Because of this fragmentation, many who reflect on the Holocaust find their task to be rethinking these three conceptual centers of Jewish history.

At the same moment that this rethinking is taking place, a new center of Jewish life has formed as a response to the Holocaust. Israel as a nation-state declared its independence only three years after the liberation of the death camps. In the wake of the 1967 Arab–Israeli War, many Jewish thinkers and activists declared Israel to be the answer to the fragmentation.

The ensuing decades have cast shadows on that judgement as the policies of Israel, especially in relation to Palestinians, have caused divisions within the Jewish community. Some of these divisions have promoted deep fault lines in Jewish affiliation and commitment. In these fault lines the issue is Israeli policies; the reference point is often the Holocaust. The twinning of the Holocaust and Israel has added another dimension to Jewish discussion that is both external and intimate – the Palestinians. *It is my view that Jews, Judaism and Jewish life at the dawn of the twenty-first century come after the Holocaust and Israel, and that the outsider/insider dimension of Palestinians, though controversial and unannounced, is central to the fragmentation of Jewish life. It may also be the key to its renewed viability.*

By surveying several post-Holocaust Jewish attempts to name the fragmentation and search for renewed viability, we can at least approach the task of the next generation. That task is to remember the dead as a form of fidelity to Jewish history and life.[1]

Post-Holocaust life is deeply problematic for Jews. Simple responses and arguments, especially through anger and challenges to loyalty, only make more difficult the formation of Jewish identity in the coming decades. These are not simple problems and they can only be worked out over time. The fiftieth-anniversary markers of the Holocaust and Israel are behind us. What lies ahead is the next fifty years, where many of these questions will be answered or at least responded to. Is there now, then, a future for Jews and Judaism? Will the covenant, so central to Jewish history and argued about in the last fifty years, be relevant to those who come after the Holocaust and Israel?

Memory, destruction and resistance

Memory is for the past, but its recovery takes place always in the present. Both point toward the future where justice, once denied, will be embraced. This pattern began in the Exodus where God, remembering injustice and the promise of the covenant,[2] forged a future of justice anchored in remembrance. The link between memory and justice has always been central in Jewish life, though the Holocaust has made it less clear, perhaps creating an unbridgeable chasm.

Still Jewish thinkers persist. One such person is Yosef Hayim Yerushalmi, the Salo Baron Professor of Jewish History, Culture and Society at Columbia University in New York. In 1977, while on sabbatical in Jerusalem, he delivered a lecture at the Institute of Jewish Studies at Hebrew University on Jewish historiography in the sixteenth century. Though the topic was specific to that time period, it encouraged him to develop a series of lectures on the subject of Jewish memory and its defining role in Jewish life.[3]

Yerushalmi finds the core of Jewish survival and identity in the bible, where a type of historical and mythical remembrance is called for by God. Exhortations to remember are numerous and are seen as a religious imperative for the entire people. Reaching a crescendo in Deuteronomy and the prophets, these books recall the wonders that God has done for the people of Israel and call Israel to remember what their enemies have done against them. The defining moment of remembrance in Jewish history is found in the bible as well: 'Remember that you were a slave in Egypt ... .'[4]

Memory, of course, is problematic; memory can be a force for justice but it can also be deceptive, even treacherous. The obligation of Israel to remember is selective, tied to God's acts of intervention in history and Israel's positive and negative responses to them. Remembrance is found within ritual and recital, and thus the narrative of Israel is both liturgical and historical. Though the mission of Israel is tied to God, it is traced through history; the covenant is a bridge between God and history embodied in Israel itself. Remembrance is central to the covenant and the security of the relationship between God and Israel.

If memory is central, the failure to remember is disastrous. More than a momentary lapse of attention or an excusable human failing, the lack of memory is fraught with tremendous anxiety, as it threatens to sever the relationship which is so important to Israel and the world. Yerushalmi points out a peculiar and revolutionary aspect of this remembrance in that God is also enjoined to remember. For like Israel, God is bound in the covenant. The remembrance found in ritual and recital is also a way of reminding God of the commitment that is jointly shared and is to be found and demonstrated in history. Memory can thus be a hymn of praise, but can become a query, even an accusation, when the promises of God are found to be wanting.[5]

Memory has rooted the Jewish people throughout history, especially in the years of exile and suffering, but the role of memory in contemporary Jewish life is deeply problematic. The dangers of memory, with its focus on exclusivity and chosenness, have traditionally coexisted with its possibilities, a sense of relationship with God and God's protection within suffering. However, contemporary Jewish life – especially after emancipation in Europe, the Holocaust and the birth of Israel – has taken on a bifurcated reality.

The result of emancipation in Europe and the U.S. and national sovereignty in Israel is that Jews have fully re-entered the mainstream of history, and yet, as Yerushalmi notes, 'their perception of how they got there and where they are is most often more mythical than real'. If myth and memory provide the foundation for action, there are myths which are worthy of preservation and reinterpretation and those which 'lead us astray' and must be redefined. Still others are dangerous, and these must be exposed and jettisoned.[6]

Yerushalmi ends his lectures without specifying which myths are worthy of preserving or which are dangerous. Nor does he specify the danger that Jewish life faces beyond tracing the rise of secular culture, a modern scientific understanding of history, and consequent decay of Jewish memory. The dangerous juncture reached in Jewish history after the Holocaust and the rebirth of a national identity in Israel seems to be defined as the vulgarization of Jewish life or its oversimplification, that is, a trend toward a superficial discussion and embodiment of Jewish life.

'Nothing has replaced the coherence and meaning with which a powerful messianic faith once imbued both Jewish past and future', Yerushalmi writes, 'Perhaps nothing else can. Indeed, there is a growing skepticism as to whether Jewish history can yield itself to any organizing principle that will command general assent.' The danger here is movement beyond vulgarization and superficiality toward assimilation. Perhaps all three trends will come together sometime in the future. Yerushalmi is honest when he states that there are no obvious solutions to the issues he has raised.[7]

As complicated as his argument is, and as tentative as his proposals for the future are, one cannot help think that he has left out an important aspect of contemporary Jewish life and with it a major element of the memory which needs to be acknowledged. Though his first lecture was delivered in Jerusalem, and though he identifies nationalism as an important part of the contemporary Jewish experience, Yerushalmi nowhere mentions the complicated history of Jews and Palestinians as part of the collective memory of the Jewish people.

If Jewish memory has become abstract, unable to bridge myth and reality or to fashion a coherent center for contemporary Jewry, is it possible that it is this lack of remembering which contributes to the problems that Yerushalmi raises? There is a history between Jew and Palestinian to record, to recite, perhaps even to ritualize in the city where these lectures were delivered. Yet if this history does not record that memory or even allude to it, then perhaps Jewish life is further bifurcated.

While lecturing in Jerusalem, Yerushalmi seems blind to the history around him, including those people struggling under Israeli domination. Or perhaps he was unable to articulate this change in Jewish history within the framework in which he was trained and sought to articulate. Either through ignorance or inability, was he actually contributing to the vulgarization, superficiality, even assimilation of Jewish life? Did including Palestinians in Jewish remembrance threaten to historicize the Jewish experience to such an extent that the traditional framework of Jewish life would be overturned? And if the Palestinians are not included, how can Jews decide which myths are worthy of preservation and which are dangerous and need to be jettisoned?

Yerushalmi is hardly alone in this deficiency. Holocaust remembrance, now so defining in Jewish life, replicates this lacuna. In fact, one way of defining Holocaust memorial culture as it has evolved is the *absence* of Palestinians. Irving Greenberg, one of the most important Holocaust theologians and formerly chair of the United States Holocaust Memorial Museum in Washington, D.C., in his book *The Jewish Way: Living the Jewish Holidays*, reorients almost the entire Jewish calendar around the Holocaust.

In his chapter on Yom HaShoah, Greenberg argues for the permanent inclusion of a day of Holocaust remembrance in the Jewish liturgical calendar. Speaking of the difficulty of retaining belief in a saving God of history after the Holocaust and therefore the difficulty of embracing the Jewish covenant in the contemporary world, Greenberg counsels Jews to learn from the ancient rabbis who lived within the destruction of the Temple. Their way was to assert the hiddenness of God as a way of calling Jews to greater responsibility. 'After the destruction of the Temple the people of Israel moved from partial participant to full partner to the covenant', Greenberg writes; 'After the Holocaust, the Jewish people were called upon to become the executive partner in the mission of redemption.'[8]

This responsibility in history extends to an image of God so desecrated in the Holocaust. Who but the heirs of the Holocaust could in fact refurbish that image? For Greenberg, the primary religious act after the Holocaust becomes the re-creation of the image of God. How is this done? 'In an age of divine hiddenness, the most credible statement about God is the creation of an image of God which, silently but powerfully, points to the God whose image it is', Greenberg writes; 'There is a quantitative dimension to this call: to increase the number of Jews, to increase the presence of life in the world. There is also a qualitative dimension to this commitment: to treat a person as a being of infinite value. To feed a starving child, to heal a sick person, to nurture the uniqueness of a wife or a husband are in themselves all sacred acts.'[9]

Jewish memory through expanded Jewish responsibility in the world is charged with ultimate significance even to the point of restoring the plausibility of belief in God. This leads to the other great religious act after the Holocaust, taking power. Greenberg sees Jewish empowerment, especially in Israel, as a 'response to the divine call to assume responsibility to achieve the goals of the covenant'.[10]

Yet, like Yerushalmi, Greenberg is mostly silent about the Palestinians and their hopes and dreams in Jerusalem. The Jewish drama of suffering in the Holocaust and redemption in Israel is enacted ritually, as if the Palestinians did not exist. Jewish responsibility does not extend to Palestinians, and the beautiful exhortations to 'treat the person as a being of infinite value' is abstracted from contemporary Jewish history where this responsibility could be exercised by Jews with the aid of power controlled by Jews.

Ironically, Greenberg's book was published in 1988 at the height of the first Palestinian uprising. News media images showed Israeli soldiers beating and killing unarmed Palestinians who were fighting for the restoration of their own dignity, taking responsibility for their own freedom and willing to suffer for it. Were they struggling, in Greenberg's words, to 'make a credible statement about God' by pointing to the God 'whose image it is'?[11]

One wonders if a third category of Jewish memory has been created, even as it remains unarticulated by most Jewish scholars. The injunction to remember God's acts in history and the peoples who have threatened Jewish existence is joined with the need to remember acts Jews have undertaken against others, in this case the Palestinian people. As with the first two injunctions, forgetting or pretending that the deeds have not taken place further ruptures Jewish history, allowing myths such as Jewish innocence and exclusive redemption to triumph. The balancing factor of history which grounds the work of God in the life of the people – in many ways the essence of the covenant – fades.

As the covenant becomes more and more mythicized, God becomes abstract or even peripheral to the people. The center of Jewish life, which is also the place of affirmation and resistance, begins to lose its force, and the people drift from cause to cause until there is only power or apathy to attract them. Religious and secular orthodoxies predominate as both refuse the tension of God and history.

In contemporary Jewish life, the Holocaust and Israel have assumed their rightful and complicated place within this void as emotional attachments to a mythologized history in which most Jews are not participants. Viewed from afar and uncritically, the

Holocaust and Israel may lose their place in history and assume a mythic status as protector of the void.

This need for revision is true for the Jewish liturgy of destruction as well. In his own work, David Roskies, Professor of Jewish Literature at Jewish Theological Seminary, explores remembrance in the context of Jewish writers and artists during the Holocaust. Roskies finds that in the midst of the Holocaust catastrophe, religious and secular writers and artists alike used the Jewish tradition of remembrance to articulate the difficulties, sorrow and anger of their predicament.

By using ancient Jewish archetypes of divine promise, election, the mission of Israel and its place among the nations, and counter-posing them to the present circumstances, Jewish writers and artists were simultaneously able to locate themselves in a history of suffering and promise over against the Nazi vision of the Third Reich *and* carry on a transcendental dispute with the God of the Jewish covenant. Here the interaction of myth and history is placed in full mobilization.

A narrative emerges which is fully engaged with the present and rooted deeply in the past. The history articulated reads almost as a liturgy, a liturgy of destruction, to be sure, but also a liturgy of resistance. An example is Yitzhak Katzenelson, a secular poet, who organized a public reading of the bible on the day the Warsaw ghetto was sealed. This was to demonstrate a continuity of history as a people rather than belief in God. At the same time Hillel Zeitlin, a modern religious existentialist, began translating the Psalms into Yiddish, and when his ghetto tenement was blockaded, Zeitlin arrived at the roundup point for deportation dressed in prayer shawl and tefillin.[12]

If the liturgy of destruction fulfills the Jewish understanding of myth and history in its deepest interaction, providing an identity, a strength, a framework for resistance and a search for meaning during the Holocaust, it also provides a space where Jewish ritual and recital interact. Memory here is recovery of an entire history, which includes myth, history, ritual and recital in a dynamic way.

The sense of collectivity is invoked within the context of individuality, transforming, in Roskies' words, 'collective disasters into individual rites of mourning and of individual deeds into a model of collective sacrifice'. What greater testimony to the strength of Jewish life can there be than the recognition of a common history, one filled with diversity and argumentation, suffering and resistance, where the collective and the individual find their place and thus plant the seeds for the continuation of the people, even in their darkest night?

The liturgy of destruction is a liturgy created by martyrs for themselves in continuity with the past and as a link to a future which the martyrs themselves will not be alive to witness. Their martyrdom is a sign of fidelity to history and the moment, to the covenant even in its shattering, and to a future that will rise from that martyrdom.[13]

The liturgy of destruction spans Jewish history, and the writers and artists of the Holocaust are heirs and innovators within that tradition. For the most part, contemporary Jewish thinkers serve as narrators of that liturgy, recovering and naming the disparate voices of the European diaspora. These thinkers enable the present generation of Jews to see the continuity of the tradition even as it seems to be shattering.

Paradoxically, the loss of tradition is the call for its survival, indeed the proof of its importance and vibrancy, if only the post-Holocaust generation will embrace it. Post-Holocaust writers and artists deal with these themes extensively, placing the traditional Jewish archetypes such as the Akedah, the Exodus, the covenant at Sinai, the destruction of the Temple and the pogrom in a radical and subversive context.

It is here that the problem surfaces. What is to be done with this liturgy of destruction and the archetypes as they are handed to the next generation? If, as Roskies states, the catastrophe itself endows the Jewish writer and artist with 'unprecedented authority', and, if, at the time when the 'traditional doctrines of redemption and retribution had lost their power to console, visual icons of Jewish suffering came to symbolize the staying power of the people', what will endow the symbols and structure of a secure and established Jewish life with purpose and meaning? Can the broken tablets pictured in Samuel Bak's *Proposal for a Monument*, or his *City of Jews*, which feature a devastated urban landscape with the tablets themselves a part of the tableaux, speak to Jews today?

In the *City of Jews* the only sign of life is a smoking chimney; the city itself is sinking under the weight of God's commandments, 'dying under the sign of its chosenness'. For Roskies, Bak's midrash (exposition and commentary) on Jewish history is as follows:

> To live as Jews means to uphold the covenant even as it is desecrated, to exist both in the shadow of eternity and on the

> brink of destruction. There is no return to the Decalogue except via Vilna and Ponar. The tablets have been broken – in order that they may be pieced together again. One cannot build them other than on ruins. The sacred symbols, though defiled, are the only ones left.[14]

The Holocaust itself has become a Jewish archetype, and this, too, is a reference point for the future. However, the Holocaust archetype is as ambiguous as it is powerful. The *City of Jews* represents a destruction which challenges the future to a depth of recollection and reconstruction which the present may be unable to bear. One cannot ignore the symbolism of dying under one's own chosenness, for it represents a deep rendering of the Holocaust experience.

Nor can one look askance at someone seeking to 'forget' that experience. For how can one 'remember' this city – which represents the collective experience of the Jewish people – without desiring to forget it at the same time? Surely there are ways of simultaneously remembering and forgetting, thus trivializing the Holocaust even as one employs the rhetoric derived from it.

Roskies sees the danger primarily in the universalization of the Holocaust which arises from the designation itself. Though the Latin word 'holocaust' refers to burnt sacrifices in the bible, the word itself is extrinsic to Jewish history. This being so, the term 'Holocaust' lacks the resonance of Jewish history and discourse and makes it available to the broader non-Jewish community, which is then free to define and redefine the parameters of the event or even compare their own experiences within that framework.

The danger Roskies sees is the diminution of the horror of the Holocaust and the loss of its particularity. This gives rise to a confusion by which the catastrophe, 'once the most private of Jewish concerns, becomes part of the public domain', with the resulting problem that 'external perceptions replace inner realities, and borrowed words and archetypes are enlisted to explain the meaning of destruction' to Gentiles but also to Jews.[15]

Here the fear of superficiality, trivialization and assimilation is raised again. The fear of assimilation is paramount as Roskies notes that the inner cadences of Jewish life are challenged by the invasion of foreign symbols, especially the Christian symbols of Christ's crucifixion found in the paintings of Marc Chagall and the work, at least in its interpretation by Christians, of Elie Wiesel. Roskies is caustic when he denotes the crossing of the boundary of Christian symbolism into Jewish life as a 'real breakthrough'.

Picturing the travails of the Jews as a crucifixion in a sense hands Christians a victory to their own claim of universality, at the same time overriding the internal dialogue and history of the Jewish community *vis-à-vis* the liturgy of destruction and the animosity between the two communities. However, the use of Jesus can also be a form of resistance, as in Uri Zvi Greenberg's statement against Jesus and the Christians who claim him, graphically laid out in the form of a cross. It can even be an attempt to speak to the Christians in a language which they can understand, forcing them to ponder their transgressions.

Still, the acceptance of Jewish evocations of the Holocaust in the non-Jewish world requires a self-censorship, an editing of particular Jewish symbols and inner dialogue. The understanding of writing and art becomes dependent on interpretations wholly foreign to the Jewish experience.

With Wiesel, this happens in the introduction of his work by the famous Catholic writer, François Mauriac, in his invocation of Wiesel and the Holocaust victims as a symbol of Christ's crucifixion. It ends by Wiesel highlighting the themes of existential doubt and the post-war isolation of the individual over the appeal to fight the anti-Semites who would consign the Holocaust to oblivion. As Roskies sees it, since 'no one in the literary establishment of the 1950s was ready to be preached to by a Holocaust survivor, existentialist doubt became the better part of valor'.[16]

The cost of this 'valor' is high, at least from Roskies' point of view. The theme of catastrophe particular to Jewish sensibility is a way of consoling fellow sufferers, and provides a message of hope and continuity; the theme of existential despair leaves the survivors in a generalized exile and breaks the dialogue between Eastern European writers and their Jewish audience. The replacement of the particular with a non-parochial message reduces the message of the Holocaust, as difficult and ambiguous as it is, to one of 'complete despair'. When Wiesel and others edit out the shared expressions of faith to concentrate on the terrifying plight of the individual, Roskies believes they embrace a cultural *rapprochement* and sever themselves from the Jewish liturgy of destruction.

The implication is that individual advancement and the larger cultural acceptance of their work takes precedence over fidelity to the family and communities that perished in the Holocaust.

Whether intentional or not, the universalization of the Holocaust carried out by Jews themselves is a form of alienation and a further exile from the Jewish ethos threatened with destruction in the Holocaust.

Implied but not specifically addressed is the most paradoxical of questions: that the near-universal attention that the Holocaust has received, in large part due to the ability of Chagall and Wiesel and others to communicate the horror of the event to those outside the Jewish world, may facilitate the loss of Jewish identification and understanding, except in the most vulgar and superficial modalities.[17]

What Roskies does not see is the possibility that Chagall, Wiesel and others might be attempting to bridge the gap between Jew and Christian for reasons other than acceptance and self-advancement. Perhaps they recognize that the shattering of the tablets represents the shattering of traditional Jewish discourse, and that the archetypes of Jewish culture and liturgy will be lost if not interpreted within a broader framework. Perhaps the danger of the Holocaust is so deeply felt by them that security takes precedence over anger; reconciliation is a necessity so that the next generation will remember the Holocaust rather than be faced with a similar event in their lives. The continuation of the Holocaust, even as an event of catastrophe much smaller than the destruction in Europe, might mean the end of the Jewish people.

The attempt to bridge the communities could also mean that these writers and artists retain faith in the possibility of the humanity of the 'other', a faith in the 'conversion' of Christianity to the plight and hope of the Jewish people through the recognition of Christian culpability in Jewish suffering. That this latter hope could come from the victims of the Holocaust who had no reason to harbor such hope seems incredible. Could the shattering of the tablets and the weight of God's chosenness mandate a final appeal for a breakthrough beyond the violence and destruction of human history?

Another possibility locates the theme of survival within the West and the birth of Israel. It could be that these writers and artists recognize that an appeal to remembrance in an expanding dialogue on the Holocaust is crucial to the post-war integration of the Jews into the West *and* the mobilization of support for Israel. The end of the Holocaust and the birth of Israel are separated by only three years, so that the emergence of post-Holocaust literature parallels the origins of the state.

As Yerushalmi and Roskies implicitly criticize this reconfigured midrash, they are also dependent on it. Yet even leaving aside this unannounced dependence, the criticism of the superficiality, vulgarization, even assimilationist aspects of Holocaust theology, remains abstract. The criticism falters when the missing connection to a life of depth is sought. There is no way back to the worlds that these authors explore.

But where is the road ahead? Or at least what paths need to be explored to create a Jewish framework worthy of the past and able to be passed on to the future? Can the myths of Jewish history even be brought into the dynamics of history so that Jewish purpose in the world will be grounded in reality? Can the liturgy of destruction be transformed into a liturgy of healing and creation?

Perhaps the answers to these questions can be found in confronting historical events which have been neglected or suppressed by the Jewish world. As Jews know all too well, on the other side of innocence and redemption lie those who are cast off and displaced, those made invisible and who are forgotten. It may be that the recovery of this history is the key to confronting the dangers which Yerushalmi and Roskies consider.

If memory is problematic, sometimes deceptive, even treacherous, does it also retain an explosive power which can transform a people's search for survival and identity? Can the memory of suffering inflicted on Jews one day come to terms with a suffering that Jews have inflicted on Palestinians? And could that dawning realization of the difficult struggle for survival and the loss of innocence propel the Jewish people into a search for life beyond being a victim or an oppressor? Perhaps such a recovery of memory can limit the bifurcation which is so much a part of Jewish life. It may also lead to a reconciliation with the 'enemy' which often as not portends a reconciliation with one's self.

For has the trauma of the Holocaust, which is remembered, recited and ritualized today more than at any time in Jewish history, led to a healing of the Jewish people? A corollary question is whether Jewish empowerment in the West and in Israel has healed Jews of fear, anger and the brokenness which post-Holocaust writers and artists have portrayed so vividly.

Through memorialization and power it is difficult to argue that Jews have finally put the era of Auschwitz behind them. One wonders if the theme of Auschwitz remains part of the landscape awaiting, at least in the Jewish psyche, a rebirth in a future scenario of destruction.

Can a healing between Jews and Palestinians become a bridge within and across the Holocaust? Is this healing the key to making Jewish consciousness whole again where now it is bifurcated? Is the desire to live with Palestinians in a renewed and transformed homeland for both peoples – the creation over time of a bi-national Israel/Palestine based on citizenship rather than ethnic or religious identification – a way of remembering the Holocaust for the future?

It is important that diverse Jewish thinkers, Yerushalmi and Roskies, but also Irena Klepfisz, Cynthia Ozick and Emil Fackenheim, point in this direction.

Irena Klepfisz is an essayist and poet. Her father, Michal Klepfisz, was an activist in the Bund and a member of the Jewish Fighters Organization in the Warsaw ghetto. In early 1943, she and her mother were smuggled outside the ghetto by her father, and he also smuggled in weapons and materials used to produce weapons later used in the ghetto uprising. On the second morning of the uprising, three days after his thirtieth birthday, Michal Klepfisz was killed while protecting other ghetto fighters as they escaped. After the war, Irena and her mother, Rose Perczykow Klepfisz, emigrated to Sweden and then the United States.

Klepfisz's experiences of the war, memories of her father and life with her surviving mother were, in retrospect, hardly easy. Grappling with the issue of Palestinians and Israeli power was no less easy, but in the end provided Klepfisz with an arena to come to a new understanding of the possibilities of personal and communal healing after the Holocaust. After traveling to Poland and Israel, Klepfisz helped organize in April 1988 the Jewish Women's Committee to End the Occupation of the West Bank and Gaza, which shortly thereafter began to hold weekly vigils in New York City at the offices of the Conference of Presidents of Major American Jewish Organizations.

The group's proposal to end the violent repression of the Palestinian uprising and to support an international peace conference and a two-state solution was often greeted with hostility. Some Jews insisted that the Holocaust precluded such political action. One Jewish man told Klepfisz that he wished she were buried in Poland like his own parents. A few Jews wished another holocaust on the demonstrators. Still others felt that their actions would lead all Jews, including them, 'back to the ovens'.

In different ways, Klepfisz and the Committee demonstrators were accused of disloyalty, of being collaborators with historical and contemporary Nazis. As Klepfisz writes: 'We were told that to give the Palestinians a state was to give Hitler his final victory, that our behavior was desecrating the Holocaust of the 1940s and ensuring the Holocaust of the 1990s, perhaps even the 1980s.'[18]

Understandably, Klepfisz experienced a mixture of shame, fear and anger, emotions she had experienced her entire life as a child of a ghetto fighter and a survivor. Still she remained resolute: 'Knowing that the world was passive and indifferent while six million Jews died, I have always considered passivity and indifference the worst of evils. Those who do nothing, I believe, are good German collaborators. I do not want to be a collaborator.' Klepfisz took seriously the admonition of a Palestinian woman whom she came to know in Jerusalem in 1987: 'Write about what you see. Write what is happening to us.'

In reflecting on the Palestinians' challenge, Klepfisz reflects on the disturbing analogies of Israel, Holocaust and the Palestinians and how they resonate in her life: '"What does it remind you of?" I ask my mother, and read her the *Newsday* article about the Palestinian men in Rufus: rounded up by the Israeli police, they're told to lie face down in a nearby field. "I know what it reminds me of", she answers and says nothing more.'

For Klepfisz, given the images etched in the collective consciousness of the Jewish people, how can this *not* remind Jews of the Holocaust?

> What is it that we have been asking everyone to remember? Is it not the fields of Ponary and those nameless fields on the outskirts of dozens of *shtetlekh* that we're all pledged to remember? Am I to feel better that the Palestinians from Rufus were not shot by the Israelis but merely beaten? As long as hundreds of Palestinians are not being lined up and shot, but are killed by Israelis only one a day, are we Jews free from worrying about morality, justice? Has Nazism become the sole norm by which Jews judge evil, so that anything that is not its exact duplicate is considered by us morally acceptable? Is that what the Holocaust has done to Jewish moral sensibility?[19]

Klepfisz extended these thoughts as she addressed a group of survivors on the 45th anniversary of the Warsaw ghetto uprising in

April 1988. Her talk begins with the idea of mourning and asks what it is that the survivors mourn. In the case of Anne Frank, for example, do the survivors grieve that she was deprived of being a great writer, or that she was deprived of the ability to nurture that which was inside of her, to explore the world around her, to enjoy the 'normal process of growing up free to experiment, to experience the pleasures of success, the difficulties of failure'.

For Klepfisz, Jews should mourn that Anne Frank was denied an 'ordinary, anonymous life'. That lost experience of the ordinary serves as a reminder and also ultimately a link to the present: 'I have come to believe that ordinariness is the most precious thing we struggle for, what the Jews of the Warsaw ghetto fought for. Not noble or abstract theories, but the right to go on living with a sense of purpose and a sense of self-worth – an ordinary life. It is this loss we mourn today.'

Klepfisz then issues her challenge specifically in relation to the Palestinian people; to apply the 'fierce outrage' of the ghetto fighters at the destruction of the ordinary life of their people to those who live on the other side of Jewish power. Jews are called upon to feel outrage whenever they see signs of the disruption of Palestinian common life:

> The hysteria of a mother grieving for the teenager who has been shot; a family stunned in front of a vandalized or demolished home; a family separated, displaced; arbitrary and unjust laws that demand the closing or opening of shops and schools; humiliation of a people whose culture is alien and deemed inferior; a people left homeless, without citizenship; a people living under military rule.[20]

In her moving address on the meaning of Holocaust memory as the sacredness of ordinary life, and by including and naming Palestinian life within the context of Jewish memory, Klepfisz implies what the Jewish community has yet to realize: that no matter what the resolution of the conflict, even were the agreements to fulfill the demands of justice and equality, the destruction of Palestinian life by Jews is now a part of Jewish history that must also be remembered.

Though Klepfisz does not state the corollary, it seems obvious that the image of the Warsaw ghetto uprising symbolizing the dignity and violation of ordinary Jewish life is complemented by the Palestinian uprising, which functions in a similar way for Palestinians.

This suggests that not only the violation of Palestinian life but the defence of that life must be remembered in Jewish history.

In this context those Jews who seek to defend Palestinians are to be remembered at the same liturgical moment, perhaps in the same liturgy, as the heroic Warsaw ghetto fighters. Klepfisz further intimates that the loss of the ordinary common life of any people is worthy of remembering, and that the destruction of that life by Jews threatens to violate the memory of the destruction of ordinary Jewish life. The fight to remember Jewish suffering is tied to the fight to mitigate or even reverse Palestinian suffering.

In Klepfisz, there is no mention of God. Her testimony, on the theoretical and theological levels at least, is more distant from God-language than that of Elie Wiesel. Holocaust thinkers are in a sharp, profound and angry dialogue with God; with many of the next generation that dialogue has ceased, been repressed or become inarticulate. Yet one wonders if active solidarity with Palestinians is an unspoken reassertion of this dialogue, a pre-theological action that represents an intuitive desire to create a framework from which speech about God may become possible again.

Is this solidarity an example of a counter-testimony to Auschwitz, a counter-testimony which the Jewish world did not expect and perhaps cannot accept? Perhaps this testimony could initiate a restoration of the image of God so desecrated in the Holocaust.

Emil Fackenheim is of importance here, for along with Wiesel he helped lay the groundwork for Jewish reflection on the Holocaust. In his early work, Fackenheim pointed to the difficulties of belief in God and the need for Jewish identification and solidarity. As for Wiesel, Israel represents the focal point for that solidarity, even as the rupture with God and the world continues.

Fackenheim understands that the answers to the pressing questions about God and the world invoked by the Holocaust are unanswerable in the present. However, the mobilization of the Jewish people cannot await these answers, as their complexity and depth can be addressed only over time in a community structure which survives the aftermath of the Holocaust. The additional covenant may provide a holding action while, over time, inquiry takes place. For Fackenheim, the threat to the community continues in the present, a threat that renders the questions mute. Only survival, especially in Israel, can provide the physical and psychological structure to continue on.[21]

Fackenheim's later work is important, as he explores the possibility of healing the rupture which came into being with the Holocaust. The Commanding Voice of Auschwitz, which for Fackenheim replaces the voice of the God once heard at Sinai, but is silent in the death camps, is the call to Jewish survival. Indeed, Fackenheim posits a commandment which issues from this voice, the 614th commandment, that forbids the handing of Adolf Hitler a posthumous victory by refusing to do whatever is necessary to survive as Jews, including and especially in Israel. This call remains, but is now complemented with the Jewish need for healing, a need Fackenheim articulates with the Hebrew word *tikkun,* meaning repair, restoration, mending.

Tikkun olam, the mending of the world, is necessary because of the unprecedented and inexhaustible horror of the Holocaust; *tikkun* is possible because of the unprecedented and inexhaustible wonder of resistance to the Holocaust among a minority of Jews and Christians. On the Jewish side, this resistance was diverse, from religious Jews who continued to hold fast to tradition and therefore to their dignity in the face of the ultimate attempt to destroy both, and those who, like the Warsaw ghetto fighters, fought the Nazis despite the odds against them. On the Christian side, there were principled protestors, like the German philosopher Kurt Huber and the Catholic priest Bernard Lichtenberg. In holding up the 'idea of man' and the 'Christian word', they forfeited their lives.

And yet for Fackenheim the greater witness came from those Christians who, without a great and noble cause, showed what in other circumstances would be considered ordinary decency: 'In the Holocaust world, a Gentile's decency, if shown toward Jews, made him into something worse than a criminal – an outlaw, vermin – just as were the Jews themselves; and as he risked or gave his life, there was nothing in the world to sustain him, except ordinary decency itself.' This Fackenheim names as a '*tikkun* of ordinary decency'.[22]

Though Fackenheim understands that this *tikkun* does not mean that ordinary decency has inherited the earth, it none the less, and like the Holocaust itself, has an ontological status. In fact, Jewish and Christian resistance to the violation of ordinary decency represents the healing of a rupture and becomes the ultimate ground of post-Holocaust thought and activity. For Fackenheim, then, these *tikkuns* ontologically root the moral necessity of the 614th commandment and the Commanding Voice of Auschwitz.

Humanist, Jewish and Christian fidelity give birth to a future philosophy, a future Judaism and a future Christianity. Though a future is possible because of fidelity in the past, post-Holocaust thought dwells between the extremes of despair and a certain faith. For Fackenheim, authentic *tikkun* is sought within the tension of despair and faith, affirming a 'fragmentariness' that is both incomplete and laden with risk.[23]

It is important that Fackenheim's understanding of *tikkun* connects the ontological with the ordinary. In this sense the retention of ordinary decency is itself a dual crossing of boundaries. The rupture of the Holocaust, ontological in its significance, creates a boundary in which the ordinary flow of life is demeaned, denigrated and made impossible. Because of this, ordinary decency is a crossing of the boundary within history and beyond; it is profoundly human and much more.

One might call the assertion of the ordinary a miracle, that is, a 'yes' to life that is being systematically destroyed. At the same time that the crossing of the boundaries is for life in its ordinariness, it is carried out with a threat to one's safety and often without the support of, or even actively against, the majority of the community. Therefore, the crossing of boundaries is a carrying of one's entire life toward others into a perilous unknown future which becomes, in an ultimate sense, a future for humankind. In a situation of utter horror, ordinary decency is found in the bonding of the ontological and the human.

The rupture, boundaries and *tikkun* that Fackenheim articulates are within Judaism and Christianity and between Jew and Christian; they are expressed by both within their commitments to Israel. In fact for Fackenheim, *tikkun* is Israel itself, the place of future life for Jews and the place of commitment to Jewish life by Christians.

Yet even this *tikkun* is fragmentary, limited in terms of Israel's size, capacity, defence and its ability to guarantee its Jewish citizens a Jewish culture or a strong Jewish identity. Fackenheim sees the enemies of Israel as implacable, attempting to renew exile for its Jewish inhabitants. Internally, the exile for the Jewish people continues with the denial of the obligation to further identifiable Jewish life in response to the Holocaust.

Fackenheim does not pursue this analysis in relation to the Palestinians and, like Wiesel, would surely object to such a proposal. One wonders if this exile which Fackenheim analyses continues because a further rupture has occurred between Jews and Palestinians, a rupture which itself is in need of *tikkun*. It could be that this *tikkun* is also both ontological and ordinary, and that only the assertion of ordinary decency in this time of trial could mend the contemporary world, a mending which Fackenheim so much desires.

It could also be that those Jews who embrace Palestinians are simply carrying on the *tikkun* of Jews and Christians in the Holocaust, and therefore preparing a possible future for both peoples. Will Palestinians write one day of the righteous Jews as Fackenheim writes of the righteous Gentiles?

Could this ordinary and unprecedented *tikkun* be a search for a covenantal framework, which in asserting ordinary decency over against political practicalities and enduring in a tension of fragmentariness, is none the less affirming a grounding that has been undermined and even in some cases destroyed? Surely these boundary crossings, though still incomplete and risky, represent a search for a *tikkun* which has evaded the Jewish world.

The 615th Commandment

Yitzhak Rabin's assassin, Yigal Amir, tried to forestall the movement toward the end of the era of Auschwitz. As with Baruch Goldstein,[24] the sense that a solidarity could be extended to Palestinians threatened the Holocaust world-view they cultivated and felt at home in.

Even the first tentative steps toward a restoration of the ordinary were seen as fundamental betrayals of the Commanding Voice of Auschwitz. Political compromise violated the boundaries of Auschwitz, as both Goldstein and Amir felt Palestinians to be the new Nazis. The era of Auschwitz, in their view, had to continue lest Jews fall into a lethargy that would allow the actual Auschwitz to be reconstructed. Continuing the era of Auschwitz is following the will of God, whose renewed voice can be heard in the Jewish settlements that spearhead the reclamation of the greater land of Israel.

In the commentary on the assassination of Rabin, the need to mute religious voices was set forth. Cynthia Ozick, a Jewish novelist and conservative commentator, sought to refute those who placed the issue of Jews and Palestinians in a utopian, transcendent framework, arguing that the issue of messianic perfectibility from the right and the left encouraged destruction and death. For Ozick, the situation suffers from a 'common arrogance' relating to this search for perfectibility: 'There are too many seers in the land, too many utopians. There are too many dreams of Eden, right and left, pious and profane. A murdered prime minister will not increase holiness. A Palestinian state will not insure paradise.'

Surely Ozick is correct; the issue is not one of messianic perfectibility. Instead, the issue of Jews and Palestinians could be one of covenantal responsibility. The removal of politics from millenarian fantasy is quite different from seeing a religious grounding and basis from which ethical and political judgements arise.

In the wake of the assassination, Michael Walzer, a Jewish ethicist and liberal commentator, also longs for a naked public square in Israel where the 'politics of calculation and restraint', a politics 'without God, without myth and fantasy, without eternal enemies, without sacred causes or holy ground', triumphs over a religious politics.[25]

The truth is that all competing parties within the Jewish narrative appeal to Jewish history and the covenant, however interpreted, for their understanding of the present and the path to the future. There is reason for such an appeal, for Israel does represent a dramatic, difficult and ambiguous unfolding of Jewish history. Rabin's meeting with Yassir Arafat was highly charged in the mind of Amir and no doubt in the minds of most Jews, for more was represented than politics in their first reluctant handshake.

The facing of the 'other' – the new 'other' of Jewish history – was recognized as a rendezvous in Jewish history. Such a facing of the 'other' should be seen in the context of the Holocaust and the 1967 war as the possibility of ending an era of history as well. The handshake represented the possibility of ending a cycle of suffering and violence which Jews have endured and now have perpetrated. When Rabin spoke of ending that cycle, one felt an opening toward a responsibility grounded in history and hope.

This opening could be the culmination of a history of suffering and violence and the beginning of a reconciliation with the traumas of Jewish history: a possible healing of the Holocaust that has not occurred through Jewish empowerment in Israel and in some ways has grown deeper through the conquest of another people.

Surely, the humiliation of the Palestinian people, which has reminded many Jews of the historic humiliation of the Jewish people, cannot heal the Jewish people. To do so would require working through the idea of the covenant itself; mobilized and militarized after the disaster of the Holocaust where God and humanity were found wanting, the possibility of healing by ending the cycle of suffering and violence is itself jarring.

For if the covenant, once given, now broken, and found again in the Commanding Voice of Auschwitz, is demobilized and demilitarized, what will happen to Jewish identity, Jewish defence, Jewish assertion and Jewish power? Could that covenant promised to and accepted by Jews, a covenant carried throughout a long and difficult history, now be renewed by sharing it in the promised land with another people?

The next step of Jewish history might begin with the realization that the cycle of displacement and death can only end with the sharing of a land and therefore a history which once featured and even now promises an aloneness and exclusivity. *The new challenge of the covenant is to find Jewish chosenness within and among those who share the land often called holy.*

Paradoxically, Ozick laid the groundwork for such an understanding years ago in an essay, 'Notes Toward Finding the Right Question'. Though this essay addresses the issue of feminism, asserting that the inclusion of Jewish women in Judaism on an equal basis with men is a sociological rather than a theological question, it may apply to the inclusion of Palestinians in Jewish life as well. After arguing that contributions to Jewish life must be valued regardless of whether they come from males or females, Ozick sees the urgency of that inclusion not with regard to the upsurge of Jewish feminism, but in light of the Holocaust:

> The timing is significant because the present generation stands in a shockingly new relation to Jewish history. It is we who come after the cataclysm. We, and all the generations to follow, are, and will continue to be into eternity, witness generations to Jewish loss. What was lost in the European cataclysm was not only the Jewish past – the whole life of civilization – but also a major share of the Jewish future. We will never be in possession of the novels Anne Frank did not live to write. It was not only the intellect of a people in its prime that was excised, but the treasure of a people in its potential.[26]

Because of this loss and the resultant mournful language, 'having lost so much and so many', for Jews there are no longer any 'unrelated issues'. However, there is a 'thick wall of scandal' separating Jews from the covenant, and, according to Ozick, this scandal is twofold. On the one hand, the scandal denies a decimated people the needed contributions of women; on the other hand, the very injustice denies women their rightful place in Jewish history, especially after the Holocaust.

Ozick's discussion of injustice is important: 'What is injustice? We need not define it. Justice must be defined and redefined, but not injustice. How to right a wrong demands ripe deliberation, often ingenuity. But a wrong needs only to be seen, to be seen to be wrong. Injustice is instantly intuited, felt, recognized, reacted to.'

The recognition of injustice gives rise to the feeling that there is 'something missing'. In Ozick's understanding, that is the reason that the written law, found in the Hebrew bible, is complemented later by the oral law found in the Talmud. The written and oral law become an extended Torah and covenant that in every instance 'strives to teach No to unrestraint, No to victimization, No to dehumanization.'

When the Torah is silent in relation to injustice, injustice calls the Torah into question: 'Where is the missing Commandment that sits in judgment on the world?' With regard to women, the question is strong: 'Where is the commandment that will say, from the beginning of history until now, *Thou shalt not lessen the humanity of women*?'[27]

When the Torah is silent on injustice, it is unable to judge. Instead it 'consorts' with the world at large. It is as if the covenant is in search of the missing commandment which will return it to its proper role in the world and remove the wall of scandal separating the people from the covenant and the people from each other. The reaction of the Jewish people to these missing commandments throughout history has been to strengthen the covenant by discovering new commandments to confront injustice. As Ozick writes, to strengthen Torah is to 'contradict injustice; to create justice, not through fragmentary accretions of *pilpul* but through the cleansing precept of justice itself'.[28]

Ozick relates the unfolding of Jewish teaching and living – the unfolding of the covenant – to the search for missing commandments. When found and implemented, these commandments are recognized after the fact as having been born of the covenant itself. The next step in Jewish life is in retrospect obvious and granted validity as the reality that it addresses becomes an acceptable part of life.

Therefore the commandment about women is within the Torah before it is spoken and recognized as it is added. The covenant unfolds as new questions are asked and answered: the covenant expands as the people and their history journey through time. The next question which demands action is in response to injustice that, if allowed to exist over time, perverts the covenant. A thick wall of scandal is erected which can only be overcome when the Torah ceases to consort with that which created the scandal in the first place.

How many Jews hear the commandment, '*Thou shalt not lessen the humanity of Palestinians*?' Did Rabin's soldiers hear it when they had difficulty carrying out the 'harsh and cruel' action of expelling Palestinians from Lydda and Ramle? Did Rabin himself hear the commandment when he wrote of this difficulty in his memoirs? Did the Israeli censors hear it when they refused to allow the inclusion of that passage in Rabin's published memoirs? Perhaps Rabin heard it again when he invoked the image of a shared humanity at the signing of the first accord in September 1993: 'We, like you, are people – people who want to build a home. To plant a tree. To love – to live side by side with you. In dignity. In empathy. As human beings. As free men.'[29]

This commandment was heard in the Lebanon war in the late 1970s and early 1980s by Israeli soldiers and Jewish poets reflecting on their actions in this most controversial of Israel's wars. In fact, this commandment was refracted in a most contentious way, through the lens of the Holocaust. James Young, a historian of Holocaust literature and Holocaust memorials, finds an inversion of Holocaust imagery in the experience of the Lebanon war. For the first time, Jews began to see themselves less as victims than as perpetrators.[30]

As Young understands it, instead of recalling traditional Jewish archetypes of Roskies' liturgy of destruction to apply to the deaths of Israeli soldiers or their bereaved families, Israeli poets 'recalled such figures more often to depict the death and suffering of others, especially that of Arab children'. As an example, Young cites the poem of Efraim Sidon who uses remembrance of the Holocaust specifically to undermine justification for the Lebanon war:

> I accuse the children in Sidon and Tyre
> Whose numbers are still uncounted
> Three-year-olds, seven-year-olds, and others of all ages,
> Of the crime of living next door to terrorists.
> If you hadn't lived near them, children,
> You could have been students today.
> Now you will be punished.

Sidon then continues in an ironic way blaming everyone in Lebanon for the Holocaust:

> I accuse the residents of Lebanon – all of them.
> For the Nazi mistreatment of us in the World War.
> Because from generation to generation, everyone must see
> himself
> As if he were destroying Hitler
> Always, always
> And that's what Begin is doing.
>
> I accuse you all!
> Naturally.
> Because I am always, always the victim.[31]

It was also heard in the first Palestinian uprising when the inversion of the Holocaust and Israeli power was even more intense. Two stories from the Palestinian uprising make this connection of Palestinian and Jewish history.

The first dates from January 1988, one month after the Palestinian uprising had begun, when an Israeli captain was summoned to his superior. The captain was given instructions to carry out arrests in the village of Hawara, outside Nablus. The arrest of innocent young Palestinians is hardly out of the ordinary, but the further instructions provided to the officer – what to do to those Palestinians after their arrest – were disturbing. His conscience would not allow him to carry out these instructions unless he was directly ordered to do so. Having then received the direct order, the captain, with a company of forty soldiers, boarded a civilian bus, arriving at Hawara at eleven o'clock in the evening.

The local *muhktar* was given a list of twelve persons to round up, which he did, and the twelve sat on the sidewalk in the center of the village, offering no resistance. Yossi Safid describes what followed:

> The soldiers shackled the villagers, and with their hands bound behind their backs, they were led to the bus. The bus started to move and after 200–300 meters it stopped beside an orchard. The 'locals' were taken off the bus and led into the orchard in groups of three, one after another. Every group was accompanied by an officer. In the darkness of the orchard the soldiers also shackled the Hawara residents' legs and laid them on the ground. The

> officers urged the soldiers to 'get it over with quickly, so that we can leave and forget about it'. Then flannel was stuffed into the Arabs' mouths to prevent them from screaming and the bus driver revved up the motor so that the noise would drown out the cries. Then the soldiers obediently carried out the orders they had been given: to break the arms and legs by clubbing the Arabs; to avoid clubbing them on their heads; to remove their bonds after breaking their arms and legs, and to leave them at the site; to leave one local with broken arms but without broken legs so he could make it back to the village on his own and get help.

The mission was carried out; the beatings were so fierce that most of the wooden clubs used were broken. Thus was born the title of the article detailing this action: 'The Night of the Broken Clubs'.[32]

The second story occurred just months after the beatings had begun when Marcus Levin, a physician, was called up for reserve duty in the Ansar 2 prison camp. When he arrived, Levin met two of his colleagues and asked for information about his duties. The answer: 'Mainly you examine prisoners before and after an investigation.' Levin responded in amazement, 'After the investigation?' which prompted the reply, 'Nothing special, sometimes there are fractures. For instance, yesterday they brought a twelve-year-old boy with two broken legs.' Dr. Levin then demanded a meeting with the camp commandant and told him, 'My name is Marcus Levin and not Josef Mengele, and for reasons of conscience I refuse to serve in this place.' A doctor who was present at the meeting tried to calm Levin with the following comment: 'Marcus, first you feel like Mengele, but after a few days you get used to it.' Hence the title of an article written about this incident: 'You Will Get Used to Being a Mengele'.[33]

Ozick states that to right a wrong demands 'ripe deliberation, often ingenuity'. Perhaps the hearing of this commandment – illustrated by spoken word and affirmed in public in ironic, accusatory, haunting and beautiful ways – simply leapt ahead of Rabin's ability to implement these words with concrete deliberation and ingenuity. Perhaps the commandment, once uttered, is so powerful that the prospects of implementation have to lag behind the recognition of the injustice itself. For if recognition and implementation occur simultaneously, the fear is that all will be lost, that the enterprise of empowerment will be undermined, and that instead of steadfast purpose, a sense of confusion and remorse might predominate. Was

Rabin balancing the hope and fear of finding the missing commandment of his own personal life and the life of his people because it was so earthshaking and explosive?

In the context of the Torah and the covenant, then, Amir's assassination of Rabin debased both. Amir thought that by murdering Rabin he could banish the commandment against lessening the humanity of the Palestinians. He was frightened of the commandment's corollary: the recognition that the covenant can only unfold with the understanding that Jewish and Palestinian destiny is a shared one, and the only question is to how that humanity and destiny will be shared. By murdering Rabin, Amir was really attempting to murder the covenant itself.

From this perspective, the condemnation of Amir by most commentators – including liberal commentators like Amos Oz and Michael Walzer who favour a 'divorce' of Jews and Palestinians – should be seen as a holding operation to isolate the murderer, and in so doing displace and manage the missing commandment which continues to surface. Amir and Walzer are, in a paradoxical way, to be seen together as guardians of a covenant that consorts, one speaking in overt religious language, the other seeking to banish that language completely.

Ozick does not analyse how missing commandments are found, who is likely to find them, or how, once found, they are to be implemented. If injustice is obvious, when does it become so? Are there stages of development when what is obvious in retrospect becomes obvious in the present? Does the community see the obvious, or do leaders understand before the people?

One wonders if the generation that recognizes injustice can also find the missing commandment. Or does that await the next generation? Do the leaders who participate in implementing the commandment do so with pure intentions and backgrounds or do they come to understand injustice because they have helped to create or maintain it? Can the missing commandment, once located, be lost again for the moment or forever, or once found is there a momentum which, like the cycle of violence, takes on a life of its own?

What happens to those victimized while the search for the new commandment takes place is another important question. Do they simply wait out the process and celebrate as the victorious community comes to grips with its own complicity? Are the victims of injustice better off with the assassins or the managers of the covenant? Are the oppressed simply suffering students, learning their own potentialities when empowerment, in the long cycle of history, finally comes their way? Or is the struggle against injustice the path toward finding the missing commandment and thus as essential to the history of the oppressor as it is to the oppressed?

This latter reality points to the interdependence of victor and victim. The 'other' holds the key through its oppression and the struggle against that oppression, and the way forward for the powerful can only be found when the 'other' is seen within the history of the powerful.

The oppressed, then, serve as a permanent reminder of the victors' capacity for injustice and as judgement on whether the found commandment has been implemented. The commandment, '*Thou shalt not lessen the humanity of Palestinians*', is a reminder to Jews and renders judgement on the Jewish past, present and future.

Helicopter gunships at the heart of Jewish history

The Al-Aqsa intifada provided another possibility to implement this commandment and yet once again the Jewish community failed to listen. In fact, Jewish leadership mobilized to make sure that any assertion of commonality between Jew and Palestinian was denied. Rather than accepting blame for the continuation of the occupation, blame was placed on the Palestinians for 'refusing' the possibility of peace.

The Israeli policy of assassinating Palestinian leaders, a strategy designed to deny the Palestinians their next generation of leadership, was a demonstration of force rooted in humiliation. The reoccupation of Palestinian areas, the virtual imprisonment of Yassir Arafat in Ramallah through the stationing of tanks only yards away from his compound, and Israel's refusal to allow Arafat to attend Christmas service in Bethlehem were more than security measures. They were attempts to further lessen the humanity of Palestinians in the eyes of Jews, the world and even among Palestinians themselves.

At the same time there were Israeli soldiers who refused service in the occupied territories and manifestos released by Israeli organizations that demanded, albeit in different language, a recognition of Palestinian dignity and the right of Palestinians to self-determination.

In June 2001, B'Tselem, the Israeli Information Center for Human Rights in the Occupied Territories, released a report detailing the human rights abuses of the Israeli military. This report covered such topics as the Israeli assassination policy, the siege that Palestinian civilians were undergoing, and a detailed map of the occupied territories including Israeli settlements, by-pass roads and security zones.

On Israel's assassination policy, B'Tselem reports:

> These killings are part of an open policy to assassinate Palestinians suspected of acts of violence against Israelis. Far from being a new phenomenon, Israel has carried out assassinations for over 30 years. Over the course of the previous intifada, Israeli undercover units assassinated 'wanted' Palestinians in the Occupied Territories as well ... The assassination policy violates the right to life, the most fundamental of all human rights, enshrined in international and Israeli law ... A country that wants to be part of democratic, law-abiding countries cannot justify such a blatant violation of legal principles and basic human values.[34]

At the same time, Gush Shalom, an Israeli grassroots peace movement, formulated and distributed a manifesto entitled '80 Theses for a New Peace Camp'. The thrust of this manifesto was that the Palestinian historical narrative of dislocation and destruction was valid not only for Palestinians, but for Israelis and Jews as well. This re-evaluation of Israeli and Palestinian history, emphasizing their historic and future interconnectedness, approached the 615th commandment without a religious sensibility.

For Gush Shalom, the inability of Israeli negotiators and decision makers to understand the perspective of Palestinians led to the demise of the Madrid–Oslo process. They state:

- The Madrid–Oslo process failed because the two sides were seeking to realize conflicting goals.
- The goals of each of the two sides emanated from their basic national interests. They were shaped by their historical narratives, by their disparate views of the conflict over the last 120 years. The Israeli national historical version and the Palestinian national historical version are entirely contradictory, on the whole and in every single detail.
- The negotiators and the decision makers on the Israeli side acted in complete oblivion of the Palestinian national narrative. Even when they had sincere goodwill to come to a solution, their efforts were doomed to fail as they could not understand the national desires, traumas, fears and hopes of

the Palestinian people. While there is no symmetry between the two sides, the Palestinian attitude was similar.

- Resolution of such a long historical conflict is possible only if each side is capable of understanding the other's spiritual-national world and willing to approach them as an equal. An insensitive, condescending and overbearing attitude precludes any possibility of an agreed solution.

This is why the Barak government, which initially inspired so much hope, failed. This is also the reason why the old peace camp collapsed with the end of the Barak government. Gush Shalom sees the role of the new Israeli peace camp as ending false myths and a simplified, one-sided view of the conflict. Gush Shalom continues:

- This does not mean that the Israeli narrative should automatically be rejected and the Palestinian narrative unquestionably accepted. But it does require open-minded listening and understanding of the other position in the historical conflict, in order to bridge the two national narratives.
- Any other way will lead to an unending continuation of the conflict, with periods of ostensible tranquility and conciliation frequently interrupted by eruptions of violent hostile actions between the two nations and between Israel and the Arab world. Considering the pace of development of weapons of mass destruction, further rounds of hostility could lead to the destruction of all sides of the conflict.[35]

It is important to see the documents of B'Tselem and Gush Shalom in the context of Jewish memory. In the face of state power, both the documents and the people who produced them are weak and relatively powerless. In terms of the Jewish community in Israel and around the world, they remain for the most part unknown.

If the organizations are unknown, the ideas they present and represent are even less known. Who among ordinary Jews knows that there are Jewish Israeli soldiers who refuse service in the occupied territories because their conscience will not allow it? How many Jews know of jail terms for these conscientious objectors?

In January 2002 a text announcing a group of officers and soldiers refusing to serve in the occupied territories was published in the Israeli newspaper *Ha'aretz*. The statement, which carried 52 reservist signatories, is worth citing at length:

> We, reserve combat officers and soldiers of the Israel Defence Forces [IDF], who were raised upon the principles of Zionism, sacrifice and giving to the people of Israel and to the state of Israel, who have always served in the front lines, and who were the first to carry out any mission, light or heavy, in order to protect the state of Israel and strengthen it;
>
> We, combat officers and soldiers who have served the state of Israel for long weeks every year, in spite of the dear cost to our personal lives, have been on reserve duty all over the Occupied Territories, and were issued commands and directives that had nothing to do with the security of our country, and that had the sole purpose of perpetuating our control over the Palestinian people;
>
> We, whose eyes have seen the bloody toll this Occupation exacts from both sides;
>
> We, who sensed how the commands issued to us in the Territories, destroy all the values we had absorbed while growing up in this country;
>
> We, who understand now that the price of Occupation is the loss of IDF's human character and the corruption of the entire Israeli society;
>
> We, who know that the Territories are not Israel, and that all settlements are bound to be evacuated in the end;
>
> We hereby declare that we shall not continue to fight this War of the Settlements.
>
> We shall not continue to fight beyond the 1967 borders in order to dominate, expel, starve and humiliate an entire people.
>
> We hereby declare that we shall continue serving in the Israel Defence Forces in any mission that serves Israel's defence.
>
> The missions of occupation and oppression do not serve this purpose and we shall take no part in them.[36]

As disturbing and equally unknown to most Jews is the media manipulation of crisis that affects the deepest aspects of Jewish history. Just after the Al-Aqsa uprising began, a briefing was held between Nachman Shai, the Israeli government spokesperson, and

Danny Yatom, national security adviser to Prime Minister Barak. In that briefing Shai underscored the need to compete in the media battle in the United States, a battle that Shai felt Israel was losing.

To counter negative reports about Israel's response to the uprising, Shai put together a committee of ten to twenty Israelis to plot a media strategy in the United States. 'And I told them,' Shai reported to Yatom, 'we are losing the media battle, and it is our job to put each of you on television to call the Palestinians liars. We have to win the media war to win the larger war.' Top aides to Shimon Peres and former Rabin people were all assigned tasks to reverse the media war. Singled out as carrying anti-Israel propaganda was CNN, which had employed two Palestinian reporters. Shai sought to pressure CNN to replace the Palestinians with 'pro-Israeli reporters who are willing to tell our side of the story'.[37]

At the very same time Eyal Rozenberg, a corporal in the Israeli Defence Forces, was making a decision based on conscience that would profoundly affect his life. That decision, to refuse to further serve his country in the IDF, was outlined in a letter that he sent to his commanding officer, Corporal Shaul Shahar. In the letter, Rozenberg outlines his struggle with the history of Israel from its creation to its response to the current Palestinian uprising.

His accusations would be seen by most Jews as extreme, yet they lay bare an aspect of Jewish history that again is almost completely unknown to most Jews. His current argument with military service is laid out almost poetically:

> A military that provides support for the construction of settlements in occupied territories and maintains them in the face of local popular resistance; a military that forcibly conscripts its citizens into its service, jailing those who refuse to work for it; a military that wins every war while planting the seeds of the next one; a military that makes use of the labor of its citizens to do business with questionable parties – whose acquisitions of military knowledge, equipment, and services is even more questionable – in transactions of nearly unimaginable scale; a military whose officers are free to ignore even its own orders without fear of judicial action by their subordinates; a military that is all this, yet continues to call itself the 'Defence Forces,' claims to have kept the 'purity of arms,' and maintains the pretense of being a 'people's army'. May no one be a part of it!

When Rozenberg initially voiced these thoughts to another officer, the officer's response stayed with him. He told Rozenberg that at the end of the day he must be able to look himself in the mirror and accept what he sees. Rozenberg's response was that the reflection in the mirror was too difficult for him to accept: 'As I continue to work for you while you slaughter a conquered people, I am living a lie, and this lie will reflect upon me from that mirror.' Rozenberg concludes, 'I may not be a person of strong character, but I can confidently state that I will never again work for the Israeli military, and that I will not be deterred by bars, locks, harassment, physical abuse, or any other sanction I may be facing.'[38]

Several paradoxes ensue. In a time when state power is controlled by Jews in Israel, there are Jews who in *their practice of life* and at great sacrifice testify to the humanity of Palestinians by recognizing their right to justice. This testimony is an act of compassion, one that disturbs an asserted Jewish consensus of unity and silence in relation to Palestinian resistance.

In a profound sense, Palestinian resistance to Israeli power stimulates Jewish resistance to Israeli power, which in turn becomes a point of reflection on Jewish history. The cataloging of Israeli human rights abuses, the drafting of a manifesto on a new sense of Jewish and Palestinian history, the refusal to carry arms against an occupied people, become forms of hope for the future. It is the foundation of a new memory related to Jewish struggle and suffering, to the events of Holocaust and Israel, in a new solidarity with those who feel the force of Jewish memory against them.

Still the question remains: who will remember this evolving memory? Who will record and ritualize these *tikkuns* of ordinary decency? Who will speak in synagogues and on holy days around the family table of this attempt to separate the thick wall of scandal surrounding the covenant? Or will these testimonies and witnesses be erased from Jewish memory and history? Will the liturgy of destruction now inclusive of Palestinians be remembered only by those Jews and Palestinians who participated in these events?

In 1990 David Vital, a historian of Zionism, wrote a fascinating book entitled *The Future of the Jews: A People at the Crossroads*. In this book he postulated that the Jews for the first time in history were undergoing what might be an irreversible separation into two nations, Israel and the diaspora. One reason Vital gives is that the experience of nationhood in Israel and modernity in the diaspora, especially in the United States, is so different that eventually these two groups of Jews will have little in common with each other. But that division, while real, is also too neat.

Vital offers a second, more telling reason for the increasing disjunction among elements of the Jewish community. In his view, geographic differences among Jews and Jewish communities are less important than a division over sensibilities and the future. In short, the division among Jews has less to do with traditional law or ritual – struggles important in the past – than they have to do with conflicting views of the 'aims, methods, and even the propriety of collective action by Jews'. According to Vital, different communities of Jews increasingly inhabit different mental and philosophical worlds.[39]

A decade later, the question seems even more urgent. Vital is correct: Jews are being split apart less in terms of their experience of Israel and America than in relation to conscience and what Jews are willing to do and what they will refuse in terms of Jewish history and memory. Instead of splitting apart around issues of geography and culture, a civil war of conscience has begun. Thus it is no coincidence that the dissenting opinions of Israeli Jews are carried to a wide audience in the U.S. by the Jewish progressive journal *Tikkun*, itself a seeker after a covenant without the thick wall of scandal.

Though many see the Jewish civil war as a battle over politics, with each side reading the other side out of Jewish history, the battle is really over Jewish memory and what that memory calls Jews to in the present. A sense of isolation, of being under assault, of being misunderstood, as always and everywhere being singled out, as always one step from a new persecution, is part of Jewish memory, to be sure.

But the struggle for an interdependent empowerment, for justice and ethics, for risk-taking to achieve what seems unachievable is also part of Jewish memory. With this struggle is the sense, again rooted in memory, of remnant, of persecutions but also new beginnings. Solidarity with the Palestinian struggle might find its deepest roots here, in this alternative history that Jews of conscience seek to keep alive as vital to Jewish identity.

Yet it is also true that memory as it resides in Jewish institutional life is clearly on the other side. And with the Al-Aqsa uprising, many Jewish moderates and even those on the Jewish left have retreated to the safe confines of the call for Jewish unity. In fact, the very call for a new Jewish peace camp is indicative of the problems inherent in Jewish peace politics and organizations, a sometimes patronizing position taken by Jews of speaking for Palestinians and setting the parameters of Palestinian self-assertion.

Most Jews in the peace camp have seen Palestinian freedom within the reclaiming of Jewish innocence, so that we as Jews could retreat to the more comfortable sense of Jewish innocence, and also see the violation of that innocence as an aberration rather than considered Jewish and Israeli aggression. What Jews have not faced in the last two thousand years is the possibility that Jewish power and the Jewish community can be mobilized for something that is not only aberrationally wrong but fundamentally flawed.

I wonder what will happen to Jewish identity if the process of conquering the Palestinian people is completed. Most progressive Jews argue for Palestinian freedom in a two-state solution, though that leaves Palestinians with less than 30 per cent of their original territory. What happens if even this disparity is not honored, if Jerusalem is not shared and if settlements, by-pass roads and security zones are maintained on a permanent basis? What if the Palestinians in whatever is declared a state are mostly free to simply police themselves, without land or resources to grow and flourish? What if most of the world and even many Jews themselves realize that an apartheid-like, ghettoized existence is the only political reality that Israel allows for the future of the Palestinian people?

Thus the more difficult questions are as yet unspoken in a generation dealing with the aftermath of the Holocaust and the rise of Israel and Palestinian resistance to Israeli power. Yerushalmi, Roskies, Fackenheim and Ozick are blind to these possibilities *as if Jews are not capable of permanently conquering another people*. B'Tselem and Gush Shalom struggle against this permanent conquering but are politically too weak to change the course of Israel.

Perhaps the Jewish tradition is not capable of handling this possibility. Certainly there are very few Jews who have thought out this possibility and considered the ramifications of such an event.

For with all our flaws and limitations as a people, I doubt that it is possible to consider Judaism without justice. Is it possible to be Jewish with helicopter gunships hovering at our center? Is it possible to be Jewish with atrocity infecting Jewish language and ritual and with Jewish ethical action permanently shadowed by the oppression of another people?

Yet the question must be posed. Is it already too late?

The accumulating evidence suggests that it may be. During the Al-Aqsa uprising Meron Benvenisti, the former deputy mayor of Jerusalem, wrote with passion:

> There is a feeling that is familiar to anyone who reads accounts of history's catastrophes – profound sorrow and impotent rage at the myopia, arrogance, stupidity, cowardice, irrelevant considerations, and sloppy thinking that sets leaders on the path to disaster. A reader painfully pinches himself – the writing was on the wall, the signs were so clear and the results so predictable that it is simply impossible to believe that the catastrophe was indeed allowed to happen.

It is then that the reader – indeed an entire people – looks for explanations. Is this present impasse inevitable?, Benvenisti asks. Does the leadership of Israel chart a new path or embrace an old one? Is there any way to reverse a process of disintegration and destruction?[40]

While Benvenisti pleads for a reversal of a policy of violence and humiliation, his earlier work, *Sacred Landscape: The Buried History of the Holy Land Since 1948*, analyses policies of Israel that speak to a longer process which continues today. In a provocative chapter entitled 'Ethnic Cleansing', Benvenisti writes of the changing circumstances of the Zionist movement as it accomplished its goal of statehood in 1948. A major theme of this chapter is how the Zionist movement – and later Jews in general – did not understand that the achievement of statehood necessitated a different relationship to ideology and to power. As a result, the war between Jews and Arabs in Palestine, like the events and tragedies of any war, took on another dimension once the state of Israel was declared. The movement from an independence struggle to state power necessitated a transition in perspective and policy formulation.

The tragedy is that this transition was never made. As Benvenisti understands the transition, Zionist policies of the pre-state period – with their symbols and perceptions of the Arab community – had to change and expand as state power was established. Yet this did not occur:

> Israel's heads of state and their agents had to learn to differentiate between the actions of ethnic leaders with no state authority – waging intercommunal war with similar groups, without government-sanctioned means of enforcement at their disposal –

> and those perpetrated by heads of state with the ability to pass laws and to enforce them by means of a standing army subject to their absolute authority.

Though the deeds might be the same, as is the suffering of the victims, the moral point of view shifts as Benvenisti believes that the 'obligations and rights of the leader of an ethnic minority without sovereignty are completely different from those of a head of state that defines itself as democratic and liberal and has pretensions of preserving universal norms'.[41]

Thus destruction of the Palestinian landscape which Benvenisti has observed before and after the 1948 war should be seen in an entirely different light once Israel was established. For example, the exodus of Palestinians before May 1948 was in the nature of 'transfer ex post facto', but the later exodus was clearly premeditated, driven by a policy that Benvenisti labels ethnic cleansing. Benvenisti concludes that the exodus of Palestinians from their physical, geographic and cultural home, indeed the re-creation of that landscape to fulfill the needs and dreams of Jews, was a policy set forth by the Israeli government – 'ongoing, interconnected processes' which continued long after the cessation of hostilities.[42]

What Benvenisti argues is that the same processes continue today and the Jewish settlements in Jerusalem and the West Bank – again ongoing and interconnected – have the policy objective of furthering that cleansing of landscape and population.

Here we return to Jewish memory in the post-Holocaust era. Jews come after the Holocaust and Israel to be sure, but this second *after* is now infected with dislocation and atrocity at its origins and most probably with a permanent occupation at its conclusion. We as Jews come after an ongoing history in Israel/Palestine that places an accusing image at the heart of Jewish history itself.

Jewish memory is therefore tainted with the suffering inflicted upon us and the suffering we have inflicted on others. At least since the biblical period, Jewish history has never faced this conundrum. What do Jews do with a memory, inevitably and in the long run in need of ritualization, that replaces innocence with culpability, ethics with atrocity?

In February 2002, Baruch Kimmerling, a professor of sociology at Hebrew University, wrote movingly of this culpability:

I accuse Ariel Sharon of creating a process in which he will not only intensify the reciprocal bloodshed, but is liable to instigate a regional war and partial or nearly complete ethnic cleansing of the Arabs in the 'Land of Israel'.

I accuse every Labor Party minister in this government of cooperating for implementation of the right wing's extremist, fascist 'vision' for Israel.

I accuse the Palestinian leadership, and primarily Yasir Arafat, of shortsightedness so extreme that it has become a collaborator in Sharon's plans. If there is a second Naqba, this leadership, too, will be among the causes.

I accuse the military leadership, spurred by the national leadership, of inciting public opinion, under a cloak of supposed military professionalism, against the Palestinians. Never before in Israel have so many generals in uniform, former generals, and past members of the military intelligence, sometimes disguised as 'academics,' taken part in public brainwashing. When the judicial committee of inquiry is established to investigate the 2002 catastrophe, they too will have to be investigated alongside the civilian criminals.

I accuse the administrators of Israel's electronic media of giving various military spokespeople the access needed for an aggressive, bellicose, almost complete takeover of the public discourse. The military is not only controlling Jenin and Ramallah but the Israeli radio and television as well.

I accuse those people, of all ranks, who order the black flag hoisted above them, and those who follow their unlawful orders. The late philosopher Yeshayahu Leibovitz was right – the occupation has ruined every good part and destroyed the moral infrastructure upon which Israeli society exists. Let's stop this march of fools and build society anew, clean of militarism and oppression and exploitation of other people, if not worse.

I accuse everyone who sees and knows all of this of doing nothing to prevent the emerging catastrophe. Sabra and Shatila events were nothing compared to what has happened and what is going to happen to us. We have to go out not only to the town squares, but also to the checkpoints. We have to speak to the soldiers in the tanks and the troop carriers – like the Russians spoke to their soldiers when they were ordered to retake control in Red Square – before entry into Palestinian cities turns into a murderous urban warfare.

And I accuse myself of knowing all of this, yet crying little and keeping quiet too often.[43]

2 Innocence, Settlers and State Policy

Throughout the years many commentators have blamed religious extremism, usually labeled as fundamentalism, Jewish and Islamic, for the violence in Israel/Palestine. This was true especially during the first Palestinian uprising that began in 1987 and continued with the Al-Aqsa uprising of 2000. Yet, paradoxically, it is within the liberal Jewish narrative in Israel and the United States that Jewish fundamentalism comes into play. Without this liberal narrative, Jewish fundamentalism would be limited in scope and ability. It would be confined to the synagogue and marginal to the political process.

And it is here that Christian and Islamic fundamentalism flourish as well. While clearly not the sole impetus for either Christian or Islamic extremism, Israel, especially with its expanded borders, plays a major symbolic and material role for all three fundamentalisms as we enter the twenty-first century.

Religion and religious identity are important in the political realm. Thus, to begin to analyse Jewish life in the present and the themes that are important to Jews and Jewish communities around the world, it is important to articulate theological underpinnings. But rather than religious extremism in the form of fundamentalism, we must begin with the work of Holocaust theologians such as Elie Wiesel, Emil Fackenheim and Rabbi Irving Greenberg. They have articulated a theology that speaks in a profound way to the Jewish people, one that has become normative in Jewish conversation and activity.

When looked at closely, Holocaust theology yields three themes that exist in dialectical tension: suffering and empowerment, innocence and redemption, specialness and normalization. Though they exist side by side, they also are sequential, the first two themes emerging at the time of the Arab–Israeli War in 1967, the third in the 1980s with the Israeli invasion of Lebanon and the Palestinian uprising against Israeli occupation in the West Bank and Gaza.[1]

The themes of suffering and empowerment came to the fore at the time of the 1967 war. In those heady times, there was a collective awakening in the Jewish community, exemplified by Elie Wiesel and

Emil Fackenheim, that is hard to describe. But the literature is clear: the experience of Israel in 1967 elicited an articulation of specific themes of contemporary Jewish history for the first time since the European catastrophe.

It is in light of the 1967 war that Jews articulated for the first time both the extent of Jewish suffering during the Holocaust and the significance of Jewish empowerment in Israel. Before 1967, neither was central to Jewish consciousness; the Jewish community carried on with a haunting memory of the European experience and a charitable attitude toward the fledgling state. After the war, both Holocaust and Israel are seen as central points around which the boundaries of Jewish commitment are defined.

Yet if the emerging Holocaust consciousness saw Jewish suffering as mandating empowerment in Israel, it also recognized some of the dangers inherent in empowerment. The lesson of Jewish suffering is indeed empowerment, but suffering also constrains the forms of empowerment. Jewish suffering is unacceptable after the Holocaust, but also no people should have to suffer as Jews have. Thus for Holocaust theologians, at least in the early stage, the Holocaust had both particular and universal meaning; the lesson of the Holocaust is that Jews and all people should be empowered to the point at which it is impossible to inflict massive suffering upon them.

Within the themes of suffering and empowerment lies the corollary of innocence and redemption, and this too developed in the wake of the 1967 war. For Holocaust theologians the victory in the Six-Day War was a miracle, a sign that an innocent people so recently victimized might be on the verge of redemption. That is, a sub-theme of Jewish suffering in the Holocaust is the total innocence of the Jewish people and thus the innocence of those who defend the lives of Jews in Israel. For Holocaust theologians, the victory of Israel in 1967 is a victory of the innocent trying to forestall another catastrophe, another holocaust, and the redemptive sign is that this time Jews will prevail.

The celebration of victory is therefore seen within the context of an earlier devastation: a helpless people abandoned by the world now ensures its own continuity and survival against a new enemy. Of course, in this formulation the transference of European history to the Middle East is complete; in so far as Palestinian Arabs and the Arab world in general attempt to thwart Jewish empowerment in Israel, they symbolize to Holocaust theologians the continuity of the Nazi drama. The 1967 war symbolizes a shift in the physical geography of the drama: the internal landscape remains the same. In the literature written immediately after the 1967 war, the feeling is clear: this time Hitler lost.

Still, there is a tension. As with suffering and empowerment, the dialectic of innocence and redemption remains problematic. Though there is no doubt about the innocence of suffering Jews in Europe and the innocence of Jews in Israel, the fully redemptive quality of victory remains elusive. Holocaust theologians stress at this point that Israel does not atone for the Holocaust, is not a fulfillment of the devastation, nor does Israel replace suffering with joy. If Israel is a response to the Holocaust, it is not an answer. The European catastrophe remains central in its horror and in the questions it raises.

Within suffering and empowerment, innocence and redemption, is the difficult question of God. Holocaust theologians are bold in asking how Jews can relate to God after the Holocaust. Can Jews believe in a God of history who allows such devastation? Can Jews relate to a God when over one million innocent Jewish children were killed? In essence Holocaust theologians conclude that there are no definitive answers to these questions and thus the religious duty of the Jewish community cannot simply revolve around belief in God. Rather, the survival of the people takes precedence, and because empowerment is crucial to that survival, empowerment takes on religious connotations.

Holocaust theologians therefore articulate a religion beyond prayer, ritual and certainty about God and place that religion in the historical progression of the Jewish people, symbolized in post-1967 Israel. In this way, Holocaust theologians challenge and ultimately replace the normative religious ideals of rabbinic Judaism, or at least provide a new focal point for rabbinic Judaism.

The third tension, specialness and normalization, exists already within the first two, but becomes more explicit as the ramifications of the 1967 war become clear. Already in 1967 the tension is felt as Jews re-emerge on the world scene in a position of power. Holocaust theologians celebrate what this power ensures: continuity and independence. Even in victory, though, they argue that the 1967 war represents a 'unique' type of victory.

This uniqueness is seen in a number of factors, beginning with the particularity of Jewish existence and history, a return to the land of Jewish ancestry, and, especially, renewed access to the old city of Jerusalem and the Temple Wall. To be reunited with those symbols of ancient Jewish heritage after a 2000-year exile, an exile that culminated in the catastrophe in Europe, is to recover the special character of the Jewish people. Thus for Holocaust theologians the 1967 war is a sign of specialness, and the description of Israeli soldiers as reluctant warriors, as restrained conquerors, is part and parcel of this special quality.

Yet it is at this point that there arises the question of normalization – what form is power to take and how is it to be exercised now that Israel is an established nation-state? For the miracle of 1967, as Holocaust theologians view it, did not carry with it the occupation of the West Bank and Gaza – or at least there is little mention of such an occupation in the early post-1967 writings. It is only in the 1980s, when it becomes obvious that the occupation is at least a semi-permanent part of the Israeli policy, and when the war in Lebanon explodes onto the front pages of the international press, that the reality of normalization takes on importance.

The arrival of the third part of this dialectic of specialness and normalization divides Holocaust theologians themselves. Elie Wiesel and Emil Fackenheim, for example, argue the themes of suffering and empowerment, innocence and redemption, but have little to say about the dialectic of specialness and normalization. That is, they argue from the European catastrophe about the need for empowerment, but their main focus is on the former.

It is Irving Greenberg who realizes that the miracle of Israel has now arrived at center stage and that the reality of Israel beyond the miracle now has to be addressed. We might say that in the 1970s and 1980s Greenberg both synthesizes the themes articulated by earlier Holocaust theologians and ventures beyond them: Jews are no longer innocent (because of the power Jews wield and the ways they wield it), and the cost of empowerment is for Jews to become more like other nations and peoples. For Greenberg, this normalization of the Jewish community is probably the most important and most difficult reality for Jews to accept. Jews who expect too much of the state, who apply the prophetic norms that grew up in situations of powerlessness, thus threaten the survival of Israel, because no state, Jewish or otherwise, can survive on prophetic ideals.

As we entered the last decade of the twentieth century, Holocaust theology reached its final articulation, having moved from a deep, almost poetic paean to Jewish suffering to an expression of international normalcy; Israel is to be measured by the same standards as any other nation. And yet the glaring weakness of this constraint that Holocaust theology has developed comes into focus with this dramatic shift.

In all of Holocaust theology there is never an attempt at a critical history of Zionism or of Israeli state policy. Jewish dissenters are rarely mentioned by name, nor are the positions they hold discussed. Thus the Jewish tradition of dissent, Zionist and non-Zionist, *vis-à-vis* Israel is lost, and the variety of lessons to be drawn from the Holocaust remain in the background or disappear altogether. The strength of Holocaust theology is also its weakness: a univocal view of history that, as often as not, is ahistorical.

It is important to understand that Holocaust theologians face constraints that all theologians, regardless of faith tradition, face when asked to legitimate state power. That is, Holocaust theologians helped to make normative – as a religious commandment – empowerment in Israel. Because Zionism existed long before the Holocaust, and the state long before Holocaust theology, Holocaust theology was, even in its own incipience, legitimating something already in existence. A further complication is that the theology that articulates a general sense of Jewish identity and affirmation in no way controls or even directly influences – nor could it retroactively change – Israeli state policy.

Thus Holocaust theologians are called upon and feel responsible to articulate and defend, or to explain as essential and normal, state policies that are presented to them. There is little question that the 1967 war was easier for Holocaust theologians to explain than the Lebanon war, and the Lebanon war was a bit easier than the brutal suppression of the Palestinian uprising. Explanations attempted by people such as Irving Greenberg are strained, and the quest for an understanding of a normalization that most Jews feel to be intensely disturbing finds an increasingly narrow Jewish audience. We might say that the first Palestinian uprising signaled the end of Holocaust theology because Holocaust theology in its inception articulated a much different sense of Jewish purpose, that of an innocent, suffering people in search of their destiny.[2]

It is within the context of Holocaust identity formation that Jewish fundamentalism comes into play. Shortly after the conclusion of the 1967 war, Jewish fundamentalism, already on the sidelines, prepared for a major role in the future of Israel. If the Holocaust was the nadir of Jewish history, was not the taking of Jerusalem, Judea and Samaria the beginning of redemption? Jewish zealots took the celebratory mood felt by Jews around the world after the 1967 victory and conquest of Jerusalem as a sign from God that redemption was near.

The return to the land of Israel brought to contemporary consciousness ancient Jewish themes, and this can be most clearly seen in the various forms of religious renewal that became commonplace. Janet Aviad documents the return of secular Jews to Orthodox or neo-orthodox Judaism, people known as *ba'alei-teshuvah*, or 'those who return'. Many of these Jews were from upper- and middle-class neighborhoods in the United States. Their feelings of loss and alienation led them to search for new foundations upon which to build a life. Many found their way to Israel, studied in Jewish houses of learning, and made their lives in a new religious environment. Whether they remained in Israel or not, it was often the return to the ancient symbols and places of Judaism that led to or helped solidify their new commitment. Clearly Yad Vashem and the yeshivas of Jerusalem became main centers of Jewish renewal, functioning as visible reminders of membership in an ancient suffering and now empowered people.[3]

One also saw the revival of Jewish religious fundamentalism in Israel as stimulated both by the crisis of the Jewish people and by the recovery of ancient myths and texts, as well as renewed access to ancient Jewish sites. Thus Ian Lustick emphasizes Israel's military triumph in 1967 as a crisis point in Israeli history that polarized sentiment and opinion on the most profound questions facing Israeli society, at the same time serving as a catalyst for the formation of religious fundamentalist movements such as Gush Emunim (Bloc of the Faithful).

For Lustick, it is ironic that the transformation of Israel, known for its unity and intimacy, into a bitterly, perhaps irrevocably, divided society can be traced to its lightning victory in the Six-Day War. By opening questions of tremendous emotional and practical import the war ultimately divided rather than united. The 'religious and emotional fervor surrounding the renewal of contact between Jews and the historic heartland of ancient Judea' introduced religious language that allowed little room for nuance and compromise. As Lustick describes it, after more than 18 centuries of dormancy, 'the distinctive blend of messianic expectation, militant political action, intense parochialism, devotion to the land of Israel, and self-sacrifice that characterized the Zealots of Roman times caught the imagination of tens of thousands of young religious Israeli Jews and disillusioned but idealistic secular Zionists'.

Biblical references abound, exemplified in the following statement by a Jewish fundamentalist:

> The commandment that pounded in the heart of Joshua and the generation who captured Canaan, in the heart of David and Solomon, and their generation, the word of God in his Torah, is thus, as it was first purely stated, what motivates us. The source of our authority will be our volunteering for the holy because we only come to return Israel to its true purpose and destiny of Torah and Holiness ... we are looking for the complete renewal of the true official authority – the Sanhedrin and the anointed from the House of David – we are those who nurse from the future, from which we gain our authority for the generations.[4]

Lustick concludes that the influence of those movements on Israeli society and government far outweighs their numbers, especially in their willingness to challenge the legitimacy of any government that attempts to withdraw from the West Bank and Gaza. By recalling the ancient glory of the Jewish people and its attachment to the land, by looking forward to the reconstruction of the Temple and the coming messianic age, and by a willingness to seek these goals through violence and, if necessary, the expulsion of the Palestinians, the Jewish fundamentalist movement became an obstacle to the pursuit of peace and justice between Israel and the Palestinians.

Though clothed in religious rhetoric, the new Jewish settlers understood their appeal was limited in an Israeli and American Jewish community wary of overt religious language. Instead, the new Jewish settlers articulated their movement to the wider Jewish public as a further breakthrough in the creation of Israel rather than a break with Israeli history. After all, the creation of Israel was through a process of settlement.

The expansion of Israel in the 1967 war was a continuation of that process. Those Jews who wanted no part of settlements in Jerusalem and the surrounding areas saw the victory of Israel in the war as necessary and a negotiated settlement that would return the territories as imminent. Here the religiously motivated also worked within the system of Israeli politics to place their new settlement ideas in the context of Jewish history and an evolving history of the Israeli state.

Appeal could be made on a variety of levels without involving diverse constituencies in overt religious ideology. Ordinary Israelis could find expanded economic and housing possibilities and secular nationalists could use the religious fervor of the settlers to accomplish their goal of an expanded state.

As has often been the case in Israeli history, security concerns that Israel was too small to defend itself were used to argue for expansion. The Old City of Jerusalem was, for most Israelis, non-negotiable from the moment Israeli forces entered the ancient walls. Could such a symbol of Jewish history ever be returned?

The forces of religious zeal were thus unleashed within a broader spectrum of war, occupation and state policies of consolidation and expansion. However, to see the subsequent decades of Israeli history only or even primarily within the context of Jewish fundamentalism is to miss the larger story. The combination of politics, ideology and religion that intersect in the expanded Israel requires a broader concept than Jewish fundamentalism.

Michael Lerner, the progressive Jewish religious activist, has suggested 'Settler Judaism' as this concept because it encompasses the diverse aspects of Israeli and American Jewish life that have led to the present impasse. Settler Judaism brings together Holocaust imagery and identity, the radical right, religious fundamentalism and liberal politics into a coherent if unexpected framework of overt and covert sensibilities that increasingly define Israeli and American Jewry. Lerner defines this combination in vivid terms as a world-view:

> Since the world is against us, abandoned us during the Holocaust, and hypocritically condemns us for violence more sharply than it criticizes others, we don't have to live according to universal morality. God gave us the West Bank as our eternal inheritance and we have the right to do whatever is necessary to hold onto it. Anyone who trusts Palestinians or assumes that they have the same kinds of human needs and motivations as Jews is naïve and likely to endanger the Jewish people. Indeed our fellow Jews are betraying us by calling for an exchange of land for peace. They are traitors and may be as dangerous to our future as Arabs. The obligations to pursue justice and love your neighbour apply only to our fellow Jews, not to non-Jews, certainly not to Palestinians and maybe not to Jews who advocate the peace process.

Lerner concludes that Settler Judaism is a 'rape of the morally and spiritually sensitive versions of Judaism that have predominated through most of Jewish history'.[5]

To analyse Settler Judaism as it has unfolded over the last decades we begin with four areas of concern and disputation: the settlements themselves, who formed them and who lives within them; Barak's 'generous offer' to the Palestinians as a way of demonstrating the continuing involvement of the Israeli government in the settlement process; Sharon's proposal for the final settlement of the Israeli–Palestinian question; and the recent campaign by major Jewish organizations to silence dissent with regard to these policies during the recent Palestinian uprising.

Instead of delving into a detailed history of Settler Judaism, I will concentrate on the post-Oslo period when the cessation of settlements and occupation were envisioned. As we shall see, Settler Judaism is alive and well today, perhaps accelerating during the post-Oslo period and even stronger than ever. As is true historically, its strength is diverse, with politics, policies and narrative at the center. Likewise historically true is the combination of Jews in Israel and the U.S. with American foreign policy that allows Settler Judaism to flourish in the twenty-first century.

This is the view of Avishai Margalit, the Schulman Professor of Philosophy at the Hebrew University in Jerusalem. With respect to the Jewish settlements, Margalit finds that the West Bank is divided into three parts or three long strips of land.

The first strip of settlements was established in the Jordan Valley. Comprised of 15 settlements, these were set up after the 1967 war and just before the war of October 1973. These settlements were developed by traditional Labor Zionist settlement institutions – the Kibbutz and Moshav movements.

The second strip, further west in the Jordan Valley, was pioneered by Gush Emunim, or the Bloc of the Faithful. These settlements were a form of resistance to the 1967 Allon Plan, a plan that sought to avoid settlements near Palestinian population centers in the West Bank. For Gush Emunim, not settling near these centers meant conceding these areas in any future agreements. Interestingly, these religious settlements had many and diverse allies: those identified with the political right, including Menachem Begin, Yitzhak Shamir and Ariel Sharon – but also those identified with liberal politics such as Shimon Peres and Moshe Dayan. Both conservative and liberal politicians wanted to destroy the Allon Plan and share joint control over the entire West Bank with Jordan.

Most settlers live in the third strip, closest to the pre-1967 border of Israel. Three types of settlers can be identified here: those seeking a better quality of life, the economically needy, and those who are both economically needy and ultra-Orthodox.

As Margalit points out: 'What the Palestinians find most worrying is the increase of over fifty percent in the number of housing units as well as the settler population since the Oslo agreements of September 1993.' Indeed, since 1993 Israeli statistics show an increase of the settler population at about 8 per cent a year, rising from 116,000 in the West Bank and Gaza to over 200,000 settlers at the beginning of the Second Intifada in September 2000. If you add the number of Jews who live in areas of Jerusalem annexed after the 1967 war, then the number of settlers increases by another 210,000 Jewish Israelis.[6]

It is within this context that Ehud Barak's Camp David proposal to the Palestinians in the summer of 2000 should be analysed. Often noted as Barak's 'generous offer', the generosity of the offer is contested. In fact it has been more often asserted than analysed. Rather than innovative or provocative, it is instructive to see Barak's offer within a continuity of Israeli policy since 1967.

In a paper delivered at the Center for International Studies at the University of Delaware, Sara Roy, Research Associate at the Center for Middle East Studies at Harvard University, offered the following analysis which I paraphrase. By the time of the Camp David Summit in July 2000, there were several processes taking place simultaneously:

- The continuing confiscation of Arab lands in the West Bank and Gaza.
- The accelerated expansion of existing Israeli settlements and the construction of new settlements on recently confiscated lands.
- The near doubling of the settler population to 200,000 in ten years, a population that is hostile and armed, with freedom of movement and the privileges of Israeli citizenship.
- The division of the West Bank and Gaza Strip into enclaves disconnected from each other by territories under the control of Israel, a direct result of the terms of the Oslo agreements.
- The paving of 250 miles of by-pass roads onto confiscated lands that run north–south and east–west. This created a grid that further bisects and encircles Palestinian areas, producing the 227 enclaves referred to by Amnesty International.

- The institutionalization of closure policy, which restricts and at times totally prohibits the movement of Arab people and goods. This closure policy locks Palestinians into the enclave structure created by the Oslo accords and makes difficult, if not impossible a functioning Palestinian economy.
- The construction of hundreds of checkpoints and barricades throughout the West Bank designed to control and further restrict the movement of Palestinians.

Roy continues:

> Barak's 2000 budget allocated $6.5 million for the construction of by-pass roads, $30 million for settlement expansion, and $51 million for the confiscation of Palestinian lands among other categories. According to the Israeli group, Peace Now, the Barak administration issued permits for the construction of 3,575 new settlement homes, and earmarked $500 million for settlements in its 2001 budget. According to official data from Israel's housing ministry, Barak's government began construction of 1,943 housing units in the West Bank and Gaza in 2000, the largest number in any year since 1992. During the final quarter of 2000, as the Al-Aqsa Intifada intensified, the Barak government began work on 954 housing units alone, up from 368 during the last quarter of 1999.

As for the Camp David proposals, Roy concludes that they lacked the following crucial elements: contiguous territory, defined and functional borders, political and economic sovereignty, and basic Palestinian national rights. Barak's offer was less than generous; it was a thinly disguised continuation and consolidation in a permanent way of the Israeli occupation of Jerusalem and the West Bank. For Roy, the problem began long before Barak as occupation was the structural and policy cornerstone of the Oslo accords.

As devastating as Roy's political and economic analysis of the Barak record and proposal is her eyewitness account of the devastation of the Palestinian territories in the middle of the Al-Aqsa uprising. She compared it with the celebratory mood she found in a previous visit early after the Oslo accords were signed in 1993:

> The images are very different now ... During the six years of the previous uprising, 18,000 Palestinians were injured. In the first

> four months since the current uprising began, over 11,000 Palestinians have been injured. The Palestinian landscape has withered, wrenched of hope, suffused in rage, and devoid of childhood. During my visit to Gaza and the West Bank, I saw hundreds of acres of razed agricultural land – destroyed orchards and irrigation systems, and felled trees, some hundreds of years old – fertile land made desolate by army bulldozers. I saw residential apartment buildings, now charred and vacant, that had been attacked by Israeli tanks and Apache helicopters, parts of their sides ripped out, their inhabitants dead or displaced. I visited camp homes whose walls, ceilings and furniture were riddled with bullet holes.

As for the people, Roy saw a marked difference in their demeanor and their expectations:

> Children no longer asked me for chocolate but for food, and they showed me their collection of bullets while their mothers brought out shopping bags filled with shrapnel they had collected in and around their homes. An elderly man in one of the camp shelters I visited broke down in tears, unable to breathe from the rage he felt as he described the attack on his family. His wife took me to their bedroom whose outer wall faces an Israeli settlement and Israeli outpost nearby. 'The only reason we are alive,' she told me, 'is that we were sleeping on the floor at the time they began shooting.' Their bedroom wall has twelve bullet holes in it and their closet has two.[7]

Rather than departing in a fundamental way, Sharon continues Barak's sensibility. As reported in the *New York Times*, Sharon's understanding of a settlement between Israel and the Palestinians conforms to his earlier sensibilities and the consensus of previous Israeli administrations. In fact, Sharon seeks to implement as a final settlement with the Palestinians the map of an expanded Israel that he, with others, helped to create.

That map is intriguing. According to the *Times*, Sharon wants to retain West Bank land in two security zones. These zones would comprise two north-to-south strips that would 'bracket Palestinian areas like the sides of a ladder'. The western zone, whose width would be three to six miles, would parallel that edge of the West Bank, the same area where Sharon oversaw the building of settlements over twenty years ago. The second zone would run through the rift valley just west of the Jordan River. This second zone, facing Jordan and beyond it Iraq, would be nine to twelve miles wide. Between the security zones would run Israeli roads that the *Times* article refers to as the 'rungs of the ladder'. The effect of the completed ladder would be the following: 'This Israeli security system would not only consume swaths of land Mr. Arafat expects to govern, it would also wall off separate areas of the Palestinian state.'[8]

Ron Pundak, an architect of the 1993 Oslo peace accords, voices the alarm of Palestinians: 'The fear is that the idea behind an Israeli interim agreement is to create facts on the ground, and transform the interim into the permanent.' Yet Pundak's fear betrays a *naïveté*: these are the facts on the ground that have been built over the years through agreements, uprisings and truces. Negotiating future agreements would have to roll back in a significant way Israel's 'advance'. What power is there to force such a roll-back?[9]

The American Jewish establishment, with minor exceptions, seeks to protect Israel from the negative images resulting from the Palestinian resistance to these facts and the Israeli repression of that resistance. With the beginning of the Al-Aqsa intifada, American Jewish groups paid for full-page statements in major newspapers around the United States. These statements call for Jewish unity and unqualified support of the state of Israel.

An example of these statements appeared in the *New York Times*. The text reads as follows: 'Be heard. You could sit home and worry silently about "the situation". Or you could stand together with Israel and make your voice heard. Come to the SOLIDARITY RALLY FOR ISRAEL.' With the slogan '**ISRAEL NOW** and Forever', the statement had the following co-sponsors: United Jewish Communities, Federations of North America, UJA-Federation of New York, Conference of Presidents of Major Jewish Organizations, Jewish Community Relations Council of New York, Jewish Council for Public Affairs, Central Conference of American Rabbis, Jewish Reconstruction Federation, Rabbinical Assembly, Rabbinical Council of America, Union of American Hebrew Congregations, Union of Orthodox Jewish Congregations of America and the United Synagogues of Conservative Judaism. Not surprisingly, the honorary chairman of the event was Elie Wiesel.[10]

At a similar rally in October 2000, more than a month into the Al-Aqsa intifada, Wiesel addressed his remarks to President Clinton. Stating that Jews stood by Israel in the present crisis 'imposed on her' by the 'intransigence' of Yassir Arafat, Wiesel identified himself as one who rejects 'hatred and fanaticism'. For Wiesel, those who consider peace as the 'noblest of efforts' have no choice but to finally recognize that Arafat is 'ignorant, devious and unworthy of trust'. After all, Arafat has rejected the 'unprecedented generous territorial concessions' offered by Barak. 'I accuse him of being morally weak, politically shortsighted and an obstacle to peace', Wiesel said. 'I accuse him of murdering the hopes of an entire generation. His and ours.'[11]

What is interesting in Wiesel's remarks is what he does *not* say or to which he makes no reference. Nowhere is the map of Israel/Palestine referred to. In Wiesel's narrative, settlements do not exist, nor do by-pass roads or security zones that in Barak's plan continue to exist and in fact are consolidated in the final plan. Wiesel's narrative does mention the Jewish attachment to Jerusalem but in a way that again mystifies its existence rather than explains its politicized nature. 'Under Israel's sovereignty, Christians, Jews and Muslims alike could pray without fear in Jerusalem', Wiesel asserts. Jerusalem is 'our capital', the center of Jewish history. Wiesel continues: 'A Jew may be far from Jerusalem, but not without Jerusalem. Though a Jew may not live in Jerusalem, Jerusalem lives inside of him.'

No mention is made of either the attempt to force Palestinians to leave Jerusalem or the overall policies of remaking Jerusalem, especially the Old City, in Jewish and Israeli ways. The strong and equally claimed attachment of Palestinians and Islam to Jerusalem is passed over without mention. The possibility of Israel and Palestine claiming Jerusalem as a joint capital, a possibility envisioned by Palestinians and more than a few Jews inside and outside of Israel, is similarly unmentioned.

In fact, as Amir Chesin, Bill Hutman and Avi Melamed report in their book *Separate and Unequal: The Inside Story of Israeli Rule in East Jerusalem*, Israeli policy has been consistent in denying these claims and in fact transforming Jerusalem into a Jewish city. This very act of transforming the city has been in place since the 1967 war, with the understanding that no matter what the competing claims, whoever physically dominated Jerusalem would determine the city's fate.

The policy has been twofold: to rapidly increase the Jewish population in east Jerusalem while hindering the growth of the Palestinian population, and to force the Palestinian residents to leave the city altogether. According to the authors, the policy has been tremendously successful: '[The policy] has translated into a miserable life for the majority of east Jerusalem Arabs, many of whom have chosen to leave the city. At the same time, Jews have moved into east Jerusalem by the thousands.' As of 1996, and this has accelerated since that time, 157,000 Jews lived in east Jerusalem – a number nearly equaling the 171,000 Palestinians who resided there.[12]

Again the policies were pursued under the cloak of innocence. 'To the world, Israel presented itself as an enlightened ruler of a troubled city', the authors write, 'In reality, while pursuing what for the Jewish state was the logical goal of fortifying its claim on Jerusalem, the city's non-Jewish residents suffered greatly.' Teddy Kollek, Jerusalem's mayor from 1965 to 1993, often told audiences of Jerusalem's movement from a provincial backwater to a thriving metropolis under Israeli control and how all its residents were benefiting from Israel's enlightened rule. Projects like the development of community centers of art and culture were trumpeted, as were the preservation and restoration of the city's ancient history.

At the same time, projects of mutual respect and tolerance between Jews and Palestinians were often cited by Kollek to international audiences. Jewish audiences from the United States, schooled in their own struggle for equality and aware of the gross inequalities between African-Americans and whites in the United States, were especially captivated by this integrationist sensibility. Again, the picture was one of beneficence and granted world Jewry the 'best of both worlds – pride in seeing Jerusalem again the center of Jewish life, and a clear conscience in being told the Palestinian minority was being treated fairly'.

Regrettably, the vision was far from reality and far from the intent of Israeli policy. The authors conclude that Kollek's liberal vision, indeed the entire presentation of Israeli rule in Jerusalem, is misleading: 'Do not believe the rosy propaganda – the rosy picture that Israel tries to show the world of Jerusalem since the 1967 reunification. Israel has treated the Palestinians terribly. As a matter of policy, it has forced many from their homes and stripped them of their land, all the while lying to them and deceiving them and the world about its honorable intentions.'[13]

Indeed the authors should know the realities of the situation as Jewish Israelis in the political and journalistic professions: Amir Chesin is a retired Israeli army colonel and was Senior Adviser on Arab Community Affairs and Assistant to Teddy Kollek; Bill Hutman was a journalist with the *Jerusalem Post*; Avi Melamed was Deputy

Adviser on Arab Affairs and Adviser on Arab Affairs to Kollek's successor, Ehud Olmert.

Amos Elon, former senior editor and columnist at the Israeli newspaper *Ha'aretz* and author of *Jerusalem: Battleground of Memory*, views the exclusive Israeli claims on Jerusalem as dubious. When the current mayor, Ehud Olmert, was asked by a reporter about the deficient municipal services in the Arab part of Jerusalem, Olmert replied that there was only a Jewish Jerusalem. Ariel Sharon, like other prime ministers before him, calls Jerusalem 'Israel's capital, united for all eternity'. When this definition of Jerusalem was originally proposed by then Prime Minister Menachem Begin in the 1980s, Elon asked Begin whether he thought 'eternity' could be legislated. Begin's response is instructive: 'In this case it can and must be.' Begin continued that in Jerusalem the 'remnants of our ancient glory are on view there. We are reviving it in our day.' To the further question of whether Jerusalem should be left for the end of negotiations of the Arab–Israeli conflict, Begin responded sharply: 'Jerusalem will never be subject for negotiation!' Elon reports that when Begin spoke of Jerusalem for all eternity, he did so in an 'ecstatic, ringing voice as though intoning an invocation'.[14]

But as Elon continues to point out, the theological theory of a united Jerusalem is haunted by the reality of its division. Throughout the years Jerusalem continued to have two of everything: two downtowns, two business centers, two public transport systems, two electric grids and two systems of social and cultural life. Kollek called Jerusalem a 'mosaic', but for Elon mosaics have a certain harmony missing in the 'united' Jerusalem.

Rather the divisions reflect a pattern of discrimination and a 'deepening chasm'. This chasm continues despite the warnings of what this division means for the future of both Jews and Palestinians. And Elon is skeptical of Barak's 'outlandish' proposals on Jerusalem to try to achieve Palestinian agreement on 'functional' as opposed to political sovereignty in parts of Jerusalem. He is especially skeptical of Barak's language about 'shared', 'vertical', 'horizontal', and especially 'sovereignty vested in God'.

Even the claim of worship without fear in Jerusalem is dubious. Since the signing of the Oslo agreements, a majority of time has seen Palestinians outside of Jerusalem restricted in their movements. The possibility of prayer in the Al-Aqsa mosque has been restricted by the same map and occupation that Wiesel fails to mention.

After the September 11th terrorist attack, Wiesel wrote a short article for the *Jewish Week*. As with many Jews, he offered condolences to those killed and thanks to those who attempted to rescue the victims, 'who brought honor to humanity'. The lessons Wiesel draws from this tragedy are lessons for all Americans. 'As Americans were counting their dead and trying to cope with the immense tragedy that struck our cities, in their camps Palestinians were jubilant. They fired rifles in the air, proudly shouting their happiness', Wiesel writes. 'They did the same thing during the Gulf War. While Scuds were falling on Tel Aviv, Palestinians climbed up to their rooftops and wanted to know the reality of their joy.' For Wiesel it is increasingly clear: 'The enemies of Israel are also the enemies of Western powers.' Wiesel ends his article with the question: 'Does the world now understand better what Israelis feel when their parents and children are murdered by suicide bombers?'[15]

Here again it is interesting what is written and what is left unstated. The 'jubilance' of Palestinians has been disputed in the world press and by Palestinians themselves. At the same time, the fact that the helicopter gunships and fighter aircraft that have attacked Palestinian territory are made in the U.S. is unmentioned. That the 'enemies of America' may in fact have legitimate grievances *vis-à-vis* U.S. foreign policy seems impossible in Wiesel's rhetoric.

Are the planes that crashed into the World Trade Center so easily equated with Palestinian suicide bombers? Could Palestinian suicide bombers be, at least for a population under occupation and closure and without an armed force that is in any way comparable to the Israeli military, the equivalent to Israel's helicopter gunships? If it is morally right to condemn terrorism of the weak, does Wiesel have the moral obligation to condemn other forms of terrorism, including terrorism carried out by the nation-state?

The arrival of Constantinian Judaism

Settler Judaism is a militarized Judaism. A militarized Judaism is a militarized Jewish world on the religious, political and narrative levels. The genius of the Israeli narrative both in Israel and the U.S. lies in the articulation of historical weakness as contemporary, as innocence in historical suffering maintained in empowerment, of political resistance to Israel's occupation as mirroring those who sought to destroy Jews and Jewish life when Jews were stateless.

A militarized Judaism and Jewish life is a Constantinian Judaism, where Jewish energies, creativity, wealth and political power in Israel and the U.S. are placed in service to the state. Again, the term 'fundamentalism' hardly suffices here. The forces joined are a militant religious orthodoxy, political power shared by liberals and conservatives, and a liberal narrative that appeals on moral and ethical levels but without the details and maps that confront and contradict that narrative.

Constantinianism was, of course, pioneered by Christianity. In the fourth century and beyond, Christianity moved from a marginal religious movement to a state-empowered religion. During the reign of the Emperor Constantine, Christianity was given free rein within the empire, at least so far as promulgating its religious vision.

Christianity was also forced to bless the state in war and peace. In this process, Christianity, especially as it accompanied colonial and imperial power, became a global religion. It also became a specialist in justifying violence and it too often blessed atrocity. At the same time, a militarized Christianity persecuted other forms of Christianity that resisted imperial state power and the accession of the church to that power. Jews were also persecuted and demeaned and the long tortuous road to Auschwitz was begun.[16]

Constantinian Judaism is relatively new and small in comparison to the Constantinian Christianity from which many Christians today flee. Here certain forms of Judaism and Jewish life are deemed 'authentic' – those that identify with the U.S. and Israel without criticism or maps – while those Jews who resist serving the state and power are 'inauthentic' and persecuted by elements of the Jewish establishment.

Those who question Constantinian Judaism are accused of weakness, of refusing to stand up as Jews, of assimilating to the broader non-Jewish world. But those who resist this militarized form of Judaism and Jewish life see another assimilation, of the establishment – to the state and power. Constantinian Islam, and the diverse world of assertion of power and resistance to it found in contemporary Islam, is little different than Constantinian Christianity and Constantinian Judaism.

The understanding of Jewish, Christian and Islamic fundamentalism as the same and as a source of the problems in the Middle East must be re-evaluated and broadened. Militarized religion in its actions and life is thus the same on many levels, but the place of each religion in their respective communities, societies and nations at any one particular time, and the relations among communities, societies and nations in terms of status and power, are crucial to understand.

Judaism and Christianity in an empowered United States need to be understood differently than Islam in a disempowered Middle East. While the tendencies toward Constantinianism may be similar in their stridency, the realities of each situation make all the difference. So, too, with resistance to Constantinianism in each religion. The context is essential to understand, both in relation to the expression of resistance and in the possibility of conscience becoming active and articulate.

The task that lies beyond the labeling of fundamentalism is a critical analysis of power and religion. Beyond this analysis is the need to break the cycle of violence and atrocity, thus allowing an investigation that critically evaluates power and religion. Surely a militarized politics leads to a militarized religiosity. Historically they go hand in hand. But just as surely, a demilitarized political situation allows for a demilitarized religiosity. The hope here is to move beyond blame and begin – with a critical analysis of maps, politics, religion and narrative – to change the dynamic of situations that lead to oppression and death.

Where better to begin than in Jerusalem? If Jerusalem is spoken about in abstract terms, as the center of Judaism or Islam or as the eternal or only capital of Jews or Palestinians, then a political and religious mobilization for Jerusalem is imperative. This is true for the victors, in this case Israel, and the defeated, in this case Palestinians.[17]

It would also be true if the victors and defeated traded places. Moreover, the claim of victory and defeat in a city and region where Jews and Palestinians are almost equal in population is an illusion. The mobilization has to be kept in place. A perpetual occupation has to be actualized and justified. Illusions such as ancient or religious claims are trumpeted over and against the ordinary needs for both populations. Freedom to worship becomes a cover for the erosion of political, individual and cultural rights. Though defined by the victors as terrorism, resistance to political injustice continues.

But if Jerusalem is seen as the geographic, political, cultural and religious middle of Israel and Palestine, if Jerusalem is seen as broken by a history of violence and a cycle of possession and dispossession, then a new claim can be made on Jerusalem. This new claim is a shared claim of Jews and Palestinians for dignity and an ordinary life.

The broken middle of Jerusalem means a sharing of a city and a land that is claimed by two peoples and that shares a history of three religions. Here sovereignty is shared and real – in politics, culture, religion and population – to live together and therefore to work out the problems of history and religion in the concrete reality of a shared life. Symbolism is downplayed as education, security, ecology, housing and governance take center stage.

Religion is also called upon to play its role. As in the cycle of violence, religion is important, legitimating political claims and counter-claims. Here militarization is foregone and the Constantinianism of Judaism and Islam is jettisoned. Rather, the side of each religion that embraces harmony, peace, justice and inclusion is emphasized. Fundamentalism begins to lose its power or even its importance, and militarization of religious values loses its audience. The assumption here is that religion responds, more or less and in real time, to the needs and aspirations of the people. When ordinary life and security is in reach, religion responds with its own values to help in this process, just as when society is militarized, religion responds in that process.

Recognizing that Jerusalem is the broken middle of Israel/Palestine means that the map of Israel/Palestine as it is today, with Israel stretching from Tel Aviv to the Jordan River and with two remnant Palestinian populations within its control, must be confronted. It also means a commitment among Jewish Israelis and Jews around the world to change that map to one of equality, either with a withdrawal to the 1967 borders of Israel and sharing of Jerusalem as a joint capital with the new state of Palestine in Jerusalem, the West Bank and Gaza, or a commitment to a bi-national state with full citizenship for Jews and Palestinians without regard to ethnic or religious affiliation. This, coupled with the confession of historic wrongs done to the Palestinian people, can move the Middle East crisis from injustice and atrocity to justice, healing and hope.

Identity here is crucial. In the cycle of violence and atrocity, identity becomes as important as religious affirmation. It is crucial to the victors, who symbolically and materially triumph, and to the defeated, who have lost all other power. Here fundamentalist religious ideas find their base, again to mobilize the victors and to protect the defeated from ultimate demoralization. Identity is frozen, seen as ancient, but is actually quite modern, responding to the context of victory and defeat.

All identity is linked to the past and throughly contemporary at the same time. Indeed the very claim of identity is always present, contextual and evolving. Clearly the identity of Israelis and Palestinians has taken root and evolved over the last century; this is also true with their understandings of Judaism and Islam.

Even more accurate is the sense that Judaism and Israel, and Islam and Palestinians have evolved together and over against one another. One might say that the dependence on a shared geography and natural resource base, along with the intermingling of culture and population, has complemented the interpenetrating of religious sensibilities. As Settler and Constantinian Judaism have evolved, a militant Islam has also evolved.

What if we were to see Jewish and Islamic, Israeli and Palestinian identities as more complex, changing, interpenetrating and evolving? Both the Israelis and Palestinians are indeed more complex. The complexity involves the following, among other, elements: Jews, Muslims, Druze, Christians and Baha'is of European, North African and Arab (on the Israeli and Palestinian sides) background intermingle: Jewish and Palestinian diasporas are energetic, traveling to and from Israel/Palestine; American and Arab politics are constantly in the air; trade and cultural influences outside of Israel/Palestine continue to affect the region.

Of course, identities are always evolving. The only question is in what direction identities are evolving. Fundamentalism is primarily an attempt to freeze identity, though, like the pretense to innocence, it serves only as a cover to disguise constant change. Settler and Constantinian Judaism and Islamic fundamentalism are thoroughly modern in their use of modern technology, of state power, even the weapons of terror.

In the end, the struggle is to seek a depth of identity in the context of the times in which we live. As with the affirmation of the broken middle of Jerusalem and the demilitarization of religion, identity formation is a choice and struggle within and among the communities we come from and live within. The context itself plays a significant role. For Jews and Palestinians, identity formation in the broken middle of Jerusalem will look quite different than it does today within the cycle of victory and defeat in a 'unified' Jerusalem that masks injustice.

Indigenous minority rights, citizenship and the new Jerusalem

For the past decades, arguments have been made for the separation of Jews and Palestinians into two states. Based on strategic, practical and moral considerations, these arguments have been supported by

Jews and Palestinians across a moderate to liberal spectrum and have been framed in terms of the rights of the indigenous people, Palestinians, and the rights of a persecuted people, Jews.[18]

Of course the two-state solution has always been more complicated than the arguments advanced on its behalf and the last decade has made such a solution impossible. If the Oslo process has brought the following reality into focus – that Israel now extends from Tel Aviv to the Jordan River with millions of Palestinians within that state, that there are two remnant Palestinian populations within Israel (with a sizeable refugee population of Palestinians outside of Israel with claims within its borders), then the two-state solution becomes a slogan increasingly void of substance.[19]

What is the future of this indigenous Palestinian population and the future of the Jewish Israeli population that also claims a right to the land in a historical and contemporary way? Is there a way beyond mutually exclusive claims or simply the imposition of power of one over another? When do indigenous claims and claims of historical attachment and suffering give way to a new arrangement mindful of the past and attentive to a future beyond the present? Does an understanding of citizenship within a state provide an avenue for the realization of the diverse needs of both an indigenous and a settler population?

The general situation of indigenous peoples and the particular situation of Palestinians raises the question of the meaning of citizenship in its broadest parameters. What does citizenship portend in the modern era? What is the role of citizenship in the modern state? What protections does it afford? Can citizenship cultivate virtue and justice? Do religious and cultural values influence how citizenship is perceived and pursued? Can the idea and practice of citizenship overcome the cycle of injustice and atrocity? Does citizenship relativize or provide a vehicle for the free evolution of identity?

Throughout the world indigenous people find themselves within the larger framework of nation-states, global economies and modernity. Often, indigenous people are beset by many forces, including modernity, capitalism and expanding world religions, such as Christianity and Islam.

Thus a colonialism once defined in terms of military empires and foreign governance has in large part given way to a colonialism defined broadly as the power of a relentless modern sensibility that invades through imposed state structures, an economic system that serves a global and local elite, and religions that often follow in the wake of dislocation and destruction. Not the least of this dislocation and destruction is the alienation of land and sacred space, the uprooting of culture and tradition, and the diminishing of specific languages and rituals.

This process of dislocation and destruction is at least five hundred years in the making. The rise of Europe and its subsequent expansion, as well as the globalization of Christianity, can be traced back to the 'discovery' of the Americas. So too the globalization of Islam has its own history of expansion, centuries in the making and continuing in the present. Here we see local religions with their roots in the Middle East moving well beyond their own locality as was true, in their own time and cultural milieu, of other world religions such as Buddhism and Hinduism.

Yet in another sense even these local religions with their specific roots and symbols were themselves born from other local religions. The birth of Christianity and Islam, like the birth of Judaism, hails from a distinct mixture of tribal religions and symbols that in their day were fought over and where the appearance and disappearance of specific cultural and religious forms became the norm.[20]

One way of looking at the history of the ancient Israelites is the winnowing of tribal particularities toward a 'superior' monotheistic belief and ethical value system. Another way of looking at this history is the forced diminishment of particular tribal systems of belief and meaning.

Looked at from this vantage point, monotheistic religions – Judaism, but also Christianity and Islam – are born in a cycle of violence of what becomes a particular religion, that violence continues within various understandings of these particular religions, with subsequent violence carried on between these religions. Thus the triumph of certain understandings of Judaism, the struggle to define Christianity over against competing forms of Christianity and over against Judaism, and the wars between Judaism, Christianity and Islam that continue in the contemporary world. Historically, the victory of dominant narratives in Judaism, Christianity and Islam are against indigenous cultures and religions, even as it sometimes today carries on assaults against remaining indigenous populations.[21]

What is important here is that the indigenous quality of the monotheistic religions and even their earlier more local versions are something other than indigenous. Is this not true for indigenous people themselves? People who are 'original' to the land are hardly that, at least in a purist sense. Indigenous people have a history – including one of migration and intermarriage – and their cultural and religious sensibilities have evolved over time. The assault they live under today may be the same kind of assault that they perpetrated at an earlier time. Few histories of any duration are innocent and colonialism is hardly the property of any ethnic or religious group.

Because of the complicated histories of all peoples in interaction with their surroundings, no history is innocent, but at the same time this does not excuse the present conquerors from their own obligations *vis-à-vis* those whom they dominate. Though the cycle of invasion and settlement may be dominant in history, the perpetuation of that cycle in the contemporary world should be called to account.

Still, the call to preserve indigenous culture is unlikely to accomplish its own mission. Rather, the understanding of the complexity of indigenous cultures may allow us to see the future as one where both the settler and indigenous culture will come into a fruitful interplay. In this interplay both cultures will change. In their future neither will survive as they exist today and both will enter a new space beyond the present.

The case of Palestinians and Jewish Israelis illustrates the complexity of the settler/indigenous framework in a particular way. Palestinians are seen as indigenous to the land and compared to the recent arrival of European Jews. Yet the Palestinians as a people are through history a varied lot, including Jews among them, but many other peoples and communities, ancient and modern. Palestinian identity has constantly shifted through history and the colonial waves Palestine has experienced over the millennia are truly remarkable. The present struggle over the land in modern-day Israel, Jerusalem, West Bank and Gaza, is actually a continuation of a struggle that has had many actors.

In some ways, the modern struggle over Palestine is much narrower and seemingly intractable, yet if history is our guide the present configuration will give way to a new arrangement in the near future. *The struggle in Israel/Palestine follows an ancient pattern of invasion and settlement, victory and defeat, but the pattern of integration and evolution of identity is also to be seen here.* The struggle in Israel/Palestine is not between outsiders (Jewish Israelis), and indigenous people (Palestinians), but between settlers (Jews of European and North African background), and those who have been dislocated from the land in the twentieth century (mostly Palestinians defined within the cultural patterns of Middle Eastern Islam and Christianity and the political patterns of a recently defeated Ottoman and British colonial rule).[22]

That the Palestinians as recently as the 1940s included Jews among them is significant for our discussion. And not only Jews. The oldest parts of Jerusalem had then and have today, among others, Armenians and Moroccans. This suggests that the recent political developments are divisive but not irretrievably so. Jews have a long history in Palestine and at different points of that history could also be seen as indigenous, at least within the broader framework of the understanding of the complexity of indigenous life suggested here.[23]

Jews who suggest that the recent settlements that comprise the state of Israel represent a return to the land where the Jewish people originated are not far off, once the cycle of settlers and indigenous people is understood. *This is quite different from the claim of some Jews that the land once settled by Jews millennia ago is by right for Jews only. The sin of twentieth-century Jewish settlements is less the desire or need for space and some form of autonomy than it is the uprooting and domination of the Palestinians inhabiting the land.* This also leaves open the possibility of a new configuration – like other new configurations before it – of reconciling contemporary reality and adjusting it so that a civil atmosphere of justice and peace can prevail.

Needed here is less the reversal of the last fifty years, an impossibility in any case, and more a vision that sees the recent history of Europe and the Middle East as time-bound and fleeting. As in previous epochs, settlers at some point become indigenous and the challenge is less the defeat of colonialism than it is the creation of a culture that recognizes the diversity of Israel/Palestine as the path to a new identity and future.[24]

The cycle of violence and dislocation should be transformed into the struggle for equal rights within a common political destiny. Here citizenship – the recognition of a place within a democratic social and political culture that is bound to neither ethnic nor religious identity – is crucial. Citizenship is the recognition that the ideal of equality under the law and shared responsibilities in the public realm limits claims, in the case of Jews and Palestinians the claims of both the settler and indigenous populations. It is a fundamental and foundational agreement that the broad structures of governance and public life will be pursued as if prior claims are secondary and primary identities are open.

To reach this stage, adjustments of laws and historic inequality must be addressed and the equalization of power between groups must begin. But this, at least in the public realm, must happen as a way of preparing a culture and politics that transcends particular communities and creates a new loyalty that allows particularities to thrive, evolve and be transformed.

Within the expanded state of Israel, indigenous Palestinian communities must therefore fight for equality within the state as a way of subverting the injustice that the last decades have brought. Jews within the state will participate on both sides of the struggle, on the one hand to preserve the dominance of Jews that is a key to their affluence and power, and, on the other hand, to pursue common interests with Palestinians against this dominance, either for moral or practical considerations or a combination thereof.

In a democratic secular state defined by citizenship, the divide between settlers and indigenes breaks down over time because the barriers themselves are false historically and in the present. History as lived rather than imagined is too complex for this division and the struggle for citizenship forces consideration beyond assumed and essentialized identities.

Clearly, a majority of Jews and Palestinians favor a separation of their communities. Jews and Palestinians have a sense of themselves as distinct in history and culture, as nationalities that combine language and religion. Behind the sense of destiny and uniqueness, both communities feel the other to be inferior and invasive, as threatening on the physical level and beyond.

Even those who see a unitary state for strategic or practical reasons most often lament this or seek a communal hegemony within that unity. Few Jews or Palestinians see the struggle for equality and polity in the land of Israel/Palestine as a good unto itself, where the freedom of movement and expression could evolve into a thriving and distinct culture. In short, there are few Jews and Palestinians who see citizenship within a democratic secular state as opportunity and possibility.

Yet citizenship free of ethnic or religious identity holds out the opportunity and possibility for normalizing life in the land by undercutting, at least in the public realm, the very ideas and attitudes that have led to the cycle of dislocation and destruction. By denying any single destiny, claim to indigenous status, or even the sense that separation is essential to identity and a future, citizenship in the democratic secular state of Israel/Palestine allows for the demilitarization of those very claims. Israel/Palestine may indeed be seen as the Holy Land by Jews, Christians and Muslims, but the politics and pursuit of ordinary life can only be achieved through a secular political system.

Citizenship is thus a disciplining of claims – political, cultural and religious – and the creation of a neutral place in which the pursuit of ordinary life takes precedence. Separated from the trajectory of any particular conception of priority and destiny, citizenship opposes the imposition of any specific claim as essential to the functioning of society.

Claims can be made, grievances posited, religious sensibilities focused, but only as contributions to an overall public discussion. *The very secularity of citizenship is itself a claim on the community, but one that binds citizens to the functioning and future of a community that has an evolving particularity within and beyond the particularities of the past.*

Here, too, a necessary discipline is entered as the particularities of settler and indigenous, Jew, Christian and Muslim, Israeli and Palestinian, have another reference point and framework through which they must pass. Citizenship as a reference point, an evolving particularity as it were, encompasses and transgresses these other particularities. Because it involves concrete issues of life, education, health, environment, security and defense, citizenship demands that previous particularities and the claims within them be subject to self-reflection and critical examination.

As the birthplace of three world religions with Jerusalem as a common home, this self-reflection could also become a base for further reflection of all those who adhere to these religions. By demobilizing the political claims of culture and religion, breaking the division of settler and indigenes, and by adding a layer to identity that transcends any one particularity and in the process becomes one itself, the demilitarization of these religions is at last within the realm of possibility. The challenge lies here: the demilitarization and secularization of the political realm may lead to a demessianization in the religious realm.[25]

As politics, with citizenship at its center, refuses a salvific role *vis-à-vis* historic claims of settler and indigenous life, so too religion, with the flourishing of ordinary life pursued in a framework outside of its own purview, must review its understanding of destiny and salvation. In a demilitarized environment where ordinary life flourishes and where bonds between people of different ethnic and religious backgrounds bear fruit, it becomes increasingly difficult to posit a religious superiority over against those of other religious or secular perspectives.

The watchword might become this: *just as the flourishing of ordinary life demands the co-mingling of individual and collective life, so too the question of destiny and salvation. Salvation at the expense of others, over against others, becoming so often a collective disaster for the ones 'outside' of this destiny and salvation (and often a disaster for those within the saved community as well), can no longer be posited as destiny and salvation.* Rather destiny and salvation are increasingly seen within a framework that, like citizenship, includes and transcends particularity or, if you will, evolves into another, broader configuration.

Citizenship is a forging of a new ecumenical political reality and religion can hardly escape this creation. Religious ecumenism follows this model, with its rhythms and symbols to be sure, but with no less consequence. Ultimate questions bracketed in public life are reinterpreted in religious life. There are many difficult areas here and the accusation of relativism, like the accusation regarding the limitations of claims within citizenship, is heard frequently. Featured also is a sometimes tortured logic of theology that seeks to provide a way of accommodation while clinging to exclusive claims.

Still the trajectory is clear: destiny and salvation become more broadly defined and less sharply focused as the 'other' is lived with and recognized as neighbour and participant in ordinary and common life. The redefinition of destiny and salvation as inclusive of all in religion is the path opened by citizenship in the political realm. Religions can hardly hold on to an exclusive definition of truth when the citizens of the community refuse this claim in the structures of their collective life.

Ecumenism on the political and religious level, like citizenship and the democratic secular state, projects values and perspectives. The disciplining of religion, the forced re-evaluation of truth, destiny and salvation – or at least the enforced refusal to allow one community's sense of ultimate truth reign in the public realm – has as its foundation a preference for inclusion and an option for ordinary life as superior to 'otherness' and the extraordinary. It is an option for the 'broken middle', as the British philosopher Gillian Rose articulated it: the in-between, the unfinished, the tension between past and future, reality and hope.[26]

The ecumenical possibility of Jerusalem, that ever-promising and too often violent symbol of messianic fulfillment, is exactly a broken middle – the geographic, cultural and religious middle of

Israel/Palestine and the place that Jews and Palestinians can meet in their suffering and brokenness. Rather than banners and symbols, the militarized language of God and messianic fulfillment which often makes Jerusalem unbearable and unlivable, Jerusalem as the broken middle seeks a solidarity in the experience of suffering and the possibility that a solidarity against further suffering may be established. Memories and grievances are brought here as are the particularities of Jewish and Palestinian identity, but the movement within and beyond both can only begin somewhere else, in a place that carries the values of inclusion and secularity.

In forging a new political space, citizenship collapses the histories of injustice and the self-righteousness that grows within those histories so that a new history can be embarked upon. Memories remain, as they should, but the new political space allows those memories to exist within a different configuration, shifting from the cycle of atrocity to a movement of inclusion that promotes ordinary life. Particularity does not disappear; rather it is transformed in the broken middle and in its transformation creates new middles.

As the broken middle continues to evolve, the lessons of suffering, exclusion and atrocity are mutually embraced and the violation of one becomes the violation of the other. Ultimately, the middle is less the 'between' of two separate and separated communities, Jews and Palestinians, the 'between' of three religions, Judaism, Christianity and Islam, or even the secularity that these religions, in their militarism, often contribute to. Rather, the 'between' becomes a place of solidarity where the ordinary becomes a gateway to the ultimate and in turn the ultimate is more and more defined and worked through in terms of the ordinary.

For how do we encounter the ultimate if not through the ordinary? How can we consider the ends of life apart from the middles of life? Separation narrows our vision and destiny as inclusion expands it. Perhaps citizenship should then rightly be considered, at least from the point of view of religious people, as necessary to a mature religiosity, as a needed discipline and opportunity, and as a gateway to something more that religious faith promises.

Here the question of indigenous peoples again comes to the fore. Within citizenship and the religiosity that citizenship helps foster, the distinctions and particularities that characterize so much of life are demystified and relativized. While particularities may contribute to the overall movement of the public realm toward justice and peace, the ontological connection of particularity and destiny is diminished.

Cultural and religious claims are relativized and seen as historically formed and contextually situated. Always evolving, though most often seen as originally given and formed, the trajectory of particularity is freed from an essentialism that seeks to freeze history and often serves as a cover for past or present tendencies toward domination. *It is only by severing the ontological claims of particularity that the strength of certain values found within particularities can surface.*

Therefore the fate of indigenous people, much like the fate of the Jewish people in Israel and elsewhere, is important in the public realm because the fate of all people is important. Whether the internal life of the people is strong or weak, whether there is a future for a people as internally projected, is an internal claim that cannot concern the larger political structure except in so far as a group of people are being discriminated against because of their identity or affiliation.

If a particular community can only fulfill its own internally constructed destiny by pursuing certain rituals and cultural ways, the community itself must pursue these needs. If the political structure cannot accommodate this or if the political structure makes it difficult to continue in a certain fashion, then the community must either argue its case in terms of the benefits it may bring to the larger polity or sacrifice to maintain certain norms and ways. The larger political structure cannot be concerned or reoriented to the objectives and claims of a particular community whether the claims are argued in terms of indigenous rights, as Palestinians claim, or historic suffering or biblical promises, as Jewish Israelis claim.

Over the long course of history the meeting of settlers and indigenous peoples involves an unexpected assimilation. Even the identities of those who claim a continuing particularity change, and most often original peoples and the settlers who come into contact with them take on the coloration and expression of mixture. They become middles themselves, who in turn give birth to other middles.

That Judaism and the Jewish people have kept a specific identity through time is written about endlessly and often without specificity. Yet recent scholarship shows the cultural evolution and distance that each Jewish culture has from an earlier one. Throughout, the center has been the covenant and, though variously interpreted and articulated, that center remains.

But just as Jews have no responsibility *per se* to pay attention to indigenous Palestinian culture, neither do Palestinians have a responsibility toward Jews and Judaism. *It is the meeting of Jews and*

Palestinians in a struggle for land and power that binds their history and future and the respect due each other is the fight for citizenship and a democratic structure that allows the preservation of particularity or its abandonment without prioritizing either.[27]

Paradoxically, it may be in the struggle to preserve and project particularity in the public realm that ultimately reduces vibrant communities and their expressions to empty postures that legitimate almost anything for self-preservation. Who could argue that the last decades of Jewish empowerment have made Jews more ethical, more attentive to others, or even more closely attached to the covenant?

Empowered, the rhetoric of the indigenous or the chosen often is used to increase and insure dominance. Then not only is the 'other' persecuted, but an internal persecution takes place as well. Those who seek to call the community back from oppressing others are themselves oppressed and often exiled from the community even as it presumes to speak in the language of God and the covenant.

Those in exile become mute, often inarticulate on the deeper issues of the very community they flee, even as they carry the values of the community into exile. Romanticizing indigenous communities can lead in the same direction: those who dissent, especially when the community gains some semblance of power, are themselves exiled. This is the fate of many Jews *and* Palestinians within the expanded state of Israel and the Palestinian Authority that exists within and under that state.[28]

The argument for citizenship over against religious and ethnic identities as defining in the public realm is an argument against a public recognition of pluralism. It is not an argument against pluralism or exclusivity *per se*. The priority of citizenship in the structuring and pursuit of ordinary life is a judgement that only citizenship can tame the passions and chasten the claims of particular communities that conquer and suffer. *Citizenship thus provides a possibility for the free expression of affirmation and dissent and an evolution of new structures, identities and sensibilities that may mitigate or even end the cycle of atrocity that afflicts humanity.*

But the option for the limitation of community claims, including the claim of being guided by God, can also be a religious claim. Here God, even the God one affirms as having a plan for a certain community or humanity itself, is limited by human agency and diversity. Messianic claims are internalized and argued for but not imposed. God can be spoken of, may even speak, but cannot determine the structure of a shared political life.

Thus a diaspora religiosity is imposed if not chosen and perhaps chosen once imposed as the place from which, at least for the religious, the word of God is spoken and heard. Organized religion and the expression of religiosity in general is relegated to a permanent minority position, or if held by the majority, remains a minority in the rule of law and governance. When the religious will *is* the public will even then the articulation must be secular in language and application.

This sensibility may encourage the realization of the new Jerusalem, the Jerusalem of light and justice, of peace, fraternity and sorority, in short the peaceable Kingdom so often alluded to in the scriptures of Judaism, Christianity and Islam. Still questions remain. Can indigenous Palestinians, realizing the historical wrongs inflicted on them, live within such a vision? Can Jewish settlers, returning to the land of their ancestors, fleeing from a burning Europe, and over time becoming indigenous to the land, accept a limitation on their own victory? It is difficult for Jews and Palestinians to accept that their own identities have evolved and will continue to evolve and that both identities will one day fuse and be transformed. Can the broken middle of Jerusalem survive and flourish with citizenship rather than messianism as its banner?

Anthony Lewis, a Jewish columnist for the *New York Times*, recently came to the same conclusion that the Palestinian intellectual Edward Said came to some years ago: that the process of Israeli settlement of Palestine has gone so far as to make separation of Jews and Palestinians impossible. Even the declaration of a Palestinian state would be in name only. Visiting Israel just before the elections in 1999, Lewis acknowledged the coming Palestinian state on parts of the West Bank and Gaza and its limitations: 'There will almost certainly be a Palestinian state ... but it will be a state of a peculiar kind. Its citizens will have to go through Israeli security checks in traveling from one part of their own country to another. In entering or leaving the new Palestine, they will be subject to Israeli controls. The state will be utterly dependent on Israel economically.' Lewis quotes Meron Benvenisti: 'All of Palestine is a binational entity, even though politics demands a different reality. It's one space.'[29]

At the same time that the viability of a Palestinian state was being questioned by Lewis, the new prime minister, Ehud Barak, prepared to build a 29-mile elevated highway connecting Gaza and the West Bank, or perhaps more accurately stated, the segmented and limited parts of Gaza and the West Bank controlled by the Palestinian

Authority. Barak's hope was to provide a way for Palestinians to reinvigorate their deteriorating situation and claim nation-state status despite the problems that Lewis and Benvenisti cited. It was almost as if a secondary citizenship was being proposed for those who will not have citizenship within the state that surrounds them.[30]

In this scenario, Palestinians in the West Bank and Gaza will have a citizenship much like the Palestinians within the pre-1967 borders of Israel who hold Israeli citizenship, a second-class citizenship that marks their ethnic and religious identity but denies them the freedom and future found among the first-class citizens of Israel who are by definition Jews. The two remnant Palestinian populations will then hold a similar limited citizenship and passports displaying nationalities that are, on the one hand, not their own and, on the other hand, void as to the real substance of nationality. Palestinian refugees remain outside the land and citizenship as the expanded state of Israel closes its borders and those of the Palestinian state it surrounds and controls.

As the settler highways for Jews on the West Bank connect Israeli towns and by-pass Palestinian towns and villages, the new connecting highways for Palestinians will by-pass the Jewish population of Israel. In any other geographic location, apartheid would be the term used for such an evolving system. And in most other geographic locations, citizenship in a democratic secular society would be proposed as the only sane alternative.

At this time at least, the question of settlers and indigenous peoples fails to address the startling creation of a state of a 'peculiar kind'. It is reminiscent of what one scholar of American slavery labeled the 'peculiar institution', a structure of oppression so unstable and immoral that it had no future. History judged that peculiar institution to be a folly, one that exacted a toll of human suffering, the consequence of which remains with us today more than a century after its demise. Is this, too, the fate of Jews and Palestinians?

Just weeks after Anthony Lewis' commentary, President Clinton hosted President Hosni Mubarak of Egypt in Washington, D.C. At the concluding press conference a reporter asked President Clinton about the fate of Palestinian refugees in the coming years. Anticipating a renewed peace effort under the new Israeli prime minister Ehud Barak, Clinton remarked: 'It will ... depend on what the nature of the settlement is: How much land will the Palestinians have? Where will it be? How does it correspond to where people lived before? ... And I would like it if the Palestinian people felt free and were free to live wherever they like, wherever they want to live.'[31]

To the uproar that followed, including the accusation by some Jewish leaders that such statements opened the possibility of the return of the refugees within the borders of the state of Israel and thus undermined the legitimacy of the Jewish state, Clinton's advisers assured the critics that his comments in no way altered traditional U.S. policies with regard to Israel.

Still the moral and practical logic to Clinton's statement increasingly takes center stage, even after the failure of the Camp David Summit. For where can Palestinian refugees return to if not Israel? The state has expanded to encompass all of what was once called Palestine. The only question is whether Palestinians who live in the expanded state of Israel and those who return will remain a remnant in an apartheid reality or whether, over time and with struggle, a civil rights movement will evolve. This movement will include Jews and Palestinians who embrace citizenship and refuse a peculiar institution that can only continue the cycle of dislocation and death.

Mapping the Holocaust and Israel

Judaism and Jewish life exist within the dynamic of a history that is both ancient and contemporary, a diaspora sensibility that is now empowered within Israel and the United States. Thus the currents and cross-currents found within Jewish life: intense religiosity and extreme secularity, a moderate and right-wing nationalism, a Jewish identity revolving around the Holocaust and Israel, a claim to innocence in suffering and empowerment. Like most ideology, philosophy and theology, Jewish commentators articulate Jewish history and its future without precise maps, especially when those maps contradict deeply held emotions and sensibilities. Or the maps referred to are partial, drawn to suit community needs and aspirations.

The map of the Holocaust is, of course, widely held and discussed in the Jewish world, but this map becomes distorted when the other map of contemporary Jewish life, the map of Israel/Palestine, is unannounced. More often, the map of the Holocaust and Jewish suffering in Europe is applied to an abstracted map of Israel/Palestine *as if the Holocaust was just ending, as if the trains to Auschwitz were still waiting, as if Israel was still in formation.*

Ariel Sharon's statement in the post-September 11th period exemplified this understanding. Accusing the United States of trying to 'appease the Arabs at our expense' – that is neglecting what Israel considers to be Palestinian terrorism to form a worldwide coalition that includes Arab and Muslim governments – Sharon recalled the policy of appeasement in the 1930s that led to the Munich Pact of 1938 and the dismantling of Czechoslovakia. In bold terms, Sharon lectured the United States: 'Don't repeat the terrible mistakes of 1938, when the enlightened democracies in Europe decided to sacrifice Czechoslovakia for a comfortable temporary solution.' Sharon concluded his comments, 'Israel will not be Czechoslovakia.'[32]

The invocation of the Holocaust world in a time of unprecedented Jewish empowerment both in Israel and the U.S. is the framework through which all other Jewish movements must be analysed. This is true of Jewish discourse in the U.S. and Israel whether religious or secular. Whatever the terminology adopted – Settler Judaism, Constantinian Judaism or Jewish fundamentalism – the context remains: a post-Holocaust Judaism and Jewish life grappling with a newfound power in the United States and Israel, yet existing in a time warp that is sometimes consciously self-serving, often operating on a raw and subconscious terrain.

One moment Jews proceed in a sophisticated, thoroughly modern way within the international nation-state system; the next moment in a pre-modern particularity with an anger and a sense of Jewish destiny that transcends the nation-state system and the responsibilities of a nuclear power. Israel's sense of itself is as a nation-state *and* as a ghetto, abiding by some international agreements and totally disregarding others for reasons of national security *and* Jewish destiny.

The danger of Settler/Constantinian Judaism is found not in its essential belief structure but in its place on the world stage. There *is* a difference between a synagogue and a nation-state, between belief and action in the world. Often, empowered Jews miss this important distinction.

Only with the map of the Holocaust, *with the understanding of our place in the world then,* and without the map of Israel/Palestine as it exists today, *with the understanding of our place in the world today,* is Judaism and Jewish life a force that can be dangerous to Jews and others. Unfortunately, those Jews who identify this second map are often branded as misguided and dangerous. They may even be labeled as traitors, self-hating Jews. Non-Jews who identify the map of Israel/Palestine are labeled as well, as innocents, as Arab-lovers, as anti-Semites.

There is a personal and professional cost to speaking of what Jews are doing in the world in relation to the map of Israel/Palestine. Politically, the cost is high. Once labeled as a self-hating Jew or an anti-Semite, one's character is undermined and distorted. Thus the fear of public speech in relation to Israel and on behalf of the Palestinians is substantial, chilling, for some, participation in what should be open, substantive debate.

Here we enter the terrain of the ecumenical dialogue, a dialogue between Judaism and Christianity in the West, but now expanded to the U.S.'s political culture, in which limits are placed on the discussion of Jews and Israel. In this dialogue, Jews and others are forced into a historical discussion of anti-Semitism as if it remains the defining aspect of Jewish life in the present. Because it is a nation-state, Israel cannot be considered only in such terms. Though Jews are one of the most empowered groups in the U.S., discussions of that empowerment are often censored.

A politicized ecumenical dialogue places the reconsideration of faith questions after the Holocaust into public life where the rules of analysis that apply to any group are suspended. The fear is the charge of anti-Semitism or the encouragement of anti-Semitism, so the secret, known by many, cannot be uttered in public discourse. That is why the ecumenical dialogue on the religious and political level has become an ecumenical deal, where the suspension of critical analysis becomes the rule and resentment toward a lack of a level playing field is buried, at least for the time being.

A recent expression of this religious ecumenism with political ramifications is the statement *Dabru Emet*, 'Speaking the Truth'. Developed by prominent Jews in the field of Jewish Studies – Tikva Frymer-Kensky, Professor of Hebrew Bible at the Divinity School of the University of Chicago; David Novak, the J. Richard and Dorothy Shiff Chair of Jewish Studies at the University of Toronto; Peter Ochs, the Edgar M. Bronfman Professor of Modern Judaic Studies at the University of Virginia; David Fox Sandmel, the Jewish Scholar at the Institute for Christian and Jewish Studies in Baltimore, and Michael A. Signer, the Abrams Professor of Jewish Thought and Culture at the University of Notre Dame – *Dabru Emet* is an attempt to affirm and articulate the changing relationship of Christians and Jews after the Holocaust. In some ways, the statement is bold, especially in its affirmation that the anti-Jewishness of traditional Christianity has significantly abated. A new partnership between Jews and Christians has been forged and is acknowledged in the following statements: Jews and Christians worship the same God; Jews and Christians seek authority from the same book – the bible (what Jews call 'Tanakh' and Christians call the 'Old Testament'); Jews and Christians accept the moral principles of Torah; Jews and Christians must work together for justice and peace.

The more controversial aspects of the statement regard the Holocaust and Israel. The statements and explanations are worth quoting in their entirety:

> Nazism was not a Christian phenomenon.
>
> Without the long history of Christian anti-Judaism and Christian violence against Jews, Nazi ideology could not have taken hold nor could it have been carried out. Too many Christians participated in, or were sympathetic to, Nazi atrocities against Jews. Other Christians did not protest sufficiently against these atrocities. But Nazism itself was not an inevitable outcome of Christianity. If the Nazi extermination of the Jews had been fully successful, it would have turned its murderous rage more directly to Christians. We recognize with gratitude those Christians who risked or sacrificed their lives to save Jews during the Nazi regime. With that in mind, we encourage the continuation of recent efforts in Christian theology to repudiate unequivocally contempt of Judaism and the Jewish people. We applaud those Christians who reject this teaching of contempt, and we do not blame them for the sins committed by their ancestors.
>
> Christians can respect the claim of the Jewish people upon the land of Israel.
>
> The most important event for Jews since the Holocaust has been the reestablishment of a Jewish state in the Promised Land. As members of a biblically based religion, Christians appreciate that Israel was promised – and given – to Jews as the physical center of the covenant between them and God. Many Christians support the state of Israel for reasons far more profound than mere politics. As Jews, we applaud this support. We also recognize that Jewish tradition mandates justice for all non-Jews who reside in a Jewish state.[33]

These two statements are controversial to be sure. For some Jews, Nazism was an inevitable outcome of Christianity, at least the way Christianity developed over the centuries. Or, if not inevitable, the combination of Christian power and anti-Semitism made persecution of the Jews, even the mass death of Jews, a permanent possibility. As for the 'Promised Land' – promised and given to the Jews – there are many Jews for which this language is, in a contemporary sense, foreign in tone and sensibility. Historically, much of the ecumenical dialogue from the Jewish partner has been the disciplining of Christian biblical claims. The Christian claim of being the New Israel, as well as the mandate to convert Jews and others – both of which can be seen by Christians as a biblical mandate – have been reinterpreted often through insistence of the Jewish community. Is it proper now for Jews to insist on biblical support by Christians for the state of Israel? Is this not a furtherance of the already powerful ecumenical deal?

In the post-September 11th period, Muslims are being invited into this ecumenical deal, but again their grievances toward Christians and Jews, including the state of Israel, must be buried as the ticket of admission. Hence the concentration on fundamentalisms – Jewish, Christian and Islamic – with those not invited to the table of ecumenical relations singled out as the culprits in a myriad of events and problems.

That Ariel Sharon – and before him Yitzhak Rabin, Shimon Peres, Benjamin Netanyahu and Ehud Barak, to name only the prime ministers after the Oslo accords – were not fundamentalists or even religious, that they and their predecessors all helped to establish the state of Israel, indeed helped to create the Israeli consensus that thought through and established the map of Israel as it exists today, is a fact almost never alluded to.

The fundamentalist option *as the problem* renders the Israeli–Palestinian conflict as resolvable if only the extremists and extremism could be eliminated. But since Yassir Arafat has been known for years, especially by Israel, as a moderate, and if the Israeli leadership truly desires peace and a two-state solution, why is it that every government from the 1967 war onward has made such a solution less and less possible? The repeated calls for settlement freezes have come and gone through the years as the boundaries of Israel have expanded. Each boundary advance becomes a 'fact' that cannot be rolled back and the mere suggestion of such a roll-back is then defined as extremism.

Within this context, Barak's offer *is* 'generous'; his plan does not take any more land than Israel has already taken and grants some symbolic sovereignty in Jerusalem where once real sovereignty was demanded but can no longer be conceded as thinkable. The failure of Camp David is seen politically as Arafat's rejection of the generous offer but it was Barak who lost the next election as someone who the electorate felt had offered the Palestinians too much. Indeed a vernacular reading of Sharon's platform was that Barak had offered up the Jewish state to a terrorist. After Sharon's victory, Netanyahu and others positioned themselves to the right of Sharon for future campaigns. Their charge? Sharon was ready to compromise the greater land of Israel.

The politicized ecumenical deal does little to encourage Israel or Jews in the U.S. to deal honestly with the questions before us. Without honesty, there is left only a bullying that I encountered in Christchurch. Yossi Olmert does not represent the majority of Jews in Israel or in the U.S., but he does represent a political climate backed by state power in Israel and the silence of American Jewish leadership. In this case, religious fundamentalists are bit players in a larger drama, aided by a liberal Jewish establishment that lacks the courage to confront a future that threatens to engulf us.

That future – a Settler/Constantinian Judaism beyond our control – is, in the long run, indefensible by any Jewish ethic Jews were nurtured within. Friends of the Jewish people do us no favours when they stand silently by or, for lack of courage, allow the Holocaust map to be brandished as the trump to any question or critique.

U.S. foreign policy is culpable as well. No matter the official positions, the United States has been the great enabler, without which the expanded state of Israel could not exist in its present configuration. U.S. foreign policy often cloaks itself in innocence and, in the case of Israel, the U.S.'s 'friendship' is explained in a different way than its friendship with any other nation. Mostly it is explained without explanation, as something to be taken for granted. But is any political alliance, especially one where strategic cooperation has sometimes been betrayed by illegal intelligence gathering, to be taken for granted, as if it goes without saying or analysis?

Blaming the current impasse on fundamentalism also serves as a cover for the U.S. If the U.S. supports its own positions on Jerusalem and the occupied territories, why then continue, even escalate, financial, cultural, political and military aid to Israel? Those who see the map of the Holocaust and Israel/Palestine deserve a response to this question from the U.S. foreign policy establishment.

In the post-September 11th period, a critical review of U.S. foreign policy is in order. The current mood in the U.S. is one that divides the forces of light and darkness, the civilized and uncivilized. But the case of Israel and the Palestinians demonstrates that such divisions are too neat. The world outside the U.S.'s borders is more complicated, as is the world inside its borders.

'Fundamentalism' is an easy category that must be evaluated against the backdrop of history, culture, religion and politics, holding to the ideals of tolerance and respect to be sure, but understanding that claims and counter-claims, the announced and unannounced maps of every place and situation, the ever-evolving maps of territory and identity, need a committed and detached spirit of inquiry. It is in Israel's interest that a vigilant and honest appraisal be made by both Jews and Americans.

Is it possible that a solidarity with Israel also demands a solidarity with the Palestinians, knowing that one community will never be secure without the other's security? A dual solidarity cannot be symmetrical at the outset, as Israel's dominance must be reversed in order to bring some kind of parity between the parties. At this juncture, 'even-handedness' is less solidarity than convenience, avoiding the hard questions and policies needed to redress the imbalance that spawns helicopter gunships and suicide bombers.

After the Holocaust and Israel, the choices before us as Jews are clear. Decisions are being made in the more sophisticated corridors of Jewish power and influence rather than by the bellicose religious minority labeled Jewish fundamentalists. As we have seen, the problem is less extremism than a moderation that is planned and expansive, backed by the power of Israel and the U.S. and framed in a liberal narrative that few, at least in the West, can argue with.

In this context, at the dawn of the twenty-first century, what does it mean to be faithful as a Jew? Arguing for the broken middle of Jerusalem is an argument against the bully in Christchurch as the future of the Jewish people. It is to say, within the complexities of Jewish and world history, that the pursuit of justice is at the center of Jewish life and that the pursuit becomes more challenging when in power than when a people is the victim of power.

Often the choice is presented to be in or out of power, as if there is no middle ground where an interdependent empowerment is struggled for. The world is presented as a place where the cycle of power rules and the effort to stay on top of that cycle is balanced only by those struggling to survive the bottom. In order to stay on top one must make sure that those over whom you have power never have the power to reverse the situation. The result is the militarization of politics, culture and religion on both sides until a war of attrition becomes the norm.

It is difficult to argue against the reality of this cycle in simple historical terms. It seems that eras of peace are followed by war. The oppressed, when given the chance, oppress others. Of course the language of power is rarely used by the victorious. Rather, past grievances and victimization, and political and religious claims to righteousness and innocence become the order of the day.

Can we claim to be Jewish if this cycle of power is affirmed as the last word? That we are either the victims of empire or the guardians of empire? That an interdependent empowerment is impossible? That the particularity of the Jewish witness must guard against the impulse toward the universal? That this dynamic of particularity and universality, so important to Jewish history and faith, must be rooted out as a danger to the survival of Jews, Judaism and the Jewish state? That to survive the language of innocence we must disguise policies of violence so that, in the end, Jews no longer understand where rhetoric and reality begins and ends?

We have reached this place of decision. The fundamental questions facing the future of Jewish life are before us. But the issue is not a Judaism or an Israeli state hijacked by Jewish fundamentalists. Nor is it a fight against Islamic fundamentalists. Rather, it is a struggle for the heart and soul of the Jewish people.

3 The Prophetic in the Post-Holocaust Era

In 1963 Emmanuel Levinas, the French Jewish philosopher, wrote an essay 'Judaism and the Present'. In this essay, Levinas discerns the central trajectory of the Judaic sensibility and the role of the Jewish prophet. Judaism, he writes, is a 'non-coincidence with its time, within coincidence: in the radical sense of the term it is an anachronism, the simultaneous presence of a youth that is attentive to reality and impatient to change it, and old age that has seen it all and is returning to the origins of things'.[1]

Of the prophetic within Judaism, Levinas writes that the 'most deeply committed man, one who can never be silent, the prophet, is also the most separate being, and the person least capable of becoming an institution. Only the false prophet has an official function.' Levinas concludes his discussion with this haunting and perceptive challenge: 'But this essential content [of Judaism and the prophetic] cannot be learned like a catechism or summarized like a credo ... It is acquired through a way of living that is a ritual and heartfelt generosity, wherein a human fraternity and an attention to the present are reconciled with an eternal distance in relation to the contemporary world. It is an asceticism, like the training of a fighter.'[2]

This summation of Judaism and the prophetic, this connection of the two, one that cannot be severed without maiming both, this particular Judaic contribution to the world, is, at one and the same time, in danger of disappearing *and* reappearing with incredible force.

At first glance, the possibility of the prophetic disappearing from the world seems unduly alarming. After all, the universities are filled with courses on the prophets and book after book of learned scholarship contextualizing and historicizing the prophets is published yearly.

On the Jewish side, readers are returning to the seminal works of Martin Buber and Abraham Joshua Heschel on the prophets as part of a revival of interest in Jewish life, even as remembrance of the Holocaust and the state of Israel become more complex and less central to the practice of Judaism.

On the Christian side, Walter Brueggemann produces volume after volume of commentary on the prophets and essays on their meaning for contemporary Christian life. Liberation theology, emanating from the periphery of world power, especially through the works of Gustavo Gutierrez, the Peruvian Catholic priest, and James Cone, the African-American theologian, has provided an activist vision of the prophetic in our time.

Though discussion of the prophetic and even the lived witness of the poor and disenfranchised – including, of course, people struggling with those on the margins – is increasing as we enter the twenty-first century, the prospects for the prophetic seem dim. We know more about the ancient prophets, their situation and psychology, even the different layers of text within the Hebrew canon, than ever before in history. Even the relationship of Jesus to the prophetic tradition has been explored and debated, perhaps for the first time since the followers of Jesus debated the meaning of his life.

Movements that carry the prophetic are alive in numbers and geographic dispersion beyond any such convergence in the last centuries, at least since the Reformation. Still, one feels time pushing on, as if the analysis has run its course, and as if the movements themselves have run into a wall that defies penetration. Even the feminist critique of power, itself a form of liberation theology, has come full circle, to a point where feminist scholars often replicate the academic careers of their male counterparts and, not unlike men, peer into a future whose movement is stilled.

How can these claims be substantiated? Surely evidence to the contrary, cited above, demands caution. What can be said with some certainty, however, is that the prophetic has fueled Judaism and Christianity from their origins, and that the canon, institutionalized and ritualized in various Constantinian arrangements through the centuries, has sought to seal the prophetic, doom it to the repetition of texts and the predictable liturgical year, and make of the prophetic demands a utopian vision that is recited in prayers and sung beautifully in hymns. And this, too, is happening in our time.

Yet a further caution is found here. Is this not the fate, then and now, of the prophetic? That it boldly proclaims itself, but then is disciplined by the powers that be? That the prophetic is taken in, transformed, written down, canonized, so that after the moment that the prophet speaks to has passed, it can be held up as the summit of a religious vision that no one seeks to live? Is this not exactly the fate that the prophet has continually experienced, announcing words and judgements that are obvious to them and within the recited and ritualized tradition, only to be told that the prophetic canon is sealed and that it is only arrogance to claim to speak in those bold tones? This experience points to a continual disciplining and eruption of the prophetic voice throughout history. Is our time any different?

Attempts to differentiate the past from the present in absolute terms often lead to overstatements and heightened claims. Upon reflection, we see change and continuity in history; the human condition has a stability that defies changes in culture and technology. Or perhaps better stated, the human condition, or at least the way we understand that condition with its prospects and limitations, changes over time.

Culture and technology contextualize the human without fundamentally altering it. The same is true for our understanding of the ultimate, the transcendent, the place of our origins and our destiny that is not observable or obvious to the eye or the intellect. Continuity and change can be found here as well, for the stubbornness of belief in God, despite the predictions of its immediate demise trumpeted at the beginning of the twentieth century, attests to this.

The prophetic is in a similar situation, appearing as ancient and modern, discernible within the biblical text and subtly changing. The longevity and evolution of the prophetic seems to suggest that, like the human condition and the search for transcendence, the prophetic is a permanent fixture of the human landscape, without which humanity would be impoverished.

Perhaps impoverishment is too weak a term for the diminution or erasure of the prophetic from the human. Although the prophetic is often seen as an outside aspect of the human and human society, rarely announced or needed, a claim can be made for its centrality, even when it is absent.

The passing of time in its personal and communal dimensions alerts us to routines of life and their importance, just as it alerts us to the emptiness of passing time when hope and expectation are held in abeyance. Life without routine is chaotic and ultimately unmanageable. Life without a dimension that points beyond itself is a boredom that can only exist by feeding itself with material objects that point, in a fetishistic way, to the same beyond.

It is no accident that modern life, though seemingly deprived of the transcendent, points beyond itself with a consumer ethic that is raised up in God-like destiny. Even the 'religious' participate in this particular idolatry of materiality. If it is true that a person and community worships what is central to its life, then the ark of the covenant in synagogues should be filled with designer clothes, automobiles and cell phones instead of the Torah. The consecrated communion wafers distributed as the Eucharist should be shaped in images of our ultimate commitments: dollar bills, plush carpeting, vacation homes. But, it is interesting, perhaps important, that even in synagogues and churches where the prophetic is routinely trivialized, the prophetic word seems to retain a value.

Life without movement, even the perfect life, defined in modernity and in contemporary Judaism and Christianity as family, affluence and power, is somehow deficient without at least acknowledging something beyond it. Is this the reason for new age movements – including ancient wisdom/new age sensibilities – that attract the affluent and the seeker?

The prophetic is many things to be sure, but it seems that a life without transcending self and the material, a life without decision that is more than self-serving, is a life that cannot be lived, even if transcendence and decision are portrayed in symbolic form. Perhaps this is the main function of religion in our time, to symbolize a reality that is, for most people, too difficult or inconvenient to even consider in real life.

This concept of beyond, or the decision to acknowledge a higher reality, is not simply or even primarily transcendent, at least as transcendent is usually thought of. It is not high above or below for that matter. Rather, it represents the possibility of breakthrough, of a new beginning, amid life, in the middle of life, where the material conditions of the world are established and the experience of the miraculous is no longer anticipated. Interrupted or not, with high drama or halting regularity, life goes on. And the realization that life goes on with and without us, that our unique sensibility and presence is appreciated *and* unnecessary to time and nature, forces us to experience life in a different way.

Over time, expectations lessen or deepen, depending on personality and vision, but regularity is established. Even loss eventually becomes part of that regularity, so that new beginnings are missed or dismissed, unnoticed or forfeited. Yet without new beginnings, there is no life. Waking from sleep to the new morning, experiencing the young, finding light in the darkness, all of these experiences are the breath of life. In each of these experiences, in each new beginning, the prophetic can be found. For is not the prophetic at its very core, the possibility that newness, companionship, awareness and love are possible? That the impossible is possible, not in the defying of nature or time, but in its fulfillment?

Levinas speaks of this moment as here and not here, as coming within the present but from a distance, existing in time and out of time. Generosity is embraced and enhanced; a freedom is granted and taken. One can never be silent about such an experience, if by silence we mean something more than the absence of words. There is aloneness in the prophetic that comes through a connection with others, a reaching out that reaffirms an essential solitude and a possible solidarity.

There is also practice; for Levinas, the prophetic cannot be learned like a catechism or summarized like a credo. Is that because the prophetic must be discerned, thought through, embraced for the duration of life rather than as a momentary feeling? Perhaps this is because the prophetic cannot be lifted out of life, examined in liturgical moments, or preserved for certain rituals or in certain texts. Rather, the prophetic is to be carved into the routine of life, just as a fighter constructs an ascetic environment in which to train.

The prophets are hardly abstract for most who write about them. Though scholarship admits little of the personal, at least directly, I noticed quickly and at a young age that the prophets attracted highly engaged scholars who led dual lives. Part of that duality was the highly trained scholar, most often in biblical studies, the other part, a person embroiled in the affairs of the world. This latter quality was no doubt personal in the sense of certain psychological properties and personal propensities that might or might not be explainable in psychological terms.

At least in the twentieth century, the prophets' gravitational pull on the person was also driven by events. Perhaps it is best to say that the personal and historical often come together in the study of the prophets which, often as not, is a thinly disguised prophetic commentary on the times in which we live.

Take Buber, Heschel and Levinas as examples of this interplay. From their earliest years, all three exhibited strengths in the intellectual and religious arena as well as strong personalities in the public arena. Also they were formed in the crucible of the twentieth century, within the Holocaust and its aftermath, as refugees and exiles.[3]

Brueggemann and Gutierrez were likewise formed in the crucible of the twentieth century, Brueggemann as a post-Holocaust Christian in the U.S. and Gutierrez as a native American speaking for the poor of Peru and Latin America. In their works, the prophets are analysed in different scholarly forms but also in thinly disguised vignettes. These individuals are men on the run, from the Nazis, religious establishments, the military and global capitalism, analysing men on the run, the prophets. The ancient prophets are respected in their historic contexts; they are also mouthpieces for a wounded humanity and individuals who see that pain and cannot be silent.[4]

When I first read Buber and Heschel as a teenager, I noticed this immediately. The ancient was being brought near in a cadence that was difficult to deny. Years earlier at Hebrew school, the afternoon and early evening variety of the 1950s, my teachers, often with European accents, would recall stories about Moses and Aaron, Jeremiah and Isaiah which were strangely discordant with the America of opportunity and promise I learned about earlier in the day at public school. These stories were far away and near at the same time.

At that same moment, Martin Luther King, Jr., a person of another religion and culture, was embracing the prophetic mantle. He, too, spoke of the prophets as if they were simply models for him and the movement he led, but I understood immediately, perhaps intuitively, that the model was an embodied presence and that the prophetic, indeed the prophet, was in our midst. Like these other students of the prophets, King was on the run from the law, a refugee in America, destined for the fate of so many ancient and contemporary prophets.

As a youngster following the civil rights movement and then entering college, the prophetic was always close to me. Weren't we all called to embody the prophetic, to be prophets in the world, in our time? My early Hebrew school training raised this possibility, though not because it was taught overtly or embodied by the community from which I learned and with whom I worshiped.

Like most American Jews of the time, my family was lower middle-class, mainstreaming into American life. In the U.S. the prophets were businessmen and inventors, those who fueled the economy and created technology that would bring about and maintain the American century of affluence and goodness. The latter, of course, was assumed because of the religious sensibility that allowed the U.S.'s economic expansion and military assertion, especially in competition with and against Godless communism.

But for me it was always more than circumstance, events and learning. From the earliest age I rebelled against the formality of Hebrew school and synagogue ritual as a form of hypocrisy and evasion. These judgements were no doubt too harsh and they were not informed by a close scrutiny of the lives of members of the congregation nor an informed reading of the prophetic canon.

This rebellion did not come from a learned or politicized family, or even a Reform affiliation that stressed the prophetic to the exclusion of Hebrew and the law. It may have been the stories of the prophetic canon as they filtered in from the background of my Orthodox, then Conservative synagogue affiliation. It no doubt had to do with a rebellious personality, but in looking back, and through all accounts that I can gather, rebelliousness was not an overt feature of my youthful personality. Quite the opposite: I was a quiet youngster, prone to reasonably good behavior, interested in sports and later public speaking and, for the most part, unexceptional.

It was the clash between the prophets and the Holocaust, an event that was being named as I entered college, that further challenged me. In Hebrew school, I had heard about the mass killing of European Jews, but the event itself was never mentioned or defined. Like the prophets, though much more opaquely, the Holocaust was in the background. It was not defining – the prophets were not defining either; rather, both hovered at the margins of American Jewish life.

Though it is difficult to understand this today with the center of Jewish life almost completely redefined, Israel, as a recently created nation-state, was on the margins as well. Perhaps the Jewish community realized, almost foresaw, the tremendous impact that the Holocaust and Israel would have on Jewish life. My teachers, no doubt subconsciously, feared the return of the Holocaust and saw Israel as central to Jewish identity and religiosity, and perhaps, again without conscious knowledge, feared even more the clash between these events and the prophetic itself.

In retrospect, the disorientation caused by the naming of the Holocaust is obvious and the reorientation that the state of Israel has forced upon Jewish life is obvious as well. But the obvious in retrospect is the inarticulate subconscious fear from the time before. The next dynamic, the prophetic in conversation with both events, could hardly have been foreseen consciously or subconsciously.

My own teacher, Richard Rubenstein, helped name the Holocaust as a formative event in Jewish history. It was a strange and defining coincidence that I sat in his classroom in the 1970s. Unbeknownst to me, his book, *After Auschwitz: Radical Theology and Contemporary Judaism*, which had been published in 1966, set off a firestorm in Jewish life. The Jewish community did not want the Holocaust to become a public discussion, either among Jews or in the wider American community. Rubenstein broke that taboo with bravado, one might even say with a vengeance.[5]

Today, the Holocaust is remembered in an almost liturgical way. But then, especially in Rubenstein's writing, the Holocaust was like a tornado that left little but devastation in its path. Rubenstein questioned the covenant with God and humanity in *After Auschwitz* because of God and humanity's silence *during* Auschwitz. Rubenstein accused Jewish theology, including Martin Buber and his teacher Abraham Joshua Heschel, the two most powerful Jewish voices of that generation, of avoiding the theological ramifications of the Holocaust. Both Buber and Heschel continued on, at least in Rubenstein's estimation, as if nothing had happened, as if the Holocaust was simply another experience of Jewish suffering.

Rubenstein thundered against this avoidance in a tone not unlike that of the prophets who railed against the Jewish betrayal of God's promise and lordship. And more. Like the Jewish prophets, Rubenstein exposed the Jewish community's hypocrisy in the silence that came after Auschwitz.

Was the Jewish community, especially Jewish leadership, afraid of admitting its own failures in relation to the Holocaust: that it was, at least in Rubenstein's analysis, through compromise, complicity and cowardice, an accomplice to the destruction of European Jewry? Were the Jewish theologies of Buber and Heschel, with their emphasis on creation, encounter, beauty and justice, rather than militarism and empowerment, also part of the problem then and now? Are the organizational and theological leaders of the Jewish people today as blind as they were then?

For these understandings, Rubenstein was exiled from his position as Hillel Rabbi at the University of Pittsburgh. He landed in Tallahassee, Florida in 1970 in a new department of religious studies; there was no organized Jewish presence in town and few Jews on the faculty, so that opposition to his thought and presence was insubstantial. I landed at the same university at the same time partly because the affluence of the Jewish world had eluded my own family and partly because students from the southern part of Florida had yet to achieve academic respectability among the more elite universities.

So there I was at 18 years of age confronted by a Jewish presence who had been exiled because of his views on the most horrific event of our century. He had been exiled as a Jew for refusing a Judaism that was complacent and assimilationist in its silence and comfort *after Auschwitz.* The peculiar, perhaps defining quality of Rubenstein's presence, at least in retrospect, was that he appeared as a prophet without God, all the time suggesting, by his very opposition, the possibility of God.

If there was one thing clear to me as I watched and listened to this impressive and difficult man, it was that the question of God was so important as to risk condemnation and exile. In Rubenstein's teaching, I never had a sense of an academic performance, of notes to be reviewed for testing, or papers to be done for evaluation. In fact, the entire process of grading was a mystery to my fellow students and me. Rubenstein paid little or no attention to this aspect of university life and the rumors were that he never even looked at the exams, only perused the papers and left it to graduate assistants to grade our efforts.

There was more to Rubenstein than this initial and groundbreaking book. During the time I spent with him he had his most fruitful writing years and book after book issued from him. His rage against the Holocaust and the silence surrounding it brought forth other volumes of boundary-crossing work: *My Brother Paul*, an inquiry into the common journey of Rubenstein and Paul of Tarsus; *Power Struggle: An Autobiographical Confession*, an account of his struggle with Judaism, Jewish theology and the Jewish community; *The Cunning of History: Mass Death and the American Future*, his attempt to place the lessons of the Holocaust within the broader parameters of modernity with its bureaucracy, social organization and advanced technology, credited with so much good, and in the Holocaust and after, responsible for so much evil.[6]

Taken separately, Rubenstein's works seem disparate – Jewish, Jewish-Christian, personal, American and global. But experiencing them together, or at least pieces of each that were delivered as a whole, the central force was undeniable. It was the rage of a prophet, pursued by history and Jewish leadership, who thought on the run, and whose exile deepened his concerns and honed his sensibility until his rage became a focused asceticism.

Rubenstein was also a rabbi, trained in rabbinic theology and practicing as a rabbi until the publication of *After Auschwitz*. His denial of the efficacy of the covenant after Auschwitz was therefore both against and within the rabbinic system. It was precisely the need to justify suffering in a theological system that drove Rubenstein from the rabbinate.

He took seriously the rabbinic sensibility of justifying Jewish suffering as punishment for the refusal to fulfill God's law, a sensibility found within and interpreted from the prophets. He in fact took it so seriously that he felt Jewish belief hinged on the ability or inability to affirm this. Rubenstein did not see his refusal to accept the covenant after Auschwitz as the abrogation of the covenant by God or the Jewish people; Rubenstein simply refused any longer to accept the terms of the covenant.

What Rubenstein argued against was the fudging on this central issue: either one accepted the scriptural terms of the covenant, instituted by God and voiced by the prophets, or one refused the covenant and thus Judaism. For Rubenstein, a pastoral option of principle and flexibility, a holding in abeyance any final parsing of the demands of the tradition, was not a strong point. Rather, Rubenstein exhibited a prophetic judgement on a rabbinic system driven to the extremity of its own convictions. In person and in thought, Rubenstein was that judgement. He embodied that extreme.

I also fought against the rabbinic system as I experienced it as a child, all the while absorbing its nuances and compromises, its fascinating swing between *halakhah* and *aggadah*, law and story, principle and outreach. In the United States of the 1950s and 1960s, strict enforcement of the rabbinic system was hardly tolerated by the community or even attempted by the rabbis. The pastoral option was exercised to its fullest.

With the mainstreaming of the American Jewish community, the impossibility of the rabbinic system itself became obvious. But that did not mean that the rabbinic system or the rabbis themselves were unappealing to me. In fact its very foreignness and inability, the very diminution of the rabbinic office and the rabbis themselves, intrigued me.

And here was Rubenstein, combining the role of the prophet and rabbi in one, heightening the challenge of both, even and especially as he disengaged from the tradition. Like the question of God, Rubenstein posed the role of the prophet and the rabbi in ways I had never encountered and with questions to which neither the tradition nor I had a response.

Yet if Rubenstein called for anything other than the dissolution of the Jewish tradition, he called for a response that brooked no compromise, or at last revealed its compromise rather than resorting to subterfuge or obfuscation. When Rubenstein spoke I never averted my eyes. He was too compelling. When I responded, I could not avert my eyes either.

There was no answer to Rubenstein's haunting analysis and no way to relegate it to the academic realm. His words were a challenge that I could not shake. How was I to respond to this prophetic critique of religion, Jewish life, and modernity? Was it true? And just as importantly, could I accept Rubenstein's understanding that without God, especially with the modern propensity and capacity for evil, only a cycle of power remained and that the choice was only to hold or be subdued by that power?

I found it impossible to disprove Rubenstein's assertions and impossible to accept them as defining for my life. There *had* to be a way out of this conundrum, or at least a place where solace and comfort could be found. If there was no way out, did I then have to join the powerful, indeed use my talents to augment that power, for my people and myself? I had never thought of myself in this way, as a corporate executive or as a political mover and shaker. Was this a failing, somehow an evasion of responsibility and calling?

It was then that I met William Miller, a southern historian, who years earlier had converted to Catholicism from a Methodist denomination. In 1973, he had published a curious book, *A Harsh and Dreadful Love: Dorothy Day and the Catholic Worker Movement*. I came across the book when Miller held a series of brown-bag lunches to discuss the movement. The Worker movement, foreign in its Catholicism and intriguing in its commitment to the poor, captivated me. But even more captivating was Miller himself.[7]

In some ways, Miller was the polar opposite to Rubenstein. Born in Jacksonville, Florida and educated at the University of Florida and the University of North Carolina at Chapel Hill at a time when the South had yet to be inundated by a more cosmopolitan northern migration, Miller was quintessentially southern. His manner was slow and soft-spoken, often hiding a questioning and brooding mind.

Where Rubenstein had a brusque and definitive manner so that there was no question of whom you were addressing and where you stood in his universe, Miller had a graciousness and openness that allowed a freedom in his presence. With Rubenstein you were always in confrontation, or at least that possibility hung in the air; with Miller there was never any confrontation or even direct engagement. It was almost as if Miller was present and absent at the same time, somewhere else at the precise moment when you thought he was where he seemed to be. Miller was always disappearing and reappearing, as I found when I asked him the questions that Rubenstein posed and awaited an answer.

There were no answers from Miller. When I talked with him, he allowed my thoughts and joined them, for the most part silently but always with a further movement that at first I could not understand. Encountering the Catholic Worker movement had been a moment of conversion for Miller. The writing of his book was so different than his previous writings, which were, for the most part, standard southern histories of the modern period; he gave up on the academic enterprise and even on the notion of progress in history. From Dorothy Day, herself a convert to Catholicism, and her subsequent life among the poor, Miller gleaned an understanding of history that transcended the cycle of power even as that cycle continued. By moving deeper into a life of faith and the demands of that faith, history was experienced at a different level and seen from a different perspective.

The key here was hospitality in the broadest sense of the term, being for others, allowing others their freedom, forsaking participation in aspects of modernity or serving the victims of that system. Intellectually, it meant a concentration on the elements of history that led to healing and reconciliation. The poor were signposts of the need for such efforts and the realization that progress in history was in large measure illusory, and at any rate not to be pursued as a race for meaning and authenticity.

Meaning and authenticity were found somewhere else, embraced at another level, pursued in another dimension. The works of mercy had a hold on Dorothy Day, the Catholic Worker movement, and Miller himself. They were the ultimate expression of a hospitality that pointed to a grace and beauty in the universe, a love that was found within the harsh and dreadful.

Looking back over the decades, Rubenstein and Miller represented counterpoints for me. Initially, they existed over against one another, as two possibilities in the world. Clearly Rubenstein's Jewishness was important for me, though his Jewishness was so distinctly different from anything I had previously encountered, I am not sure that I identified with Rubenstein for that reason. Miller's Catholicism, as a religious belief and ritual, was not a reason for my attraction to him; Catholicism was more than foreign to me, it was an unknown. Their attraction to me as counterpoints to one another no doubt came because those counterpoints were inside of me. I could identify with both of the worlds they presented to me because they existed inside of me.

I wonder now, again with hindsight, whether Rubenstein and Miller represented for me two warring sides of a Judaism that I encountered in my youth, but now raised to an intellectual standard unavailable to me in Hebrew school. The Jewish world was entering a phase of its history where hospitality and power were at war. Choices were being made, mostly without being articulated, that had profound consequences for the future.

Coincidentally, or perhaps providentially, Miller spoke to me about a part of my own tradition that was disappearing. Distant as he was from Judaism and Jewish life, Miller could not have directly understood this. Or perhaps he did understand this sensibility from his own conversion to a post-Vatican II Catholicism that emphasized compassion and hospitality.

Over the years I have come to accept that this internal dialogue that Rubenstein and Miller represented are more than two warring sides within me. Looked at from a certain perspective, they are two options in the world. But from another perspective, they are two aspects of a world where answers are elusive, confining, lacking a flexibility and nimbleness essential to life. For me, at least, these world-views are present and demand a practice that joins them as a life response to the world I live in. More than assent or denial, these worlds demand a commitment that involves the world of power and hospitality in a dynamic that takes on diverse configurations at different times in history. Is this the challenge of the prophetic in our time? Has this always been the challenge of the prophetic, adjusted for time and place?

The worlds that Rubenstein and Miller brought to me – the Holocaust and hospitality, the end of the Jewish covenant and service to the poor – led me, perhaps inevitably, to Maryknoll and the world of liberation theology. If my university formation had been different, if I had been trained for the academy by those who thought it was the pinnacle of the intellect and the engine of progress, I would never have been drawn to Maryknoll or accepted what turned out to be their invitation to travel the world and experience cultures and theologies that were foreign to me.

Teaching at their headquarters in New York, at a seminary-turned-school of theology that served its worldwide mission of conversion and justice, I met many students, visitors and theologians from

Africa, Asia and Latin America. In the 1980s and 1990s, Maryknoll was something like the Catholic Worker had been in the 1970s, a magnet for Catholics and people of other faiths who were searching for a faith that held together belief in God and works of justice. The Catholic Worker community had become almost a site of pilgrimage for those on that search, as I found Maryknoll to be as well. And for these seekers, Maryknoll carried some of the same contradictions as the Catholic Worker.[8]

Both communities were traditional in their foundations and their spirituality and yet were pioneering new ways of being faithful in the second half of the twentieth century. The people who came on pilgrimage often combined these two aspects themselves, but were unable to articulate them and most often experienced a tension between these two sides in their own lives. It was almost as if a civil war within the Catholic community was in evidence, seen from the outside but also found internally as well. The church as institution had nourished the person, especially the post-Vatican II church, but that very same institution was receding in importance, relinquishing its leadership and, as time went on, becoming a regressive force.

Maryknoll was explosive because it brought these tensions to the surface, exposed them and, at least for a time, provided an institutional base for dialogue. It was a public expression far beyond its Catholic borders. When I arrived at Maryknoll, the wars in Central America were raging and U.S. attempts to quell the popular uprisings were in the national and international media. Nicaragua, Guatemala and El Salvador, only dimly recognized countries to the American public, were becoming central stories on the nightly news. Of course, Maryknoll knew of these countries as they had had missionaries in the region for half a century.

If the American public was being educated about the region, Maryknoll was being re-educated; for some time the native catechists they trained to carry the word of God to the people had encountered difficulty with the governments of the region. More recently, some of these catechists, sent to the outlying areas, were not returning home. Some went over to join insurgent forces to fight for justice; others were murdered because their mission was deemed by the government to be subversive. And in 1980, the year I arrived at Maryknoll to teach at their school of theology, two Maryknoll sisters were brutally murdered in El Salvador.

It was in this ambience that I first was introduced to liberation theology and its practitioners and theologians. The national spotlight on Maryknoll increased with the death of the sisters and at Maryknoll the shock of these deaths was personal as well. The women were known to almost all of the people at Maryknoll, and some for many years. They had been in spiritual formation, taken their vows, and made retreats together.

Though Maryknollers served in many parts of the world, their experiences, though diverse in continent and culture, were also shared. In their deaths, the sisters became icons to millions of people. They were derided by some on the political right and elevated by others on the political left, but at Maryknoll they were also persons, flawed and committed, who held up a mirror to those who lived the missionary vocation. The women's fate was almost too awful to contemplate; it might also be the fate of any Maryknoller, tomorrow or another day.

At Maryknoll, liberation theology was less ideological than vocational. This theology had grown up in the last decades in parts of the Third World and some Maryknollers became aware of and sensitive to it. Native priests, trained in European seminaries, the very fruit of mission activity and schools, were the engines of this theology.

Returning from Europe and having internalized European post-Vatican II theology, a theology that saw the signs of the time – that is, the contemporary world as vitally important to religious life – they simply applied that theology to the countries and regions from which they came and to which they were now returning. Theology dominated by Rome, emanating from Europe, and recovering the roots of Christianity and the church, roots that were less institutional and dogmatic, provided the foundations for an evolving theology in Latin America and elsewhere.

Liberation theology evolved within the contemporary situation of the Third World, too often one of grinding poverty and political repression dominated by global and domestic elites. It was pushed also by communist movements and a Marxist intellectual framework that saw faith as an opiate to the masses that provided legitimation to the powers that be. But it was also pushed by the experience of the Nazi years and the silence of the church during the Holocaust.

Dominant European Christianity provided the seeds of the Holocaust and the silence during the Nazi era. Christian institutions were complicit; Christian martyrs were few. Was this the same Christianity that had come to the shores of Latin America in the fifteenth century and to Africa and Asia in Christianity's global outreach?

Were the legitimation of anti-Semitism and the silence of the church during the Nazi era the same legitimation of anti-nativism and the silence of the church during the plunder, slavery and exploitation of the Americas and Africa?

After the sisters were murdered there were memorial services at Maryknoll. The pews were filled with family members, Maryknollers and the media. The liturgies were considered and dignified; a constant refrain was remembrance of the anonymous thousands who had died in the region without benefit of North American religious affiliation or the media.

Maryknoll was generous in its hospitality by emphasizing those others who had died and by drawing attention away from itself and pointing to the injustices that continued to fuel the civil wars in Central America. There had been many martyrs and would be more in the days ahead unless justice was pursued. The death of the Maryknoll sisters raised the issue to a new height, but this would only be important if it drew attention to the cycle of violence that was enveloping Central America.

I remember attending the liturgies and wondering about the meaning of these women's lives and deaths. What was their witness? Did it differ in death? Or was their witness found in life among the poor? Was their witness to the truth of Christianity and, were they, like martyrs before them, the seed of faith and the church? Was theirs a testimony to the Christ of faith and a path, perhaps through intercession, for others to find that same faith? And what was the meaning of their lives and deaths to others outside the Catholic church and even outside Christianity?

Here, mission, as traditionally conceived, had little place. A Maryknoll priest suggested that the sisters, indeed all missionaries, were evangelized by the poor. Did this form of evangelization among those who did not know Jesus as Christ have a place of priority in its mission and teaching that the missionaries themselves were lacking? If the poor were Christians, did they practice a Christianity that well-trained missionaries could learn from and embrace?

Reverse mission was also emphasized. The poor and the marginal could teach the affluent from the core culture of Christianity, wealthy enough to send missionaries to the poor, that the Christianity they practiced and the political and economic systems the church often legitimized were hardly Christianity at all.

The Christianity of the poor was revolutionary, overturning the systems of oppression and religious institutions funded by those systems. I wondered whether reverse mission was the reversal of the history of Christianity, moving backward through the centuries, before the Reformation and mediaeval times, before the Inquisition and the Crusades, before the Constantinian synthesis of church and state.

Where did this reversal find its stopping place? Could it stop at the early Christian communities, the revival of basic Christian communities that was part of the contemporary world of the poor and articulated liberation theology? Would it jettison Christian history completely and embrace an evangelical Christian piety of personal engagement with Jesus as Christ? Or would it move back before the messianic claims attributed to Jesus and the councils that defined who Jesus was in his life and for the believing church?

Maryknoll, the liturgy itself, the priesthood, the convent, the missionary vocation, even the very structure of the church where the service was being held, spoke to layer upon layer of that history. Did martyrdom attest to this history or reverse it? Was martyrdom a moment to behold the core of this history only to re-embrace a faith and church of the everyday, the compromises with power and comfort? Or was martyrdom the chance to begin again, to embrace a freedom beyond institution and certainty?

Martyrdom was hardly a foreign concept to me. In some ways, I was raised on the theme. The story of the first-century Rabbi Akiva refusing to bow to the Roman idols and being hacked to death for this refusal was related often in Hebrew school; before them the Maccabees held out against King Antiochus and the desecration of the Temple.

The Maccabees fought as guerilla warriors, though this was hardly emphasized when I was a child. What was emphasized was the refusal to eat pork and to worship the idols that the Greeks placed in the Temple. Those who refused were killed. Akiva went to his death reciting the Sh'ma.[9] The Holocaust was an event of mass martyrdom, at least the way some have interpreted it. Before the categorization of the Holocaust, however, the story of Jews being rounded up and killed, dying with the Sh'ma on their lips, was known to Jews of my generation. I heard these stories as part of the learning of what it means to be Jewish.

So sacrifice, even unto death, was part of our legacy. The refusal to sacrifice unto death, or more accurately, the fight to prevent death, even if the fight itself led to death, came later. The Maccabees as guerilla warriors, accounts of Masada as the place where Jews held out against the Romans in the second century and committed suicide rather than surrendering to them, were foreign, at least to American Jews of the 1950s and 1960s. Some now denigrate the idea of martyrdom completely or the idea of dying without a fight, as if physical defense is the center of dignity and life.

As a child I had no sense of shame about the martyrdom of Akiva or even of the Holocaust stories I heard; I felt a strength and a wonder when these stories came to me, a strange defiance of the world and power that caused me to embrace my identity as different and deep. At Maryknoll, I found this same wonder, even amidst the gory details of rape and murder. My community, for understandable reasons, has refused martyrdom as an option for itself and in the process created martyrs among Palestinians. Christians had created so many Jewish martyrs; now they were suffering a martyrdom of their own.

What is this martyrdom? What does it mean? Does it prove Judaism or Christianity to be the truth or the way? Is martyrdom faith until death, a faith uttered in life and at the moment of death? Are the martyrs to be followed in faith because of their faith even unto death? Should martyrdom become a force, a power that says never again should those of the martyred community be without power? Do martyrs die for their community and faith, or do martyrs across particularities share a common tradition? Are Jewish and Christian martyrs, separated by time and creed, also bound together? If their respective martyrs are bound, does this also mean Jews and Christians are also bound together?

As I sat during the liturgies at Maryknoll, the triumphant quality of the Mass could be heard. Resurrection was the overwhelming theme; following the way of Christ was another. The Sisters as martyrs had joined a communion of Catholics who died for their faith and joined with others to usher in a world of justice and peace. The ritual was beautiful, and yet there seemed to be no dissonance, a failure to face squarely the horror of death, with no elevation of the depth of anxiety or commitment in its human dimension.

In short, the prophetic aspect of martyrdom, as a projection of the human search for meaning and justice, while not completely absent, was absorbed into a larger umbrella of ritual and history. During the service, the prophetic was left as one possibility, perhaps for those who could not see the larger picture. But the question of whether these women were in their lives and at the hour of their deaths prophets themselves was left unanswered. Indeed, the question was not even asked.

Should we ask that question? If asked, how should the question be framed? In what language or symbol structure? What boundaries are there to the prophetic? In what sources do the prophets find their voice? Does the very canon that gives voice to the prophet also seal that voice in the present? Does the prophetic tradition as carried at least by Judaism and Christianity render a suspicion so deep that the prophet who appears after the canon is mocked and trivialized? If we understand that the prophetic is alive and that prophets are among us, how are they to be discerned and acclaimed? Is the prophet then separate from us, a witness to be heard on the periphery of others' lives? Or is the prophetic within all of us, a place that is called forth by those who embody more fully the prophetic call?

My own journey has convinced me that the prophetic is within each of us and that the prophet is a singular expression of that broader phenomenon. Martin Buber and Abraham Heschel, Dorothy Day and the Catholic Worker movement, Gustavo Gutierrez and the Maryknoll sisters killed in El Salvador may have been more focused, more decisive, even more intelligent than most, but are they fundamentally different? They grew up among us, fully and only human; but then how does one account for their vocation?

Often, of course, the prophetic is pushed away as a vocation for others. Most often the prophet is so far away from consciousness that the idea that the prophetic is a vocation is not even considered. If there once was a prophetic vocation, there is none today. I wonder if this lack of category for the prophet in contemporary culture represents a deep loss of vocation in general, or perhaps the understanding of vocation in life has undergone a renewal, yet the claims of the prophet seem too distant, beyond reach. After all, the call to be a nurse or a doctor, the call to be a teacher or a public servant, seems attainable, even laudable.

The call to be a prophet seems arrogant; the claim, that for whatever reasons one is drawn in that direction and over a lifetime embodies that vision, seems egotistical. But the burden of this calling, the suffering it often entails, mitigates the haughtiness of the claim and disciplines its place in the world. For the prophetic should not be confused with the whole of life or the understanding of truth in its entirety. The world cannot function as if there is only one vocation, the prophetic, nor continue without the prophet. The prophetic is neither a higher calling than others' callings, nor a lesser one.

Could it be that the prophet calls others to their own depth, placing before them the center of their own vocation? The prophet does not live in a vacuum, outside human need or limitation. The radical call of the prophet exposes the connection of one to another and the limitation of all, including the prophet. It is dangerous to point to the flaws of others and society, for to do so exposes the critic to an accounting, sometimes an angry and emotional accounting, precisely for having uncovered that which may need to be hidden.

In its deepest moment, the prophetic calls for a mutual accounting that will help all, including the prophet, confess our limitations and transcend them. And if the call is not to transcend the faults and limitations, since the prophet points to a world and a history that features betrayal, then it is to create structures and belief systems that help us travel a more just and peaceful path.

Though the prophet is usually seen as a person with an immediate judgement in mind, and is often contrasted with the more methodical and sober personality so prominent in modern society, this contrast misjudges the prophetic. Most often the prophet is outside the institutions that might carry out the changes that the prophet calls for; the prophet may even condemn the institutions themselves as unworthy and corrupt. Yet the prophetic calling is to reform in a deep way, embodying justice at the core of society and its institutions.

The prophetic in the contemporary world

My own life suggests these questions and prompts these reflections. They haunt me in a way that is personal rather than distant, contemporary rather than ancient. From my early disaffection with synagogue life, to meeting Rubenstein and Miller and my journey with the Catholic Worker and Maryknoll, thus virtually my entire life, I have wrestled with my own calling and limitations, as have others.

Often, especially after I became a writer and public lecturer, and especially in regard to my stand for Palestinian rights to freedom and dignity and criticism of Israeli policies and the silence of Jewish leadership in the U.S., I have been elevated by some and denigrated by others well beyond what I deserved in either direction. On the negative side, I have been referred to as a traitor and a self-hating Jew; on the positive side, I have been called rabbi and prophet.

Over the years it has been easy enough to deal with the negative appellations; they circle around me as if they are referring to someone else. When hurled with invective, especially when Israeli policy is in the news and impossible to defend, I experience the taunts almost as an out-of-body experience. I often ask myself to whom these critics are referring.

The possibility that I might be a rabbi and a prophet has been much more difficult to deal with, perhaps for the obvious reason that the titles convey a specialness and a burden that seem more appropriate for others. It is perhaps because of this that I have had trouble accepting this naming. I have always made it clear that I am not ordained as a rabbi, lest the official rabbinate claim that I am pretending to a title I do not deserve, and I have distanced myself from the prophetic, often suggesting, sometimes in jest but with a serious tone, that it is impossible for a prophet to arise from North Miami Beach, Florida.

I have often wondered why these labels are attached at all. Is it because people are hungry for a word from a rabbi that they can identify as in line with the justice and peace instruction that is expected from the Jewish tradition?

Being called prophet has many layers of meaning as well: it gives people a way of acknowledging thought and activity that is important, but not to be done by them; it allows people to listen to a message and then dismiss it as utopian, as if it is too extraordinary for life lived in the real world. The prophetic can be an occasion for assent and dismissal at the same time as the prophet is elevated and then sent on the way.

The lack of speech and action in the prophetic line is part of this naming. Over the years I have asked myself if my denial of what others see in me is contributing to this cycle. What the world needs to hear remains unsaid: the people who claim the mantle of leadership do not speak the prophetic word and condemn those who do. People who are hungry for the prophetic vision call those who provide it prophets; those very people dismiss the claim as too high and beyond their own calling in life.

Is there a way out of this cycle, where the prophets are consigned to ancient texts and the contemporary world, so in need of prophets, denies the claim as egotistical, and those who might be prophets deny its attribution because of feelings of inadequacy?

There are distinctions to be made. Superlatives are used so often in modern life that they tend to lose their meaning. Celebrity distorts the very measure of significance and depth. The academy in many ways distorts the intellectual and prophetic life, functioning as part of the educational industry and skewing learning and scholarship toward résumé building and tenure rather than decision making and community building.

Critics abound everywhere; livelihoods are derived from instant analysis; there are constant critiques of power, as if only criticism can be entertained as significant thought. This only encourages the critique of the critique, reactionary criticisms that only bolster the power of the powerful. Is it any wonder that a general cynicism about power abounds? The cycle of critique itself becomes corrupted. It emerges from a void. Is it any wonder that the respondents also operate from a void?

Then there is the wariness to religious speech in general. Or the uncritical embrace of religiosity, boldly announced by political candidates and religious media personalities, but that ultimately lacks substance. Here the prophetic word is heard within a chorus of skepticism and assertion, both blind to the deeper significance of the prophetic vocation in the world. Does this skepticism and assertion mask a cultural, political and economic civil war, one that is unable to break through to another foundational level?

Perhaps, adjusted for time and place, this is always the plight of the prophet. Located between factions and struggles for power and status, entangled in religious and cultural claims and counter-claims, always feeling that the religious traditions have failed and are coming to an end, the prophet hesitates, is humbled, anxious about the consequences, aware that the world will not heed the prophetic word. Why embark on such a career? Why accept such a vocation?

Indeed my own life and the lives of other Jewish dissidents exemplify this difficulty. The accusations against us have been many, success fleeting. The world has gone its way. On the specifics of speaking to the Jewish tradition, and by doing so forcing Jews to look again at what we have done to the Palestinian people, demanding a confession and a reversal of the policies of exploitation, dislocation and destruction, failure is clear and constant. The warning – that these policies in the name of Jews and the Jewish tradition are bringing the Jewish tradition as we have known and inherited it to an end – has fallen on deaf ears. At least at the outward level, the Jewish community thrives and its power is almost unlimited. A security and affluence pervades Jewish life that is startling and instructive.

Assimilation to power and the state is an attempt to prevent communal suffering and promote communal affluence. Can anyone blame Jewish community leaders for choosing that path after the Holocaust? And if Jews did not choose it for themselves, would not others choose it for their own interests? If Jews refuse assimilation to power and the state, do we place ourselves beneath and under the power of those who have no qualms about such a choice? Can Jews, by listening to the prophetic voice after the Holocaust and with the nation-state of Israel, actually choose a path of renouncing privilege and power, thus opening the possibility of suffering for values that the world denigrates?

Suffering here seems key and hence the connection with martyrdom. The prophetic seeks justice and in doing so sides with those who are on the margins of society and power. The hope is for the restoration or creation of a relational and just engagement with one another, as a way of witnessing to foundational values of tradition, community and life. Suffering is neither courted nor suggested. The reality, however, is that such a view is bound to cause suffering for the prophet; the very risks entailed for the community are real.

Individual and communal life is always risky, always on the verge of experiencing suffering or causing others to suffer. A way is being pursued, so inactivity or neutrality is not an option. The option is often disguised: how often do we hear that though the way is difficult there is no alternative?

The prophet suggests another way as a risk outweighed by the risks of the present. For in alleviating one's own suffering but causing other suffering has freedom been achieved? Or does the cycle await its next turn in which the victim turned victor becomes victim again?

In victory, what is achieved? In victory, held up at the expense of another people, what is left of ethics and justice? Today, Judaism and Christianity are spent forces, if we take seriously the ethical demands of each tradition as they have been lived out. Is it then another layer of difficulty, to claim to speak in the prophetic voice that both traditions claim but rarely live out?

Today, the experience of the prophetic is ecumenical. Who can deny the prophetic insights, indeed the prophetic lives, of Martin Buber, Dorothy Day, Martin Luther King, Jr. and Gustavo Gutierrez? Who could relegate Mahatma Gandhi to a category other than the prophetic because his religion was Hindu rather than Jewish or Christian?

There is thus no denying the cross-fertilization of the prophetic in our time. Buber was influenced by Gandhi; Gandhi was central to King as was Buber; Day was inspired by Buber, Gandhi and King; Gutierrez, following the evolution of this prophetic community, read and reacted to Buber, Gandhi, Day and King and others as well. How many today that stand in this prophetic line were struck at an early age when reading Gutierrez' *A Theology of Liberation*?

The ecumenical quality of the prophetic voice as it developed in the twentieth century bequeaths a situation paradoxical to that of the twenty-first. As the religious traditions fail and their force dissipates, the prophetic voice emanating from different religious backgrounds and geographic areas increases. After a while, the prophetic voice is seen as a communal one, with the boundaries between the communities from which these voices emanate fading in importance. Distinguishing characteristics of each tradition that help shape the voice and discipline of the prophet, while embodied in each person, are less and less important to others who are influenced by them.

To most Christians who find Mahatma Gandhi's witness compelling, his Hindu background, the particularities of Gandhi's discipline that flow from his birth tradition, are inaccessible and unimportant. That Dorothy Day is a Catholic is, for most who come into contact with her writing and witness, of only tangential interest. So, too, is the case with Martin Buber's understandings and his Jewishness. Buber's ideas relating to I and Thou are perhaps the most referred to concepts in contemporary literature, most often without attribution to Judaism or even to him as a person.

This ecumenical prophetic community is a sign of the times. For some, the loss of particularity lessens the message of the prophet or even distorts it. Can a Catholic actually embrace Buber's Jewish witness? Can a Jew seriously contemplate Gandhi as a prophetic figure to emulate? Has King become whitewashed, embraced by white Jews and Christians, without his African-American heritage, thus undermining his radical and more pessimistic criticism of American racism and power?

For others, the ecumenical embrace of prophetic witnesses around the world is a source of freedom, breaking the boundaries of influence so that the boundaries of separation and division can be broken as well. The chances of a Catholic refusing Buber, a Jew seeing Gandhi as distant, and King being unavailable to whites, are minimal today because they did not refuse one another, or see each other as distant and unavailable and because their witness is in the public discourse, framing questions that confront us all in the twenty-first century.

Those who lament the loss of particularity have their points to be made. To see those who rise within certain communities as interchangeable runs the risk of universalizing the prophetic out of existence. The foundations from which that voice arises and the particular dynamics that help define the prophet are important historically. If all politics is local, as some have said, the real life of the prophet is as well. The universalizing of the prophetic voice has its locality and particularity as well. Though each of these prophets were birthed within a certain community and struggle, the twentieth century transformed locality and particularity onto a world stage.

The prophetic message, tried in one form of community, was also heard in another form of community. Indeed, the prophetic message is heard in both places, continuing to be resonant in the original situation within which the contemporary prophets lived, while also heard beyond those situations in a new particularity and struggle on the global stage. Perhaps this is one of the marks of the contemporary prophet: to be heard in the original particularity and locality *and* the evolving world scene, a new particularity and locality evolving within the globalization process so discussed in economics and politics.

This dynamic is an ancient one. The Jewish biblical prophetic tradition moved beyond Judaism two thousand years ago, and in the expansion of Christianity has been a global force since the fourth century. This globalization continued primarily through colonialism and imperialism, and Christianity was transformed in this process not only through its power but also, and perhaps in the long run most significantly, by the spread of the witness of the prophets in Christian texts and ritual. Christianity of empire has been challenged from the beginning by Christianity of community, primarily through the prophetic line featured in the Hebrew bible and in the figure of Jesus himself.

Beneath and around the messianic claims attributed to Jesus, the prophets have consistently appeared. Contemporary liberation theology is impossible without the prophetic Jesus, but that theology is also part of the universalizing of the prophetic message. Historically it has many heirs, including aspects of Reformation theology, the struggle to abolish slavery and the civil rights movement. On the one hand, these movements can be seen as civil wars within

Christianity, a struggle over what Christianity means in relation to the social and political order. On the other hand, the historically contested issues are greater in scope and have released worldwide movements that address these issues. The cumulative effect is beyond Christianity. And once the struggles were noticed and recorded, they were drawn on, as indeed they are still today, by people around the world.

The universalizing process continues and will accelerate in the twenty-first century. The ecumenical prophetic community is part of this process, and while certain particular elements of the prophetic will be de-emphasized, perhaps even lost to history, the expansion of the prophetic terrain is important. Each tradition attempts to seal the prophetic within its own particularity; crossing boundaries and traditions at will and, in so doing, unsealing the prophetic, freeing it from constraints that the prophets fought. The prophets were, in a certain sense, guerrilla warriors against the state and the power of their time, both of which were legitimated by religion.

Should the ecumenical prophetic community, by respecting the canon as defined by each tradition, grant a posthumous victory to the powers that write and interpret their lives? Perhaps the dynamite of the prophets, always available in the texts of these traditions but always guarded by orthodoxy and religious leadership, is now being freed and exploded by the ecumenical prophetic community?

This ecumenical situation has been in place for some time and yet it remains, even at this late date, unnamed. A tradition has grown up within a myriad of traditions; its place and witness is as strong, perhaps even stronger, than the traditions from which this ecumenism is drawn. In the main, this new tradition stands over against the older ones, in their particularity *and* in their universality. For it is not only the prophetic community that has crossed boundaries in solidarity, the ancient traditions have formed new understandings to buttress their traditional articulation.

The rise of neo-orthodoxy is a case in point, where the orthodoxy of one community is cited as a reason for the orthodoxy of another. While this is often trumpeted as a survival and revival of ancient particularities, particularities that not only opposed and persecuted each other historically but also condemned each other to the outer theological reaches of damnation and hell, in reality the acceptance of an alliance around orthodoxy buries the rough edges of their particularities.

It should not surprise us that the globalization process has also affected those who claim orthodoxy. In the end, the struggle now seems to be between the ecumenical fraternities of the prophetic and the orthodox, those who seek to free the prophetic voice and those who seek to seal it.

But if this is just a replay of the struggles within each tradition between the free prophets and the sealing of the prophetic, albeit on a new and broader stage, does it actually moves us closer to religious truth, discipline and action? Is this ecumenical prophetic and orthodoxy simply a replay of a cycle that is always with us?

Perhaps it is and perhaps it is not. If it is true that the prophetic is disappearing and reappearing in our time; this has probably always been the case. The ancient Jewish prophets, of course, were not themselves Jewish; they were Israelites or, more specifically, they arose within an evolving tribal confederacy. It is more appropriate to name the claiming of the prophets by Judaism as an interpretation of these tribal confederate voices, not much different than the later Christian claiming of the Jewish prophet Jesus. Both reside in what looks to be, retrospectively, an evolving tradition; the prophets, however, spoke their truth to power in light of the promises and provocation of a God who chose a people rather than a religion.

The gathering of the prophets into a tradition or, as the case might be, traditions, is retrospective, to be sure, and introspective as well. The formed religion, a religion that takes at its center the prophetic and the sealing of the prophetic, shapes disparate witnesses of different time periods and situations. Arising within contexts of power and duress, at home and in exile, the prophets were many though only a few survive in the text. At the same time, the writing and rewriting of the prophets may only represent the original words of the prophets tangentially.

Clearly, there are a number of voices layered within each of the prophets that have been preserved. The tradition, as it evolves, gathers, signifies and disciplines the prophets: but are we on safer ground to understand the prophets as those persons who emerge unexpectedly in history, at the margins of time and power, and then disappear, some to oblivion, others preserved in compilation and through editing, voices that gnaw at the edges of consciousness?

There is an anarchistic quality to the prophets even as they are preserved in the canon. Though defined and structured, the haunting quality of prophetic freedom remains. Who can tame completely the power and weakness of Moses or turn a blind eye to the tragedy of his death, when he was allowed only a glimpse from afar of the promised land?

The anger of Jeremiah and Isaiah when confronted by injustice is countered by the poetic beauty of their vision of reconciliation and peace. This is true of Job as well. He is an ancient figure, not counted among the prophets, and outside of the evolving tribal confederacy. But he carries forth what is to become a Jewish tradition in the rabbinic period, that of discussion among peers and argument with God about the meaning of justice and life in general.

In scripture, these prophets are placed side by side, and the time frame and the contexts of their lives are blurred. Biblical scholars spend their lives separating time periods and layers of texts, but the reader, if unaided by religious leadership, is simply introduced to the books to read and meditate upon. Thus, even though ultimately sealed by the text as interpreted by the rabbis, the prophets exist in the text as anarchistically as they existed in life. What is introduced is a dialogue among the prophets in relation to power, suffering and justice, which then reintroduces itself periodically in life, following the paths these texts have traveled.

The religious establishments that have canonized the prophets are forced periodically to deal with a new outbreak of prophetic thought. But, with time, religious leadership can usually institutionalize the prophetic to an extent that its disruptive message is contained. The parameters of the prophet are circumscribed so that even those who embody aspects of the prophetic do so within a managed system. If the parameters are respected, the prophetic voice becomes an agent of renewal of the tradition, that is, after the rough edges are rounded.[10]

In a fully functioning religious system, the prophets' agreement to operate within those parameters is unnecessary, for the system is powerful enough to do this of its own accord. Here, suspicion of the claims of the prophet operates initially, then the religious system harnesses the power of the prophetic into a safe house of religious idealism with a nod to the ancient prophets as a recognition factor that indeed the prophet, correctly interpreted, is within the approved religious framework.

The proliferation of the traditions that harbor these voices within them, the arrival of rabbinic Judaism, Christianity with its march toward denominationalism and globalization, the arrival of Islam and its missionary thrust, all provided an expanded audience and increased terrain for the prophetic word. Though the prophetic in these religions is controlled, in Judaism through the introduction of the Talmud, in Christianity through elevating Jesus to the messianic, and in Islam through the final interpreter, Mohammed, the end points of interpretation are always unstable. This is so for a variety of reasons, not the least of which is that the prophetic is included in the Talmud even as it is disciplined. The messianic claim of Jesus transcendentalizes the prophetic message found in the parables of his life. The same is true in Islam where the prophetic aspects of Mohammed are disciplined by the claim that he is the last prophet. There is only a small step in these religions from unsealing the prophetic from the interpreters and from the major figures of the religion itself.

These religions, with their communities formed around ritual and text, have crossed paths in the past and are often in close proximity today. This leads to cross-fertilization and borrowing. Obviously, this has happened in the borrowings that are the foundations of the traditions themselves; the prophets are brought into Judaism through the rabbis, are imported wholesale by Christianity, and then reimported by Islam. The origins of these communities are bounded by this borrowing and thus divisions are set in place so that the borrowings are essentially disguised.[11]

Judaism, Christianity and Islam are presented as wholly different in their trajectory, carrying a salvation history that separates the communities on an eschatological and thus earthly plane. When living in close proximity, cooperation on the earthly plane may be necessary, though it remains strictly provisional and, for the most part, strategic. While living together may appear to be a sharing of traditions, and while the traditions themselves may also appear so close together as to be difficult to distinguish without a theological guide, religious leaders convince the community that, despite appearances, separation is the reality. This notion is carried on despite the origins, life together in communities, and the frequent philosophical, theological and cultural interchange that has occurred historically and seems endemic to the intellectual and theological traditions of the modern age.

Ecumenical understandings, therefore, are hardly new, nor is the meeting of worlds that have had little or no relation to one another. Indeed the opposite would seem to be the case: separation is in need of discussion as well as how the ritual and dogma of religions and religious communities have come into being.

Though the ecumenical discussions of our time are highly touted and often generate great controversy, most often their discussion of particular and common ground hides, perhaps intentionally, their true commonality in the prophets, in the prophetic voice, and in the sealing of that voice by the very representatives who meet in ecumenical discussion.

Does this ecumenism of the religious authorities represent a final effort to seal the prophetic and rescue the traditions themselves from a new borrowing of the prophetic, the formation, if you will, of a new community around the prophetic, that crosses boundaries and borders? Surely, the eruption of the prophetic in the twentieth century accompanied a renewed ecumenism among the traditions.

One possible interpretation of ecumenical renewal is that it is only strategic, gathering strength against the tide that seems ready to sweep aside all religious institutions and hierarchies. Another possibility is that contemporary history has shown the limits of institutionalized and ritually centered religion and that those who people the hierarchies have these limits as well, not only strategically but also in terms of their own faith.

No doubt both strategy and faith are in play and here another division is found, a civil war, if you will, over the future of religion and religiosity. In many traditions and their denominational centers, the rereading of the bible in light of contemporary history has caused a rethinking, a new accounting of history and the role of faith in history. The transcendent is being rethought, reimagined and even played down as the locus of faith. With this change, the question of fidelity is being asked again; what fidelity is, to whom or what fidelity is owed, how fidelity is embodied in the world.

When the transcendent is reimagined, life is emphasized and the social, political and economic spheres become more important to the life of faith. The very notion of fidelity itself is an opening. Where closure once reigned in a view of the transcendent that emphasized completion outside of history, and therefore only duration on earth, process and practice take their place in fidelity. The transcendent remains, however it is chastened and open to question. Testimony rather than finality is heard and testimony is free, coming from many places, most often in unexpected ways. The course is not yet finished; humanity becomes again a partner in a joint venture.

The evolving covenant within history

Here the covenant returns in an evolving sensibility. It is initiated in circumstances that have been defined by ancient texts and continues evolving in other contexts. Though religious communities claim the covenant as their own, history challenges that claim through the very behavior of the community.

After Auschwitz, covenantal claims by Christians are more difficult to assert as given; after Israel, covenantal claims by Jews are challenged. Challenges to the covenant throw religious legitimation, institutions and hierarchy into a cycle of disconfirmation until even the hierarchy begins a search. The covenantal question, once safely tucked away in the transcendent sphere, now reintroduces the prophetic. For is not the core of the covenant the prophetic?

In canonical religiosity, the prophets, when they are called upon, exist as counterbalances and correctives to wayward piety. The covenant is static, outside of history, given for all time and in force for eternity. The reactors of Deuteronomy are classic in this sense, as are writers of the gospels themselves. Both attempt to achieve the same goal, to capture and define a covenantal moment in and outside of time and history.

Moses and Jesus lived and no doubt were prophetic at their core. However, their more obvious respective missions, as a liberator in Egypt and beyond and as a charismatic leader within a Roman colonial occupation, hide a deeper reality of God's providential plan and sacrifice. The prophetic at the heart of the covenant with its moment and context is thus removed in a transcendence that lessens the drama on earth or, perhaps more accurately stated, transfers the initiation of the drama from the human to God.

Is the covenant at its very foundations prophetic, embodying a dialogue between humanity and God that can only be tested in the everyday of social, economic and political life? The background story of each of the ancient prophets is found in this dialogue and test. The covenant can be found here as well.

One could say that the covenant is both dialogue and test, in an evolving history that is ecumenical from the beginning – between and among the tribes of Yahweh, Egypt and the peoples the tribes encounter in the wilderness and the promised land, but also wherever Jews, and later Christians and Muslims, take root and travel.

Though each context and community proclaims and carries the prophetic, and thus the covenantal language, the larger questions and challenges move beyond the particular in their importance and the very possibility of any particular community encompassing the message. The very mobility of the prophets, shuttling between God and society, the personal and historical, enhances and defies particularity at the same time. The prophets have never been contained, hence the need for texts and religious authorities to seal them. The power of the covenant, prophetic in its message and mobility, also defies that sealing.

The covenant's continual return to history, like the return of the prophets, is unpredictable in its time and appearance. Its very ecumenism, already evident during its time and increasing in the future, shows a propensity for arriving in the least expected places and among the least expected peoples. The Israelite tribes first, marginal among the power of Egypt, those who were marginal within the confederation – the widows, orphans and strangers – then new communities, Christians for example, who were marginal in the Roman empire and so on.

Since the covenant, like the prophets, is not first and foremost a religious assent to a transcendental proposition, but a focused dialogue on God and the social order in which both parties find a vocational bond and a pattern of communication, the particular and universal are from the beginning in a tension that cannot be contained. Even those communities that feel that they have transcended particularity, for example the Christian claim to universality over the narrow particularity of the Jews, are ultimately surprised by claims that follow that same pattern, as in Islam, that a broader universality has been established.

A further surprise, one that has been developing in the last centuries and will surface in its importance in the twenty-first century, is that the covenantal bond will increasingly be found outside of any of these religious carriers. At least in the West, but in other places as well, the religious covenantal ideas without rhetoric or ritual have permeated secular society and have found a new particularity, a new home as it were, no doubt destined, as were the earlier carriers, to find another eruption of the covenant and the prophets in unpredictable and uncontainable ways.

In some ways religious and secular particularities are the new agents in a long history of dialogue. Like previous particularities, the secular is proud and defining, placing its case before the world as transcendent in its purpose and destiny. The religious and the secular also seek the covenantal and the prophetic to bow before their power and naming, demanding that religion, ostensibly the carrier of both, legitimate the policies of state and power.

By preaching a canonical version of the covenant and the prophetic, a deal is brokered between church and state that resides in the very sealing of the canon's dynamic tension. In this deal, the force of a dialogue between the religious and the secular is given over. Dissent, with possible homes in the religious and/or secular worlds, becomes homeless.

Or perhaps its new home is between and among these worlds, once again repeating an ancient pattern. Here the question of fidelity returns to the center. The covenant and the prophetic, now translated in time and language, begin between the religious and the secular worlds. God demands recognition, even a cultic place of worship and power.

However, that recognition of worship and power is tested in the social and political order. The constant re-emergence of the widow, orphan and stranger present the essential test of fidelity, as witness to the essential act of deliverance from Egypt, where God became known and was experienced in the community, itself another constant refrain in the biblical text; together these join what we know as the religious and secular into one. Fidelity in this evolving tradition of the covenantal and prophetic affirmation is never simply belief *or* justice, assent *or* attention to the marginal, or the reverse, but rather a life inclusive of all, as if both are found together or not at all.

What then is fidelity in the covenantal and prophetic tradition? The ecumenical quality of both sensibilities has evolved over time. Are the words and concepts of the first affirmations binding and in need of repetition? Do God, promise, exile, punishment and return also remain in their naming and sequence? If translated in language and imagery, does particularity survive in the ecumenical, at least the particular formations of assent and justice? Has the constant movement of these particular carriers of the covenant and the prophetic toward a Constantinian synthesis vitiated their claims to embrace God and justice? Can the secular that has absorbed so much of these understandings be left on its own to interpret and embody these callings? In the compromises of the secular, have the covenant and the prophetic voice fled their own temples?

Alone, the question of fidelity seems isolated. Completely surrounded in other realities, the covenant seems to disappear. A spoken ecumenism with particular communities that also seeks broad contours of commonality can be superficial, very much like a liberal secularity that perceives itself as open to everything but is closed to decision and a critique of its own foundations.

The superficiality of both the religious and the secular when embraced uncritically is startling and instructive. Both claim history and function as if history is theirs to be interpreted and inherited as a claim on the present rather than as a subversive memory of challenge and critique. It seems that particular carriers of language and culture are also carriers of politics and economies; when the covenant and the prophetic are claimed they become subservient, almost as servants of that particularity.

What if there is a broader tradition of faith and struggle, one that carries the covenant and the prophetic along with it, sealing and unsealing its dynamic, burying and raising up its power, dampening and exploding the dynamite of its message? Take the case of communities that formed around and yet distance themselves from the covenant and the prophetic, even as they codify and claim both. What if these communities are challenged from within or from others in different communities that have gone through the same process of assent and denial in other times and circumstances? What if fidelity then is a certain stance in relation to the covenant and the prophetic, at any time and place, and sometimes at the same time and place? Orientation then would be defining, rather than being the outward manifestations of language and ritual. The sealing of the covenant and the prophetic would always be confronted at some time and place by its unsealing. The confrontation would be contemporary and historical in the present.

How would this unsealing be rooted? Would the unsealing itself be a kind of rootedness? What would be the practice that accompanies such an unsealing, one that points to and uncovers the sealing of the canon and the prophetic? A traveling practice through time, culture and geography seems tenable, but only if there is also a place and community in the present. The covenant and the prophetic are never fulfilled perfectly nor is endurance its special quality.

Rather, vigilance is necessary to ensure that the warning signals are understood and observed, and that, in dire cases, transformation can be envisioned and struggled for. The aim, of course, is neither permanent revolution, so that ordinary life with its joys and suffering is unendurable, nor an unjust status quo where the ordinary is violated repeatedly.

Permanent revolution and an unjust status quo signify an uneasiness about ordinary life, where community, secure and flourishing, with hospitality as its hallmark, is looked down upon. The desire to overcome the limitations of life, including the flawed quality of personal and communal existence, is to be avoided as an assault on our humanity. Here, roots in the present become crucial and a practice that derives from particularity is essential.

Though seemingly contradictory, the need for roots is hardly antithetical to the broader tradition of faith and struggle. Roots in the present can free the person and perhaps the community to embrace others in history and in the present as embodying and bequeathing elements of fidelity that are essential to our own struggle to be faithful. Our own struggle is then in harmony with those who have come before us and with others in the contemporary world, known and unknown to us, who struggle now.

Fidelity, like the covenant and the prophetic, is therefore contextual. How could it be otherwise? The practice needed to guide our fidelity is likewise contextual and must be ours, that is, available through inheritance and searching. Inheritance is our grounding, our roots. Yet, by extension in time and place, by extending our terrain of embrace, that rooting becomes deeper. This sensibility helps avoid a superficial uprootedness or a rootedness that is stuck in contemporary life.

A dynamic is created that is particular and ecumenical in the broadest sense, one that humbles claims on all sides. Past and present have their importance and their limitations; likewise, particularity and universality are valued without claim beyond context and an ordinariness fundamental to human life. Ontological claims of any community are disciplined, even as particularity is valued. The seeming uprootedness of modernity, with its claim to universality, is similarly taken to task as a false naming. Modernity is a rootedness as well, with its claims and counterclaims, no better or worse than other particularities.

The covenantal and prophetic dynamics are real ones, moving across borders and boundaries of culture, geography and religions, within and beyond particularities, and in dialogue with systems that claim that they are beyond either. This dynamic tempers ontological claims all around, but does it allow any claim?

The covenant and the prophetic are claims in and of themselves. What are these claims and how can they be made? From where do these claims issue? Are the claims binding or voluntary? What are the consequences for living out the covenant and the prophetic? Are there consequences for refusing to live it out? Finally, are the claims personal, both for those who embrace the covenant and the prophetic and those who refuse to do so, or are they communal?

The ancient prophets are often invoked as a category when quoted, but they are cited selectively. The same is true with the covenantal drama. The dramatic story line is featured and the liberation of the slaves remembered. Told to children in religious schools and read in synagogues and churches, the drama *is* the lesson that a faithful God fulfills the promise of care and concern for the people God has chosen. That promise remains for those who hear the story and assent to the wonder contained within the canon.

Yet the other side of the story, the violence against the oppressors and the violence within the community en route to liberation, the violence directed by God through his messengers in the Exodus story and the violence threatened in the prophets, is most often skipped over or read allegorically. The sheer volume of repetition in the Hebrew bible is also left behind, as are the passages where other gods appear and, of course, the references and events that cannot be deciphered or verified.

Creating a canon and investigating it historically are complex realities. Reading and absorbing the canon, the very interpretation of ancient texts, represents another level of complexity. Layer after layer of difficulty is found. The canon or the historical investigation, the reading or interpretation, none can be taken at face value and none can be taken for granted.

As testimony, shaped and rewritten and presented in the form of a canon, the Hebrew bible is impressive, outrageous, affirming and deceiving. It alternates between extremes: at times the narrative is unduly pessimistic about humanity and the destiny of Israel; at other times it is widely optimistic about both; at times the two are rendered in startling combination.

Paradoxes abound. Chosenness and promise is a gift; chosenness and promise have to be earned; chosenness and promise can never be revoked; the revocation of both is often threatened; God is a God of love; God is a God of vengeance.

The elaborate instructions for guarding and maintaining the Tent of Meeting are seemingly endless; justice is the center of the covenant and without it worship is worthless or, worse, an abomination: the servants of God are chosen and protected; they are often tried with difficulty beyond their ability and sometimes executed by an angry God for transgressions that seem deserving only of rebuke. The stranger is constantly invoked as in need of protection and inclusion, and the treatment of the widow and orphan are signposts for God's favor or judgement. To carry out Israel's destiny, entire communities including the stranger, widow and orphan are annihilated, an act commanded and sometimes led by God.

The ancient covenant and the prophets are shadowed by actions and beliefs that are difficult to accept and are certainly impossible to project today. The questions of idolatry and justice, of chosenness and promise, remain as categories that define parameters of the covenantal and prophetic in our time.

However, what do we make of the specific content of the origins of these defining frameworks? Judgement is dramatic in these ancient narratives. Plagues of locusts and the slaying of the firstborn are featured, along with the mass slaying of those at Sinai who dared invoke other gods. The ecumenical is found also, especially in the formation of the tribal confederation.

The demands of tribal particularity are listened to and often heeded, but the gods of these tribes, even if Yahweh is at their head, meet with resolute condemnation. Idolatry is configured in a fascinating way, centered around faith in the one God and the building of a just society that mirrors that faith. Is the destruction of those who have other gods as well or those who veer from justice as conceived by Yahweh proportionate to their crime?

It is telling that many of the arguments surrounding the claims and actions of God and the Israelites are preserved in the canon. Reading the Hebrew bible, one cannot help but be struck at the attempt to end the discussion about these themes and how the texts themselves refuse that closure. If read from a postmodernist perspective, and in some sense the rabbis read these texts in a similar way, the narratives contain infinite possibilities of interpretation.

Yet the seriousness of the issues, the construction of the canon as a real rather than fictional history of God and God's people, belie this possibility. Rather, it seems that the oral testimonies across generations, when gathered together in writing as a founding document of the community, are too complex to simplify. Through their canonization the testimonies take on a trajectory that, when seen individually, is only partly evident.

The canon itself is far from clear in its parts or even as a collective. When the Hebrew bible ends, it is a history become constitution. Who the interpreters are to be, what the community will be in history after the document, how God will manifest himself in the future, or even if that manifestation will continue, is left up in the air.

With the ecumenical, conscience becomes essential. With history, conscience is honed. The canon is formed and the community, then communities, carry the message forth. But the message is proclaimed in different circumstances, with power and without, and those on the margins hear the story in new ways. The covenantal takes on a life of its own, so that at some point the canonical narrative is almost left behind, or at least it is only referred to in certain ways, lifting out themes, ignoring passages, returning to them.

The struggle against idolatry is a harsh one, and in the canon a patriarchal God is strong in punishment. Do we accept that punishment today? Condemnations fill Jeremiah and Isaiah; Amos is little different. Moses and Joshua before them are compassionate and brutal; Aaron witnesses the death of his children through an act of God and is silent. Do we accept the death of three thousand Israelites for the sin of building and dancing before the golden calf?

The rabbis interpreted these passages as if they were not history. Instead they became texts for interpretation, for speculation, for the most part practical and sometimes mystical. That everyone in the promised land would be put to the sword so that the Israelites would possess the promised land, a command of God to be carried out by Joshua, can be thought about in interesting ways by the rabbis, and in other ways by contemporary settlers in the same land. Yet does not the text itself bear a responsibility, a fearsome quality, that is difficult to read today without wondering if the God portrayed there is a God that can be worshiped today? Does conscience need to address the canon as it addresses the present? Or does the canon itself make this assertion of conscience today more difficult?

Here, the covenantal and prophetic are key. By invoking the prophets do we invoke also God's wrath? In the prophets, an anxiety about naming and bowing before the one true God, as if straying to other gods is the greatest sin, is a prevalent theme. Does this anxiety betray a compulsion, an inner fury directed against the very ecumenical that is so crucial in the contemporary world?

The covenant itself is narrowly focused, at least in the choice of one people who will carry it in the world and to the world. That particularity, tied to a fidelity that promises power and land, is challenged by the prophets, but mostly within this same promise.

Having read these narratives, is it possible to suggest that the covenantal and the prophetic do not contain the promise of power and land? Within the canon, and even adhering to the covenantal and the prophetic dynamic, promise cuts two ways. On the one hand there is the promise of power and the land; on the other, the promise of exile if power and the land are abused. Is it possible today to argue that either one is real or desirable? Should fidelity, however defined, be the price for privilege and status over others? Should betrayal, however defined, be cause for exile from place and culture?

It seems that a critical reading of the text, even in liberation struggles over the years, gives one pause. Of course, the Christian reading of the Hebrew bible as one of violence and wrath, a constant temptation, especially when compared to the brief parable stories of the Christian bible, is disingenuous. To have a more replete understanding of the Christian canon we would need to read the 2,000 year history of Christianity as its testament. Would this testament, moving from Paul to Auschwitz, yield a more faithful witness to the covenantal and the prophetic? Or would it simply repeat the rhythms of the canon Christians inherited and thought was fulfilled?[12]

The new Israel seems, at least from the reading of history, to live within a similar dynamic to the one that Christian theologians have painstakingly argued has been superseded. Though God's judgement seems to have been limited to Jews and others who did not accept the messianic promise, the penalty for refusing is the same that befell the ancient peoples who were in the way of the incoming Israelites. Conquering, looting, murdering, this on a scale made global and enduring over many centuries.

And the cycle of atrocity engendered by the canons of Judaism and Christianity continues. Or is this a cycle that has only adopted the Hebrew and Christian canon as cover for its assertion of power?

At this point, the threads of argument are difficult if not impossible to untangle. Disengaging Judaism and Christianity from the use by each of their own canons is interesting and provocative, as is the attempt to disengage Judaism and Christianity from their own history. In the end, however, the origins and the carrier, and those who use both for their own ends, are joined together.

To go back behind canon, religion and history is impossible. To move beyond them, separately or together, is also impossible. For the claims made in canon, the religious territory staked out by Judaism and Christianity, and the history that fulfills and transforms both do not vanish. And the moment a critical appraisal is made and a new venture is embarked upon, another side of the venture emerges.

The cycle of atrocity may be fueled by the canon and by a general hunger for power, or may be opposed by those who pledge fidelity to that narrative and by a general human desire for good and justice, but the cycle seems ingrained in history. It is almost as if atrocity, like justice, has an eschatological thrust to it, a steadfastness that provokes a continual civil war in human history between the forces of empire and the forces of community.

The canon and the dynamic of history that flows from and around it are part of the struggle to be faithful; they inform the broader tradition of faith and struggle with questions and humility. Does the broader tradition break the cycle of atrocity, this congealing of power and promise, simply through its critique? In seeking to break this cycle, does it simply ready it for another turn at another time?

Placing oneself in the service of community rather than empire does not guarantee the triumph of community, or if community does win out, it does not guarantee that victory will keep community from becoming empire. Since the covenantal and prophetic voices speak in strident tones, buried and amplified in a canon that is also at times strident, the establishment of community can justify atrocity and injustice. The history we inherit becomes even more complex when the community contribution to atrocity is understood and acknowledged. Community and empire are at odds, to be sure; they are also implicated in similar dynamics and histories.

So those who embrace the covenantal and the prophetic must also ask serious questions about the broader tradition of faith and struggle. If the particular, the exclusive, the ecumenical and the pluralistic unite in the other, 'night' sides of the positive aspects of tradition and culture, and if the canon, with the covenantal and prophetic, in different ways contribute to that night side, should all of it simply be jettisoned? Should a new start for humanity be envisioned? Does conscience demand such a reckoning that the traditions we inherit, no matter how they are interpreted and acted upon, must be consigned to the dustbin of history?

The question of strategy enters here: since these canons and communities abound, should one hold fast to, or at least argue within, the community traditions, if only to fight off the power of empire proclaimed in God's name?

Though strategy is part of life, the longevity of such a discussion is limited. Fighting in the name of realities no longer maintained are holding actions that are destined to be swept aside. Generations that come after battles and rhetoric not believed in do not adopt that same strategy, for even the superficial adherence to language and ritual is no longer available to the next generation. A rote recital of claims and slogans is impossible for those whose inheritance is a strategic one.

Surely, abandonment of the canon and the dynamics that have flowed from it is constant where people are free to do so. The flight from religiosity, at least as defined by Judaism and Christianity, is in direct proportion to the achievement of cultural, economic and political freedoms. Modernity is a lure. It becomes almost a system of religious piety, because it promises that freedom. And though religious people and communities often chide the superficiality of the new belief system, it is precisely because of the superficiality of the old that the new is greeted with such fervor.

Of course, the old canon is simply replaced with a new one; the promise is transposed from a specific people and land to a universal territory of acquisition and consumption. Atrocity continues, as does injustice and poverty, and this is hidden in the religion of modernity as it was in Judaism and Christianity. Power is still prized, the affluent still rule, but the language and the symbols have changed. In most cases, the struggle between generations and between faiths – the struggle between traditional religions and the religion of modernity – is one of canons that disguise their real history of practice. Both hide the births of their histories and their complicity in the ongoing cycle of atrocity and injustice.

The covenantal and prophetic are deeply flawed. Does that mean the replacements, offered in each generation, are pure? The cycle of atrocity is clear and is fed by many streams of thought and religion in every generation. Does that mean that the cycle will stop simply because certain streams are emphasized or renounced?

Strategies to bring the cycle of atrocity to a close are important and will continue. But strategies themselves are doomed in this endeavor because a war among strategies, all claiming to be the answer, is also our inheritance and part of our future. Strategy and purity are both illusions, if by them is sought a circling around the questions within history or a frontal assault on the struggles in history.

Rarely is community or empire achieved and, if it is, the downfall of both is immanent. Opposition to community and empire has within it its own contradictions and instabilities. While at times important to state that opposition, even to act upon it, the reaction is always flawed.

The rhetorical call for change is always distant from the reality of that change; flaws of purpose, intent and implementation are always found, even in the noblest of efforts. If this is true today, it is likely that it was found in the giving of the covenant and the emergence of the prophetic voice.

The covenantal and prophetic traditions that continue to speak to the world in the twenty-first century can only be humbled by their own history as evidenced in the canon and the history of those who have carried the canonical texts over the millennia. This failed tradition, with its own internal contradictions, limitations and flaws, exists among other failed religious and secular traditions, with their own internal contradictions, limitations and flaws, and they are often fused together in an eclectic, even confusing tangle.

Is it possible in Jewish life today to separate the strands of culture, ethnicity, religiosity, nationality and polity or even to separate definitively what is distinctly Jewish and what is borrowed from other cultures and religions? The same surely applies to Christianity and any other religious tradition that is ancient and surviving.

The evolution of all things human denies an origination, separation, or even connection of realities that have been mixed from the beginning. Already in the canon, specification and separation are difficult if not impossible. The narratives surrounding the covenant and the prophetic are themselves shrouded in mystery. The identity of Moses is problematic, including his birth and upbringing. His wandering outside of Egypt before his return to lead the Israelites is recalled even in the canon only in bits and pieces. The story of the wandering in the desert is both truncated and expanded within and beyond the allotted time-frame; the story of Moses' last testament and death is so heavily redacted that one can feel the heroic diminished and inflated for reasons that are extraneous to Moses' life.

So much has been lost to the canon of these years of the Exodus; this is as true with the prophets themselves. Among the prophets that are preserved, how many are lost to history? Why were those in the canon preserved and those who are absent lost? Was it simply accident or with purpose? Were the words of the prophets preserved their words?

Here the story of Jesus is instructive. Decidedly and only Jewish, a practicing Jew who himself read and was throughly influenced by the prophets, a Jew who cannot be understood outside the parameters of the covenant and the prophetic, Jesus was jettisoned by the community that he was birthed within and adopted as the center of a new community. In his reading of the prophets, Jesus developed his own prophetic practice, a practice that was related to the prophets he read and was something different as well.

Was Jesus' prophetic understanding only authentic in so far as he imitated the ancient prophets – if indeed this was possible – or was his prophetic understanding authentic in so far as he developed and lived his own prophetic practice? Almost immediately after his death, the community that gathered around Jesus sought to imitate his life and teachings and began to depart from them. Jesus as a prophet underwent the same canonization process as the earlier prophets; the community that created the canon sealed his witness in a way similar to the Jewish community, which the Christian community then condemned for its sealing of the messianic.[13]

From that time on the division between Judaism and Christianity evolves. The division as articulated by Christianity is centered on Judaism's sealing of the messianic. Yet it seems, from traces in the Christian canon and from fragmentary historical evidence, that the initial dispute revolved around prophetic claims that have a messianic eschatology.

There are ways of seeing Jesus that involve the apocalyptic, to be sure, but the situation of occupation and displacement suffered by the Jews of his time points to words of comfort for the people and judgement on political and religious authorities that can only be situated in the covenantal and prophetic traditions. Surely for the people and the authorities, and perhaps for Jesus as well, the messianic comes later, if at all. Could the assertion of the messianic in the gospels be the equivalent Christian canonical sealing of the prophetic as the earlier canon sealed the Jewish prophetic?

If Jesus is seen within the covenantal and prophetic, he is rejected by both the community he was born within and the community that adopted him. The sealing of the prophetic continues and perhaps is crystallized by the formation of Judaism and Christianity in the following centuries over against one another. In doing so, the troublesome continuity of the prophetic is doubly sealed with Jesus, and the rejection and definition of his career/mission become the center.

Judaism denies Jesus as a prophet, thereby freezing its own history of the eruption of the prophetic voice; Christianity elevates Jesus beyond his own inheritance and, in so doing, places him above history and the prophetic, thus sealing the institutional church and its hierarchy from the prophetic challenge of Jesus or any other prophet that comes after him. Jesus then stands for Christians in a similar way that Moses stands for Jews, as the summation of the testaments and covenants. In Judaism, the history of the prophets is to be read and interpreted. In Christianity, the history of the prophets is to be read as announcing the messiah who has come and now is to be worshiped.

The prophetic today

Still we are left with the question of how the prophetic can be applied to the questions of the twenty-first century. To many the very discussion of this religious theme may seem anachronistic. And yet everyday the choice of community or empire is being made and as often the choice of community within empire. Whether announced in religious terms or not, the prophetic choice is always before us. Yet it is haunting that the choice of the prophetic is rarely one that is successful, at least in the immediate term. We are then left with a further difficulty. If the prophetic choice often entails sacrifice *and* is often unsuccessful, why choose such an option?

So often it is the religiously oriented themselves that soil the prophetic. If the prophetic is found within Judaism and Christianity, and the leaders of those faith communities often legitimate or are silent about injustice, why embrace a call that involves sacrifice, is unsuccessful and is perverted by those who *know* the tradition itself?

Perhaps this is why so many of the prophetic voices in the twentieth century were either secular or religious in a self-critical way. And that is also why the prophetic community in our time is made up of people from various traditions and cultures. Such a community contains diverse peoples and traditions, from Mahatma Gandhi, a Hindu, and Martin Buber, a Jew, to Martin Luther King, Jr., a Protestant Christian, and Gustavo Gutierrez, a Latin American Catholic.

With regard to the subject of Israel/Palestine, Jewish dissent has often been prophetic in its search for community. At the turn of the twentieth century, for example, Zionism was a decidedly minority movement among Jews, opposed by most religious and secular Jewish organizations in Europe and the U.S. Even during the Nazi period and after, significant portions of Jewish life remained either indifferent toward or actively opposed to the creation of a Jewish state in Palestine. Opposition to a Jewish state was carried even by Zionists who opted for a cultural or spiritual understanding of a Jewish homeland.

Judah Magnes, Martin Buber and Hannah Arendt belong to those who understood a Jewish homeland within Palestine as important to a Jewish future. However, they opposed the creation of a Jewish state because they believed that such an entity would militarize this homeland and Jewish life itself.[14]

For Magnes, Buber and Arendt, creating a Jewish state would force a displacement of the Arab population of Palestine. Displacing Arabs in Palestine would mirror the displacement of Jews throughout history. It would also mirror the creation of religious legitimated states and the narrowing of intellectual and cultural life that accompanies such states. A Jewish state would ultimately be no different than other nation-states.

Though Jews do not always articulate their connection with this evolving history of dissent, and often do not even know that such a tradition exists, it is here that contemporary Jewish dissent finds its own tradition and rootedness. And it is here that a historical way of understanding the condemnation of Jewish dissent can be found as well.

Judah Magnes, a Reform rabbi and an American-born spiritual Zionist, was the first president of Hebrew University. Yet just before he died in 1949, he personally lobbied United States Secretary of State Marshall and President Harry Truman not to recognize the recently declared state of Israel. He also recommended the presence of U.S. soldiers in Jerusalem to prevent the division of Palestine. Who today among ordinary Jews or Jewish leadership speaks of Magnes' position? Who actually knows of these positions?

Martin Buber, a world-renowned Jewish theologian, biblical scholar and philosopher, was forced to leave Germany in 1938 and lived in Jerusalem until his death in 1965. Like Magnes, Buber was a spiritual Zionist. With Magnes, he also opposed the creation of Israel, proposing instead a confederation of communities in the Middle East.

In this framework a particular vision and way of life as well as a universal understanding of humanity could be developed. While Magnes talked forthrightly with powerful figures in the U.S. government, Buber held a series of debates on these subjects with leading Jewish politicians in Palestine and later in Israel. This included a series of sharp exchanges with Israel's first prime minister, David Ben-Gurion. Buber's understandings, again like Magnes', are largely unknown in the Jewish world or, if known, are dismissed as naive and utopian.

Such disregard for Buber's understandings by Jewish leadership is interesting at the very least. Buber was a refugee who was forced to flee Nazi Germany; he lived his later years in the increasing turmoil between Jews and Arabs in Palestine. While ultimately accepting the Israeli state, he argued his positions within a Jewish context where he was often vilified and where his ideas had consequences for Jews in the land and for his own family. Is it possible to ignore his witness as utopian when he lived through and within the two formative events of contemporary Jewish life?

Finally, the case of Hannah Arendt is instructive. Herself a refugee from Nazi Germany, Arendt spent a significant part of her adult years organizing Jewish refugee relief efforts and was one of the first intellectuals to write of the tragedy that befell European Jewry. Her own writing included two of the major and most controversial books written about the Holocaust before the subject was considered worthy of academic consideration.

Like Magnes and Buber, but from a more secular perspective and with some modifications, Arendt was a bi-nationalist on the question of Palestine. She also thought that the Holocaust had to be analysed in historical, philosophical and political terms. Her reporting on the trial of Adolf Eichmann in Jerusalem was deemed insufficiently condemnatory of the evil intent of the Nazi regime, and so this part of her work was chastised rather than forgotten. The campaign of vilification against Hannah Arendt stands as the quintessential attack on a person's Jewishness rather than dealing with the Jewish tradition of dissent which she embodied and distinguished.

But we need not identify those who have left a record of achievement and notoriety to witness the demise of the Jewish tradition of dissent in our time. Since the creation of Israel, there have been a variety of dissenting actions and speech that address the hopes and aspirations of the Jewish people – a people which has certainly struggled and suffered in the throes of violence legitimated by religion and nationalism – to end the cycle of violence and atrocity.

One thinks here of the soldiers under Yitzhak Rabin's command in the 1948 war who, educated in 'cosmopolitan' ways, refused to cleanse Arab villagers from areas that would become part of the new Israeli state. These same soldiers, seeing Palestinians being displaced and forced across the borders, remembered the Jewish exile from Spain as an image which they glimpsed within the Palestinian catastrophe.

The record of dissent continued during the Israeli bombing of Beirut in the 1980s, when some Israeli soldiers refused to serve in Lebanon. It accelerated during the Palestinian uprising when other Israeli soldiers saw, in the policy of might and beatings, images of Nazi brutality once carried out against Jews. For many Jews a transposition had taken place in Jewish life: were Jews, in denying the rights of Palestinians, acting like those who had denied Jewish rights across the millennia?

Like much of Jewish history, past and present collapses into a multi-layered reality. In this sense, the prophetic is non-linear, available at any moment, and the echoes of an earlier dissent can be heard in a later dissent.

4 A Jewish Witness in Exile

In 1998, the fiftieth anniversary of Israel's independence was celebrated. The mood was quite different from what would have been expected. Some of the celebrations were modified to include a more sober acknowledgment of Israel's past and future. Some of the celebrations were cancelled altogether.

There were also counter-celebrations, designated 'commemorations'. These commemorations took notice of the Palestinian catastrophe associated with the founding of Israel and raised the question whether celebration is possible in the context of occupation and settlements. At that moment, the Oslo process was stalled and the assassination of Rabin and inauguration of the Netanyahu years had taken a toll on Jewish hope.

Jews were found in all of these venues and weighed in on the issues surrounding Israel's birth and future. Would Israel come to terms with Palestinians by granting a limited autonomy in the small and segmented areas of the West Bank and Gaza not yet settled by Jews?

Or would Israel see another way, recognizing the Palestinian need for a secure and expanded land base to rebuild Palestinian life? Would Jerusalem, so central in religious, cultural, political and economic terms to Jews and Palestinians, be shared? Or would Israel claim the city as its own and further divide Jews and Palestinians?

On the surface these seemed purely political questions to be resolved in the political arena through negotiation and ultimately through power. As victor, Israel makes its claim and the Palestinians, as the weaker party, appeal to the mercy of the victor.

Will that appeal be heard now after the collapse of the Oslo process? Is that appeal more than political? The issue seems less about the past than the immediate context. Politics is often played out in the forum of the immediate. The long range is secured by decisions in the present, especially if they benefit the people or the nation. The nation seeks security, expansion and affluence. All nations that are victorious think that the future is theirs.

And so it may be. But the thinkers we have analysed suggest a past that haunts the present almost as an accusing image.

Those who reflect on the Holocaust see disjunctions in contemporary Jewish life that have not been bridged by empowerment. The nation of Israel has brought pride and sometimes shame on the Jewish people; with its nationhood secure and normalized, its symbolic hold on the Jewish people is already diminishing. Future generations will see Israel in the framework of the international nation-state system. The power of the Holocaust to mobilize the Jewish community is likewise receding. In the future it will be less and less connected in the Jewish imagination with Israel.

Hence the arrival of Operation Birthright, the program that seeks increased travel to Israel, especially among Jewish youth. This program, and others like it, teaches Jewish youth the connection between the Holocaust and Israel and the connection of both these events to their own lives. What was once obvious to a generation that witnessed the Holocaust and the birth of Israel is no longer self-evident.

The bifurcation of Jewish life, experienced by those who lived through those years, then analysed by those who lived after the Holocaust and the formation of Israel, appears to be increasingly accepted as the norm of Jewish life by the next generation. The possibility of a strong and integrated Jewish identity, when bifurcation is at the center, is difficult to imagine. Jewish identity, like Jewish memory, will exist in a mythic form, abstracted from the difficult details of life.

The challenge then is the next fifty years. What will Israel look like then? Will the Holocaust be remembered and, if so, how? There will be those who identify themselves as Jews. What will the content of that identity be? Will the missing commandment be found, or will it fade into a distance that obscures the violation itself?

If the missing commandment is found by a few, what will they do with that commandment? Will their voices be heard? Will they speak a language that allows that voice to find its place in the long history of the Jewish people? Will the covenant be spoken about, but its substance lost, and be held up even as its ability to challenge the people who claim it is diminished?

Against their own political positions, Yerushalmi, Greenberg, Roskies, Fackenheim and Ozick propose a way forward. The next fifty years could signal a recognition of the historic wrongs done to Jews in Europe *and* Palestinians in Palestine. This recognition could bring some Jews and Palestinians together across the borders that are now being sealed. A movement for civil rights in the expanded state of

Israel and among the Palestinians within and in between Israeli sovereignty could bring the missing commandment into view. The *tikkun* of ordinary decency is likely to be the unannounced motivation in this movement toward the sharing of the land and equality. Klepfisz's plea will be heard in less emotional circumstances as a claim upon Jews that desire for others what they desire for themselves, an ordinary life which would be, if both peoples find it in the next fifty years, extraordinary.

The Holocaust will recede in its ability to mobilize Jews and Jewish identity, but it may become even more powerful for those who cannot reconcile themselves with the norm of bifurcation. The Holocaust will move from a memory to mobilize Jewish empowerment to a subversive memory that critiques those forms of Jewish empowerment that institutionalize injustice.

That memory will seek an interdependence of justice and equality and will operate within and around state power. The *tikkun* of ordinary decency will move across borders of state and community, Israeli and Palestinian, and Jew, Christian and Muslim. It will create a common homeland for Jews and Palestinians. Then the mourning of the Holocaust will find its place in a Jewish identity that laments and is hopeful, aware of death and the possibilities of life.

The boundaries of our destiny

To analyse the future of Judaism and Jewish life within this context is to ask about the borders of the state of Israel and the boundaries of Jewish life. Are the boundaries of the state today the boundaries of our personal and collective identity as Jews? If these are in effect the boundaries today are they the boundaries of Jewish destiny?

Since Israel, like any other state, will take whatever land it can, all the while employing the rhetoric of suffering, innocence and security, and if there is no countervailing power in word or deed, as indeed neither seems to be in sight, then Jewish identity, politics, culture and religiosity will be worked out within these boundaries. Paradoxically, those who have struggled against these boundaries of the state and Jewish identity must surrender their opposition now and recognize that the continuation of a rhetoric of two states – *as if the map of Israel will be reversed* – is to participate in an illusion that deceives Jews and Palestinians alike.

Some of the consequences of the boundaries of Israel and Jewish life on the threshold of the twenty-first century include:

- Palestine, as it existed before the founding of Israel and even before the 1967 war, has been destroyed. Israel has conquered and controls Palestine even within the prospect of some autonomy or even a rhetorical statehood. The Jewish tradition, with its emphasis on ethics and justice, is alive only where the immediacy of Jewish interest and power is absent. *In the destruction of Palestine, the Jewish tradition as it has been known and inherited – a tradition that emphasized ethics and justice – has come to an end.*

  At the same time, a new realization may emerge within the destruction: that Israel has not and will never exist by itself. Even in its destruction, Palestine has existed and continues on within Israel in geography, memory, architecture, culture and population.

- The struggle over the next fifty years is less the establishment of a Palestinian state next to Israel, for that could be a state in name only, than the struggle within Israel to recognize its dual population throughout the land, Jews and Palestinians, as equal in dignity and political rights. The goal must be citizenship without reference to ethnic or religious identity and the evolution of a new political and social identity that involves the particularity of Jewish and Palestinian history while transcending both.

  As that identity evolves, Palestine will assert itself within and then with Israel so that the true reality of Israel as Israel/Palestine or, if you will, Palestine/Israel, will be recognized. For Zionism, the implications are obvious: the ideological structure that gave birth to the state and to the destruction of Palestine, an ideology that emerged within the context of the crisis of nineteenth and twentieth century European Jewish life, will come to end. In the twenty-first century, Judaism will return to its diaspora sensibility but in a transformed way.

- The end of Judaism and the Jewish tradition *as it has been known and inherited* precludes a return to a diaspora whose ethical tradition has been damaged by the militarization that the formation and expansion of Israel demanded. However, a new diaspora will emerge that includes Jews and those of other peoples and cultures, including Palestinians, who are in exile because of force or choice.

Those who search out this new form of Jewish life will be Jews who refuse today the borders of Israel as the boundaries of Jewish destiny. Many of these Jews have, at this very moment, crossed over into solidarity with the Palestinian people. They are in exile preparing the future of Jewish life, a future that can only arise when the land of Israel and Palestine is shared.

Why is the future of Jewish life only possible with a sharing of Israel/Palestine? Because only then will the suffering that Jews have caused be truly acknowledged and confessed. With that confession and the movement to redress grievances, a mature sense of identity can be embraced with honesty and determination. The struggle to build Israel/Palestine will itself be a marker on the road to renewal. For can Jews proclaim their identity, can a future be built, while oppressing another people?

What will that future be like when a new normalcy enters the life of Jews and Palestinians? What will be salvaged from a Judaism that failed in its moment of crisis? Only the next fifty years can provide the answer.

Judaism in its mainstream variety may continue. In such a configuration, Jews will continue to enter and serve American and Israeli society. Constantinian Judaism will be consolidated – where Jewish activism, thought and theology will serve the American and Israeli states. The mainstream here includes those identified as religious – Orthodox, Conservative and Reform – and secular. Though both groups will drift farther apart in their understandings and lifestyles they will share a fundamental assimilation to the state and power. The bond between religious and secular will be found in this assimilation.

Renewal Jews in America, those who find Arthur Waskow and Michael Lerner to be leaders for the next generation of Jewish life, will dissipate into the categories above. For the most part they or their children will drift back into the areas of Jewish life that their parents came from originally. The experiences that galvanized their parents, including the struggle to reclaim the innocence of the Jewish people by allowing the creation of a viable Palestinian state alongside Israel – a state that is founded on the once occupied territories after the 1967 war with its capital in Jerusalem – will be unavailable to them.

The end of this vision of Palestine accomplished, few of these children will find relevant the struggle to recreate Israel/Palestine. Without this struggle and the charismatic leaders that emerge within it, the children will be faced with the crisis that their parents eluded by commitment to an Israel they continued to hope would respond to Jewish ethics and by an evolving mysticism and ritual that lent meaning to affluent lives at the end of the twentieth century.

The void of Jewish life, skirted in the previous generation, will become unavoidable to the next generation. Overall, the response will be apathy, drift and ultimately assimilation to power and the state.

Israeli Jews, already split into religious and secular in a more divisive and substantive way than American Jews, could conceivably normalize their existence in the expanded state of Israel. Having conquered Palestine, Zionism will end and Israeli society will consolidate itself. Secular Israelis will follow the model of the West; religious Jews will continue to foster messianic expectations. Secular Israelis will deepen what one Israeli sociologist has called their 'Hebrew-speaking Gentile' mentality. Jewishness and any link to Jewish history will continue to atrophy just as religious Jews in Israel see themselves more and more as the final and messianic product of that history.

At one level, remnant Palestinians will serve as a reserved and cheap labor pool for Israel and both religious and secular Jewish Israeli communities will use them to enhance their standard of living, regardless of the rhetoric of civil rights or religion. Thus Palestinians will be the African-Americans or Latinos of Israeli society in the production of affluence and their limited share in the affluence they help to create.

However, there will also be movements among Palestinians and among some Jews in Israel, especially in the secular camp, to lift living standards among Palestinians and even to accord equal civil rights to them. From the Jewish side this will be done out of necessity – international pressure and opinion – and from personal, economic, political and cultural interchange. Living side by side and with Palestinians will cause two trends: to further repress Palestinians *and* to open society to equal participation to facilitate harmony and economic growth.

For the mainstream of Jewish life in the U.S. and Israel, the expansion of affluence and land, consolidation of advances and societal structure, assertion of Jewishness and power, and avoidance of the accusing images that the destruction of Palestine places at the center of Jewish life can continue unabated. Those exiled from Jewish life in both countries because of their solidarity with the

Palestinian people will become increasingly peripheral, almost invisible, to other Jews.

Jewish history, when recalled, will be silent on these exilic Jews because no category exists for them in an assimilationist community. This is part of the end of Jewish history: the inability to remember the contemporary prophets who prepare a future. The future is in process – the witnesses to a new life of repentance and inclusion, to a revolutionary forgiveness where confession is coupled with activity on behalf of justice – but that future will be lived and remembered in another historical framework.

In the Middle East, will the memory of those Jews who have crossed over into solidarity with the Jewish people be preserved by Palestinians in their suffering and struggle? In the U.S., will that same memory be preserved by Christians who have committed themselves to a future of Christianity beyond oppression, anti-Semitism and silence?

Yet another possibility foresees a revision of identity, something not easy to predict, especially when those identities are forged in suffering. Pride of place is foremost when a people have just emerged from suffering; pride of resistance is essential when a people are under occupation. Of course, a singular identity is always an illusion as is a monolithic sense of purpose. Identity is more complex and diverse.

Even the inheritance of identity is often romanticized, as if a continuity exists from ancient times until the present. Understood in this way, changes in identity are difficult to contemplate or understand, as if such an understanding – that identities are formed and unformed, that they are eclectic in the past and in the present – is itself a betrayal of the struggle of suffering peoples.

But is it true that *a* Jewish or Palestinian identity existed historically or exists today in the present? To posit identity as if it is static is to condemn communities and peoples to a cycle of violence and militarism, to a ghettoized mentality that continues in victory and victimization.

The crossing of boundaries of Jews and Palestinians in their homeland of Israel/Palestine and in their various diasporas will increase in the next fifty years and will provide a context for the evolution of both identities into a new configuration. This evolving identity will combine aspects of both particularities in their diversity and will fashion a new particularity which will also be diverse. The dual movement of repression and openness in Israel/Palestine and the assimilationist trends among Jews in the West will find more and more Jews and Palestinians sharing perspectives and hopes.

Finally, these remnant Jews and Palestinians are a growing minority and they can face majorities in each community whose primary focus is status, power and affluence or simply getting along in whatever situation exists. However, the conscious minority will have the advantage of realizing that cultural and political integration is not only necessary for the flourishing of Jewish and Palestinian life in the homeland and the diaspora, but that it is essential for the healing of the sufferings that have frozen Jewish and Palestinian identity in a false way. Because they are a minority becoming more and more conscious of the cycle of violence and the contradictions within both communities, because they will realize more and more that the expansion and evolution of both Jewish and Palestinian can only occur when both identities are embraced *and* transcended, this minority will find itself forming a common front in the next fifty years.

At some point, and there is evidence of this beginning to take place now, a solidarity based on inherited and often romanticized identity groupings will give way to an identity in formation characterized by shared values that emerge in a common struggle for the possibility of ordinary life and human flourishing. In this sense mutual respect, coexistence and equality – values in their own right – can only be achieved in the homeland and the diaspora when these sensibilities are used to affirm and overcome the division between Jew and Palestinian.

With the loss of every culture and tradition, the human spirit is diminished. Sometimes it is easier to mourn these losses than to commit oneself to the birth of a new reality that may or may not carry that history into the future. At the end of Jewish history *as it has been known and inherited,* Jews mourn their dead in synagogues and public places as if by remaining in the past Jews somehow affirm life. But when that mourning is the cause for another mourning, then the dead, Jewish and Palestinian, are murdered again. A cycle of death and destruction, once experienced, is renewed until mourning itself becomes a way of life and, finally, there is no one left to mourn.

On the threshold of the twenty-first century, it is time to bring that mourning to a close. The next fifty years await decisions that will give birth to a future worth bequeathing to the children of Jews and Palestinians. That future will be neither Jewish or Palestinian in the way these peoples are known today.

The memory of those who struggled at a critical historical moment, who opted for life without thought of betrayal or grandeur, will live on in the place where the refusal of the final assimilation to power and the state takes hold, and with inclusion and justice as its watchword, will grow strong.

This strength requires a steadfastness and a vision that is deeply rooted and is open to a future that incorporates and transcends the past. The dream of Jews to a secure and just existence and the dream of Palestinians to a restored Palestine will one day occur, though in an unexpected configuration. The next fifty years are a time of waiting and working, a time when all will be tested in their fortitude and hope. In the twenty-first century, through struggle and loss and a solidarity that crosses boundaries, a new dream will arise.

Reinventing Judaism and Jewish life

Though traditions are usually seen within the framework of broad continuities, the reality is quite different. In fact, traditions, whether they be political, cultural or religious, are most often characterized by unannounced discontinuities. As disconcerting as this might seem – that in fact a modern Jew has much less in common with Jews of antiquity than religious and community leaders would like to acknowledge – discontinuity has its bright side as well. It allows space for continual reinventions, rethinking and repositioning and thus the flexibility for a future beyond the impasse of the present. A recurring theme of Jewish history, hence a continuity in that history, is this capability of reinvention.[1]

Reinvention is different than the original creation, though when investigated the creation itself is a reinvention of a previous religious outlook. The ancient Israelites were borrowers and synthesizers, as were those who were exiled to Babylon. Those who returned to Jerusalem after the exile as well as the rabbis after the destruction of the Temple and Jerusalem, invented what we know as Judaism.

The Torah was not only written after the events it reports on, it was redacted, edited again; it represents a selection that is then re-interpreted through teachings later brought together – and, yes, redacted and edited again – in what we know as the Talmud.

Jewish philosophy and theology, and in the modern era Holocaust theology, represents a further reinvention of Judaism and Jewish life.

In the early part of the twentieth century, anyone suggesting that Jewish identity would be formed around the events of Holocaust and Israel would have been consigned to oblivion. It would not have been seen as possible.

Thus the end of Judaism as we have known and inherited it in our time is hardly a radical statement in the broad sweep of Jewish history. What is remarkable about Jews and Jewish history is not the continuity of the people and tradition but rather the ability of the community to continually reinvent itself as it has done and is doing in our time. What has disguised the change over the last two thousand years is the relative continuity of institutional structure in synagogues and community councils.

The appearance of the nation-state dominated by Jews and a thorough modernization in the West has stripped this veneer and the transition appears more like the one at the close of the Temple era and the rise of the synagogue, that is, the transition from Temple-centered Judaism to Rabbinic Judaism. Even this transformation was disguised by the continuation of Temple themes in the rabbinic system. As the rabbis became dominant they kept alive the image of the Temple, reinventing Judaism as a waiting period for the return of the Temple that the rabbis had no investment in wanting to reappear.

The genius of the rabbinic system was the ancient imagery it retained and redeployed. Thus the genius of the Judaism revolving around the Holocaust and Israel in our time: though rabbinic Judaism as it knew itself is hardly recognizable in the new theology, the remnants of this system have been retained and retrained to function within the new era.

But the Holocaust and Israel have overpowered that which survived in these earlier transformations and the dissent that informs the civil war over these same issues has further distanced Jews from the Temple and the synagogue. While Jewish renewal movements have attempted to revive textual study and creatively adjust Jewish ritual, this has occurred within and as a resistance to the dominance of the Holocaust and Israel.

Through affirmation and dissent the Holocaust and Israel have been affirmed as defining of contemporary Jewish identity. This places Jewish identity in a waiting period of unknown duration. The Holocaust and Israel cannot forever provide the identification sufficient to mobilize Jewish energies and there is no way back to previous symbols, no matter how deep within the tradition or invention and reinvention.

Without a way back and with no discernible path forward, what is left is a struggle against the final assimilation. Not surprisingly, this struggle is led by those without 'religion' and religious language, Jews like Noam Chomsky. Is it any surprise that the most vehement and relentless critic of state power in the world is a religionless Jew who takes up, in our time, what other Godless Jews, like Karl Marx and Sigmund Freud, did in their time?

Perhaps Chomsky, like his previous soulmates, does not speak in religious language because he knows that the forces he struggles against only use religion to mask their desire for political power. By critiquing state power, especially in the U.S. and Israel, Chomsky unmasks that which is cloaked in religious rhetoric. Where the American and Jewish establishments use the language of innocence and entitlement, Chomsky uses the language of maps and abuse of power.

With Chomsky we must also add the late Israel Shahak. Shahak was a survivor of the death camps and then a citizen of Israel from 1945 until his death in 2000. A lifelong human rights advocate, Shahak was relentlessly critical of Jewish religion as exclusionary; he wrote extensively about the roots of Jewish chauvinism and religious fanaticism in Israel as being rooted in classical Judaism. In his seminal work, *Jewish History, Jewish Religion*, Shahak's subtitle sums up his sense of Jewish tradition: 'The Weight of Three Thousand Years'.[2]

Shahak's understanding is that Judaism has been and continues to be a burden to Jews and to others, in the present day to the Palestinians, and therefore needs to be jettisoned. Though Shahak's analysis is itself at times burdensome, his central insights are important to consider. Two quotes will suffice here: 'Religion is not always (as Marx said) the opium of the people, but it can often be so, and when it is used in this sense by prevaricating and misrepresenting its true nature, the scholars and intellectuals who perform this task take on the character of opium smugglers'; 'Only when a historiography becomes – as Peter Geyl put it so well – a "debate without end" rather than a continuation of war by historiographic means, only then does a humane historiography, which strives for both accuracy and fairness, become possible; and then it turns into one of the most powerful instruments of humanism and self-education.'[3]

Taken together, Chomsky and Shahak provide a barrier and border for religious consciousness, a warning about the reinvention of

Judaism and Jewish life. With them in mind, state power and religion in service to the state – the hallmarks of Constantinian religiosity – must be opposed, lest those who reinvent Judaism become, in Shahak's words, 'patriotic liars'.[4]

But if these political and religious borders are respected is it possible to reinvent Judaism and Jewish life? Is this a venture worth dedicating one's energies to? Even if it is desirable to reconstruct a religiosity and a culture, such a reconstruction will need an institutional framework that may, once reinvented, become like the structures it replaced. One wonders if the next Jewish establishment would be any different than the one it replaced.

Shahak's 'debate without end' is important here. On the one hand, the covenant once given and the prophetic once announced survive independently of their original carriers. Both survive even those who claim to carry that message today. And since the covenant and the prophetic are always contextual, the manner, speech and activity required to embrace both are always changing. This independence that characterizes the covenant and the prophetic alarms the religious and secular alike. For it means that nowhere is the covenant and the prophetic to be expected and in the least expected of places they may be found.

Still, the articulation of this independence as well as the general framework through which the covenant and the prophetic can be recognized is important. It is the combination of the prophetic's existence in the world and its articulation that radicalizes the possibility of justice and the search for community in the world. And it is through articulation that the possibility of a broader coalition comes into view.

Here we return to Levinas. The Judaic sensibility is a prophetic one and Levinas sees this as a 'claim to a separate existence in the political history of the world. It is a claim to judge history – that is to say, to remain free with regard to events, whatever the logic binding them.' For Levinas this is part of the eternity of Israel and the reason for its survival. 'It is not because it miraculously survived that it assumed a freedom in the face of history', Levinas writes, 'It is because, from the beginning, it managed to deny the jurisdiction of events which it maintained in itself as the unity of consciousness throughout history.'[5]

Of course, it is clear now that the eternity of Israel is the Judaic sensibility in the world that travels among and within peoples and has no definitive home. While raising up the Judaic sensibility as a prophetic and covenantal understanding of the world and articulating it in a particular beautiful way, Levinas makes the mistake of too easily identifying it with Jewish texts and their study.

For after this recent history of suffering and struggle and as important a history of dislocating and humiliating another people, Jews can hardly claim to embody the prophetic and the covenant simply because our texts point to these realities. In fact, it seems dubious, if not impossible, to claim even these texts as our own. They are now the inheritance of all peoples. At the same time, we also inherit the texts of other peoples which point in their own way toward a prophetic and covenantal sensibility.

On revolutionary forgiveness

A little more than a decade ago in Ireland, I taught a week-length course on prospects for the development of a Jewish theology of liberation. On the second day of the seminar, the subject of forgiveness was broached in an unexpected and almost violent manner.

Having spent the first day lecturing on the Holocaust, I started the second day in like manner. A Catholic sister from California attending the course became angry with the subject at hand and, in reference to Adolf Hitler, blurted out the following: 'You hate Hitler in your heart, don't you?' Her tone was almost bitter, as if my personal opinion or heart-feeling about Hitler overshadowed the Holocaust event itself.

Behind her words and tone lay a vast tradition. Christians were those who forgave their enemies; Jews were those whose hearts were hardened. And in their hardness of heart, Jews had crucified Jesus. This same hardness of heart lay at the root of the refusal of Jews to forgive those who persecuted and murdered them.

I felt the violence behind her words, as if I was implicated in the crime of deicide. My refusal to forgive was equated with the horrible crimes of the Nazi era.

I was stunned into silence by the force of her words. Did I hate Hitler in my heart and, if so, was this itself a crime? Was her ability to forgive Hitler counterbalanced by her inability to forgive my feelings of distaste and condemnation? What struck me at that moment was that I actually had no feelings toward Hitler at all. When his name was mentioned or I spoke of him it was as if a vast emptiness enveloped me.

For what seemed like an eternity, I stood silently in front of the class. Then I noticed another student, a Sudanese priest, rise. Being unable to respond myself, I waited anxiously to hear what he had to say. Recalling his own community's struggle with Sudanese of Islamic background, he offered the following comment as a defense of my position: 'I refuse to forgive as well. If a Muslim comes into my village I will take a gun and blow his brains out.'

The contrast was so startling as to provoke a further silence. A religious woman whose violence against the Jewish people is spoken of in an internal language of the heart is confronted by a priest whose imagery of violence is so blatant as to picture the brains of another person spilling at my feet.

The assault and defense rendered me unable to continue the lecture. Excusing the class, I felt drained and at a loss. I felt like weeping.

That confrontation remains with me to this day and the image of forgiveness and murder presented by the sister and priest still resonates in a painful way. She, of course, had never experienced violence on a mass scale, nor had she inherited this suffering from her ancestors. He had experienced violence, perhaps would experience more in the days and years ahead, but seemed unable to offer an alternative path. As a Jew, I was caught in the middle, assaulted and defended without consultation and without probing. I could not endorse either position as stated and felt distant from both.

Still the issue of forgiveness continues to present itself in other fora, as I am asked often by Christians if it is not possible to forgive Hitler, the Nazis, the German people and in a particular sense Christians themselves. Yet I am struck by a fated irony: the tradition of the sister who assaulted me and the priest who defended me helped to create the violence I am called upon to forgive or perpetrate. A cycle of violence has enveloped Jews, one that we are now accused of or encouraged to continue.

The previous year I embarked on two projects that now related to this encounter in Ireland. The first was travel to Germany; the other to Israel. In Germany I spent time with Germans who were repenting their country's involvement in the Holocaust and the subsequent inability of their fellow citizens to come to terms with this historical event. In Israel I met Palestinians who suffer displacement and exile at the hands of Jewish Israelis who, often as not, use the Holocaust to justify their military and expansionist policies.

In Germany the theme was a repentance without a desire for forgiveness, for how, my hosts conjectured, is forgiveness possible when the Holocaust is buried by German affluence and the desire to embark on a new history without guilt? Remarkably, the people I spent most of my time with in Germany are Christians themselves, part of the large and growing network of Pax Christi members who, with the end of the war, and after the mass slaughter of each other and the Jewish people, determined that a chastened and pacifist Europe was a necessity.

The Israeli–Palestinian conflict is less a historical than a continuing, even escalating event: the Palestinians ask for justice and the Israelis, even those in the peace camp, are far from the desire to confess their transgressions. For the most part, Jewish Israelis feel today that their cause is justified and the suffering of the Palestinian people is secondary to the struggle of Jews to find their place in the community of nations. But in meeting Palestinians and journeying with them through checkpoints and under occupation, the question of justice is tempered by the call for confession.

Palestinians call on us as Jews to confess. One day we will ask them to forgive us. What will that confession and forgiveness look like and lead to?

In one sense, the challenge of Israel is greater than the challenge of the Holocaust, as Jews and Palestinians face one another and thus there is still time. The Holocaust is alive only in memory and Germans have the added challenge of dealing with the memory of Jews who have been eliminated from their country. This renders the most horrific crime into an abstraction that none the less gnaws at the heart of German history. In these two journeys I ask if confession, forgiveness, even reconciliation are possible without a living community at the very place of violation?

Thus at the heart of an evolving Jewish theology of liberation stand these important issues: the Christian ethos that still pervades the West and indeed large areas of the globe; the wounds of the Holocaust which remain open and unhealed; the ongoing tragedy in the Middle East which is both a response to the violence of Christianity and the Holocaust and a furtherance of violence against a people that have not been involved in the historic suffering of Jews.

A triangulation of history and contemporary life has evolved which, if it continues, threatens the healing of these histories – Christian, German, Jewish and Palestinian. Is there a way forward and if so can that way forward be found in the very confrontation that rendered me silent in Ireland? A Jewish theology of liberation, written during this time, could only begin to touch on these points, weaving together the seemingly disjointed histories of peoples and religions within the context of their historic and contemporary struggles.[6]

Surely we as Jews cannot move forward within the present impasse. Jewish empowerment, so necessary in light of the Holocaust, has not healed us as a people. When I visited the hospitals in Jerusalem in 1988, just months after the beginning of the first Palestinian uprising and the policy of might and beatings instituted by then Minister of Defence, Yitzhak Rabin, and saw the Palestinian children lying in beds from which they would not soon leave, some paralysed for life, others brain-dead, existing on antiquated life-support equipment, the point was driven home.

Instead of the healing and normalization of the Jewish condition, the force of Israel has deepened our wounds. In a paradoxical way, by externalizing our pain and inflicting it on another people, we are becoming more distant from the sources and resources of our own possible healing. By seeing power as the only way forward, by feeling that with power comes dignity and respect, by projecting power as the only line of defence against a further violation, another holocaust, that very power unraveled the tradition, culture and religion that had itself been violated.

What the Nazis had not succeeded in accomplishing – the undermining at a fundamental level of the very essence of what it means to be Jewish – we as Jews have embarked upon. I witnessed this in the hospitals and in the streets where Palestinians, struggling to assert their own dignity, were being systematically beaten, expelled and murdered by those who had suffered this indignity less than fifty years earlier.

As I was thinking through this seeming conundrum, I came across a book of feminist reflections on Nicaragua with the provocative title *Revolutionary Forgiveness*. Published in the same year that the Palestinian uprising began, and read in light of the confrontation in Ireland, my travel to Germany and the witnessing of the Palestinian children, this book had a strong impact on me.

As with my own writing on a Jewish theology of liberation, *Revolutionary Forgiveness* is also part of a journey. Carter Heyward, an Episcopal priest and professor at Episcopal Divinity School, with a group of her seminary students, traveled to Nicaragua in the 1980s at the height of the U.S.-financed war against the Nicaraguan government. Expecting to find hatred against citizens from the country that was financing this costly war that had produced so many casualties and hardship, they found the opposite: a welcoming of those American citizens who opposed their government's policies and who risked traveling to a country in the midst of war. Instead of vilifying Heyward and her students, the Nicaraguans they met were open to those who confessed the sins of the American governmental policies and sought a way beyond the cycle of violence these policies furthered.

When forgiveness was sought by one of the students it became clear that such forgiveness could only come within a commitment to justice. 'People cannot simply "forgive" – invite back into their lives on a mutual basis – those who continue to violate us', one student wrote:

> Otherwise 'forgiveness' is an empty word. Forgiveness is possible only when the violence stops. Only then can those who have been violated even consider the possibility of actually loving those who once brutalized and battered them. Only then can the former victims empower the victimizers by helping them to realize their own power to live as liberated liberators, people able to see in themselves and others a corporate capacity to shape the future.[7]

It is in the ending of injustice and the journey toward a mutual and just future that forgiveness becomes revolutionary.

This understanding of revolutionary forgiveness, though Christian in inspiration, is also Jewish in its demand for justice. By placing forgiveness in motion, the static and superficial request – even demand by the powerful – to be forgiven *without embarking on a new social and political project of inclusion and justice,* is placed in perspective. In Heyward's sensibility, forgiveness is less the end of the matter than it is a process of conversion to a future different than the past.

Being in right relation allows a forgiveness that is not devoid of memory. Rather, memory of past injustice becomes a shared memory of victim and victimizer. This memory, coupled with the desire to create a society beyond injustice, allows a new societal foundation to evolve. In revolutionary forgiveness, a new freedom is found, a freedom that also evolves over time into a new social and political identity. No longer victim and victimizer, both parties are freed to become whom God calls us to be.

Thus a personal transformation is accomplished as well: in the movement toward justice, people are freed from having to assume the role of victim and victimizer, a role that cuts to the heart of human dignity and potential. Beyond the cycle of violence is the embrace of the human, flawed and finite to be sure, but flourishing in a new social and political order where right relation is struggled for and attained.

Revolutionary forgiveness is far from the teachings of my mentor Richard Rubenstein. For Rubenstein it is not so much the existence of God, but the kind of God one can posit after Auschwitz. If God exists, where was God in the Holocaust? If God is all-powerful, an essential belief in Jewish history, why did God refuse to act? If God is not all-powerful, if God is unable to rescue a suffering people, why worship such a God? As for the traditional Jewish belief that suffering is punishment for neglecting Jewish law and God's teachings, who can hold fast to a God who reckons such disproportionate suffering from the people God chose and promised to protect? Were those millions who perished in the Holocaust guilty of a crime? If so, did the punishment hardly fit the crime?

So Rubenstein's response to the Holocaust is disbelief, a defiant agnosticism or atheism if you will, that is, a refusal to believe in the God of Jewish history, and this disbelief has social and political ramifications. If God is not to be relied on, who is? The solidarity of God with the Jewish people has been irrevocably broken. On the human level, solidarity is also deeply questioned, for if God was absent from the Jewish people during the Holocaust where was humanity?

Thus both the solidarity of God *and* humanity cannot be relied on and only power, the power to protect and punish, can be efficacious in our world. Theories of the righteousness of God and the goodness of humanity – the prospect for revolutionary forgiveness – for Rubenstein are blinders to the reality of the world. After Auschwitz we know better: those with power flourish and those without power are condemned to the margins of society, segregated into ghettos, and sometimes threatened with annihilation.[8]

Listening to Rubenstein, first as a college student, later in discussions at conferences on the Holocaust and, in 1992, at Auschwitz itself as part of a delegation on the future of the Auschwitz camp site, I experienced almost a mirror image of the Catholic sister and Sudanese priest I encountered in Ireland. After Auschwitz, internal and external violence has merged into a protective shield that allows little room for exploration. Views of the world outside of power are relegated to the periphery, as if to entertain these views is a form of violence itself, *as if contemplation of a world journeying toward revolutionary forgiveness can only lead to another Auschwitz.*

The views of the Catholic sister conjure up the world of Catholic and Christian piety, often experienced by Jews as a form of violence, and the need of the Sudanese priest to defend through murder the integrity of his people provokes the memories of a world collapsing around the Jews of Europe. On the one side, a forgiveness that can only come from an internal violence against the Jewish people; on the other, a struggle that starkly places the future of a people at risk.

For Rubenstein, after Auschwitz only the organization of an empowered state can shield Jews from both risks. It is only in the power of the state, a power used to exclude the Jews of Europe, that Jews can protect themselves. Instead of revolutionary forgiveness, a forgiveness that raises the question of solidarity and God in right relation and justice, Rubenstein feels compelled, despite the risks, to choose the power of the state. The struggle for power is all and the winners take all: Jews and Jewish leadership, indeed the leadership of any community, has the responsibility never to lose again.

In *After Auschwitz*, but even more so in *The Cunning of History*, Rubenstein cites the writings of Hannah Arendt. Arendt's *The Origins of Totalitarianism*, with its sweeping survey of contemporary European history and the crisis of values and traditions she finds there, are crucial to Rubenstein's political argument and conclusion. The whole of Western civilization has come 'toppling over our heads', Arendt writes, and the lesson of our century is that those on the margins of society are declared superfluous and condemned. Rubenstein takes these themes and expands upon them; as a theologian, he also explores the culpability of theology and God. But the social and moral reconstruction that Arendt envisions in *Origins* and pursues in her later work is absent from Rubenstein's analysis.

Yet it is almost as if Rubenstein is stuck in the absence of God and solidarity. With this absence the cycle of power can only continue on its foreordained path. While Arendt, herself a refugee from Europe, analyses the horror and then embarks on a reconstruction of the values so violated in the Holocaust, Rubenstein is not so inclined. Perhaps Arendt could not afford the break that Rubenstein sees as so definitive. As a refugee rather than an American analysing the effects of the Holocaust, Arendt had to construct a world for herself in another place.[9]

Thus it is not surprising that the possibility of forgiveness is present in Arendt's work, though it is only peripherally connected to the question of God. Arendt rarely writes about God, for her main theme is a social and philosophical reconstruction of a world where the death camps are still visible and the Cold War is in full bloom. Even her discussion of Jesus of Nazareth as the 'discoverer of forgiveness in the realm of human affairs' is couched in non-religious language. Arendt's view is that too many contributions from religious thinkers and actors have been lost to contemporary public discourse because of their religious nature. Her point, especially on the question of forgiveness, is that the contribution itself, even when shorn of its specific religious nature, can assist in the reconstruction of the public realm after the catastrophe of the Nazi era.[10]

What does Arendt mean by forgiveness? What role can it play in personal and public affairs? To begin with, forgiveness is linked with promise; both are seen in the context of the ability to create and secure a stable public realm. Both forgiveness and promise, while often thought to be in the private realm, are, for Arendt, also public in nature.

Here the concept of respect rather than love is the currency, and the private realm where love may indeed suffice is transcended. For Arendt, respect is defined by the Aristotelian *philia politike,* a friendship without intimacy and without closeness, 'a regard for the person from the distance which the space of the world puts between us, and this respect is independent of qualities which we may admire or of achievements which we may highly esteem'. Love, often thought of in regard to the Christian aspect of forgiveness, is, when transported into the public realm, dangerous. 'Love, by its very nature, is unworldly', Arendt writes, 'And it is for this reason rather than its rarity that it is not only apolitical but anti-political, perhaps the most powerful of all anti-political human forces.'[11]

If forgiveness is public because of the distance it allows so that people may function in the public realm, promise is also public in nature because it creates the possibility of meaning and stability in a world where neither is self-evident. The unpredictability of human affairs and the unreliability of human beings necessitate a 'promise' into which 'certain islands of predictability are thrown and into which certain guideposts of reliability are erected'.

Forgiveness and promise come together because without either, the dynamic of finitude and the search for meaning and coherence collapses. Though both forgiveness and promise are never assured, both are necessary if we are not to become lost in violation or in uncertainty.

To create order means to allow people and institutions to transcend their natural tendency toward inwardness and selfishness. This is an ongoing process of trial and error, for action in the world is unpredictable. Only through a willingness to risk, to promise, can a future be envisioned; but only with a willingness to forgive can the risk, stymied by error, be taken again.

Since trespassing is an everyday occurrence and is directly related to the establishment of new relations within a broader web – Arendt's definition of the constantly evolving public realm – trespassing 'needs forgiving, dismissing, in order to make it possible for life to go on by constantly releasing men from what they have done unknowingly'. For Arendt the role of punishment can be seen together with this dynamic of forgiveness and promise, as the act within the public realm that reminds the person and the community of the frailty of the human enterprise and the ability, once the punishment has been carried out, of the person to re-enter the process which sustains life.[12]

Forgiveness and promise interact in Arendt's system of thought as a way of responding to and insuring the essence of human activity, that is, new beginning. All acts are themselves beginnings, and the way those acts interact with other acts are, in their unpredictability, also beginnings. Our acts soon have a life of their own or, better stated, assume a different life as they intersect with other acts.

Chains of action and speech evolve, and since both determine identities, identities are always evolving. Identities are therefore constantly being formed and unformed. That is why the interaction of these three elements is so crucial. Adi Ophir, a Jewish Israeli historian and philosopher, explains the dynamic of Arendt's understanding:

> The one who forgets cannot forgive, but the one who forgives (or is forgiven) is free to forget; forgiveness unties. Similarly, he who fulfills promises is free to let his memory loose and untie the knot that promise creates. Before forgiveness, or before the fulfillment of a promise, forgetfulness acts like a virus in the network: it prevents the untying of old entanglement and loosens ties necessary for successful coordination and cooperation among actors. After forgiveness has been granted or a promise fulfilled, it is memory that becomes the virus: it infects the network with

> unnecessary ties that block new beginnings; it distorts identities; and it increases the burden that the past and the others who represent it exert on unforgetful actors.

Arendt's view of forgiveness, promise and new beginnings coincides with her view of the structural elements of human action and the public realm in which it occurs. Ophir describes Arendt's vision in this way: 'Plurality, new beginnings, open-endedness, uncertainty, the weaving and unweaving of flexible, loosely structured networks of interrelations embodied in the spaces of mutual visibility, in which identities are never fixed, and no pre-established teleology resides.'[13]

This question of forgiveness haunts the contemporary world as does promise, the twin complex that Arendt believes makes possible new beginnings in a fragile, humanly constructed and meaningful world. Throughout her work, the limitations of life are stressed; teleologies when brought into the public realm signal totalitarianism. Instead, Arendt stresses plurality, interrelation, visibility. New beginnings mean that the old is neither to be swept away nor preserved, and traditions are constantly being remade even as they are being proclaimed as eternal. Her watchword is a freedom born of commitment and restraint; memory, like commitment, evolves.

The anchor of memory, especially the memory of violation and suffering, is waiting to be brought into a new relation with the wider public realm. Only by releasing one's hold on this memory, by forgiving through accepting a new promise, can one's horizons open again. The freezing of memory, the inability to forgive and accept a new promise (as one is forgiven and welcomed back into the arena of promise as well) betrays the very structure of social existence. But even more important it betrays the promise of life, for without forgiveness and promise there is no future.

At the same time it is clear that Arendt believes that certain acts cast one outside of this structure and therefore make one unfit to participate in the public realm. Eichmann, one of the masterminds of the Final Solution, is one such person. Arendt believed that through his actions he disassociated himself from the rest of humanity. As Ophir points out, for Arendt there is a point beyond which forgiveness is impossible, 'for *what* one *does* destroys whatever is left of the respect for *who* one is'.

Here we encounter radical evil, an evil that can only be fought with violence. This struggle with radical evil, especially as routinized and legalized in the modern state, must be systematically opposed *as a crime against humanity and the future.* Thus by inference the memory of radical evil against individuals and communities cannot define the possibility of life experience. Radical evil takes place within the world but is also outside of the world of discourse and action that can support meaning and life.

To define the future by the radical evil experienced in the past is to delimit the possibility of new beginnings; it is to bury the possibility of forgiveness and promise that unleashes that which is static and old. The way out of these memories is not to forgive the perpetrator or to dwell on him. Rather it is the acceptance that life is more than radical evil and those within the public realm can, through struggle and compromise, create a future beyond that evil.[14]

Here Arendt and Carter Heyward join their respective analyses. A new beginning is possible if the promise – to enter into the public realm with a sense of mutuality and justice – is authentic. Though there are no guarantees in the future, the ability to move forward, to transpose the memory of injustice into a call to freedom, is dependent on a commitment to move beyond past violation and crime. When the crime has removed the individual or community from the ability to participate in the public realm, then others must be found who will carry on. Even in the darkest hour there are those who refuse injustice or repent of past injustice. Those who are violated must also recognize the possibility of a new beginning in those former persecutors.

To break the cycle of violation and memory, forgiveness and promise must be engaged by both parties. Risk is inherent, of course, and there are no guarantees that a new configuration will not arise in the future that seeks to dominate the same or other individuals or communities. And as Ophir points out in relation to Jews in Israel, his analysis of Arendt has contemporary significance. Citing Arendt's lifelong fight against totalitarianism and the presence of totalitarian elements in contemporary life, Ophir quotes Arendt and then follows with his own provocative comment: '"Totalitarian solutions may well survive the fall of totalitarian regimes .... " Indeed, they have survived, even in the State of the survivors.'[15]

Thus revolutionary forgiveness, found in right-relation and the commitment to justice, with memory and promise joined in a dynamic that allows new beginnings, is always haunted by reversion to injustice, by abrogated promise, by a memory that refuses to risk. So revolutionary forgiveness is always provisional, prone to movement in unanticipated directions, hopeful, risky, challenging identities and theologies so often thought to be unchanging.

Forgiveness is revolutionary in that it allows new beginnings, but in its constantly evolving status it refuses the totalitarian impulse, or rather is constantly in battle with that impulse even when it arises from the former victims. New beginnings are shadowed by totalitarian fragments and solutions that survive the end of one configuration of totalitarian rule.

What does this analysis have to do with the question of faith and faith communities? Is revolutionary forgiveness possible with faith or without it? Can forgiveness take place, can promise take hold in secular or religious communities? Are new beginnings illustrative of faith or in contradiction to it? Do particular secular or religious communities lend themselves more readily to forgiveness and promise, to open teleologies and new identities? Do others lead away from these possibilities?

Surely those mentioned and analysed from the Christian community – the Catholic sister, the Sudanese priest and Carter Heyward – and from the Jewish community – Richard Rubenstein, Hannah Arendt and Adi Ophir – are diverse in their understandings, beliefs and directions. They also cross boundaries.

Could it be that, in this instance, that it is the religious Christian, Carter Heyward, and the secular Jew, Hannah Arendt, who help us see the possibility of a forgiveness that leads to justice? Is it simply coincidence that perhaps the most haunting statement of religious reconciliation in the post-Holocaust era has been made by Johannes Baptist Metz, a German Catholic theologian heavily influenced by the Frankfurt School of Jewish secular thinkers? Metz writes the following of a new beginning of Christianity: 'We Christians can never go back behind Auschwitz; to go beyond Auschwitz is impossible for us by ourselves. It is possible only together with the victims of Auschwitz.'[16]

Metz names this a 'saving alliance' and refers back to the origins of the Christian community when both Jews and Christians were 'outside' the Roman imperium. But what can be said today when so often Jews and Christians are 'within' the imperium? Is it possible that those Jews and Christians who affirm their religious faith and those who are secular in their orientation are often divided, some outside and others within the new imperiums?

Surely religious identification, Jew, Christian, or for that matter, secular, agnostic or atheist, does not tell us where individuals place themselves with regard to revolutionary forgiveness. As Ophir correctly points out, totalitarian solutions can survive among the survivors and violence as I experienced it in Ireland can be expressed by those who see forgiveness as the center of their faith. Theologians like Rubenstein can deny the possibilities of new beginnings while Arendt, as a secular philosopher, can place it at the center of her philosophy.

Often as not these boundary crossings are seen as fascinating engagements and/or contradictions; they are explored for a while and then forgotten. The lines of Jew and Christian, secular and religious, are then redrawn incorporating these insights *as their sources and significance disappear or are rendered invisible.* For Christians these influences become invisible when, for example, a theology of the cross is explicated. Jews are guilty of the same offense when Jewish particularity is asserted.

Who remembers the tremendous influence of Reinhold Niebuhr on Will Herberg, Abraham Joshua Heschel, and Irving Greenberg, or the influence of Karl Barth on Michael Wyschogrod? The separation of religious and secular is equally as interesting, for the theologies of liberation and renewal are significantly impacted by secular thought and justice movements. One thinks here of the influence of Marxism on the initial writings of Peruvian liberation theologian Gustavo Gutierrez, the Black Power movement on the African-American liberation theologian James Cone, and the civil rights struggle on leaders of Jewish renewal such as Arthur Waskow and Michael Lerner.

Does the interdependence of religious and secular thought and the interpenetration of Jewish and Christian theology ask of us a new articulation of what it means to be created, to be human, to forgive and to promise, in short to engage in revolutionary forgiveness? Does, then, the crossing of boundaries raise the question of God?

A Jewish witness in exile

As the Al-Aqsa uprising continued in 2002, Sara Roy, whom I quoted earlier on her analysis of the Barak proposals and her eyewitness account of the continuing devastation of Palestinian life and culture, wrote a short opinion piece for her local newspaper. Her title: 'The Revenge Must Stop'. Though deemed 'too personal' by the editors, and thus remaining unpublished to this day, Roy's writing testifies to the complexity of the issue of Israel/Palestine for Jews.

A child of Holocaust survivors, Roy tells the story of her mother and her mother's sister who had just been liberated from the concentration camp by the Russian army. The Nazi officials and guards who ran the camp had been captured and the surviving inmates were given free rein to do whatever they wanted to their German persecutors. Many survivors threw themselves upon the Germans, injuring many and killing others.

Roy's mother and aunt witnessed this revenge and fell into each other's arms sobbing. Roy's aunt, who had trouble standing, grabbed 'my mother as if she would never let go', saying to her, 'We cannot do this. Our father and mother would say this is wrong. Even now, even after everything we have endured, we must seek justice, not revenge. There is no other way.'

In her moving portrait of her mother and aunt, Roy reveals in an intimate way the struggle that Jews undergo to find their voice of dissent. Roy crosses the most intimate boundaries of personal violation when she suggests the meaning of her story: 'Peace for Israelis and Palestinians has a price: an end to occupation, an end to Israeli settlements, the establishment of a viable Palestinian state, Jerusalem as the capital of both states, and a mutually acceptable resolution of the Palestinian refugee issue.' Without this, Roy concludes, 'the violence and revenge will continue with more shedding of innocent blood on both sides. As my aunt said long ago, "There is no other way."'

The victims of violence can react in different ways and certainly the desire for vengeance, the vivid scene of Holocaust survivors beating and killing their former tormentors, is understandable. Who could judge such a reaction? And yet the haunting scene of two women struggling to hold themselves upright physically and psychologically is breathtaking. Justice, not revenge, is the way. The lesson of the Holocaust is to end the cycle of violence and atrocity. There is no other way.

One hears in Roy's anguish, as the next generation, as a child of Holocaust survivors, that the cycle of violence and atrocity continues. Could it be that Roy seeks the end of this cycle as a way of somehow bringing a healing to her mother and aunt, whose only solace could be that their suffering was not in vain?

Another Jewish voice is the Israeli journalist Amira Hass. Writing for the progressive Israeli newspaper *Ha'aretz,* she is the only Israeli journalist who lives in and reports from the Palestinian territories. Like Roy, she perceived Barak's offer as far from generous, for it kept 'intact the largest Israeli settlements and their connecting roads'. The overall consequences of decades of Israeli settlements are for Hass clear, allowing Israel to 'create the infrastructure of one state, stretching from the Mediterranean to the Jordan River'.[17]

Hass details the result of these policies: 'Alongside the flourishing green and ever-expanding Israeli-Jewish outposts – well maintained by Israeli policies and laws – is a Palestinian society subject to the rule of military orders and restrictions, its dense communities (including those in East Jerusalem) squeezed into small areas, served by miserably maintained roads and an insufficient water supply system.' Like Roy, Hass is a witness to the occupation and provides a warning that has already come into being. 'Anger has accumulated in every Palestinian heart', Hass writes, 'over the scarce water, over each demolished house, over the daily humiliation of waiting for a travel permit from an Israeli officer. A small match can cause this anger to explode, and in this past year, it has.'

But Hass has something else in common with Roy. Like Roy, she is a child of Holocaust survivors. In fact, Hass was formed by the stories of the Holocaust she heard from her parents as a child. Of all the many accounts, one stood out:

> On a summer day in 1944, my mother was herded from a cattle car along with the rest of its human cargo, which had been transported from Belgrade to the concentration camp at Bergen-Belsen. She saw a group of German women, some on foot, some on bicycles, slow down as this strange procession went by and watch with indifferent curiosity on their faces. For me, these women became a loathsome symbol of watching from the sidelines, and at an early age I decided that my place was not with the bystanders.[18]

In the end Hass' desire to live among Palestinians stemmed 'neither from adventurism nor from insanity, but from the dread of being a bystander, from my need to understand, down to the last detail, a world that is, to the best of my political and historical comprehension, an Israeli creation'. For Hass, the territories represent the central contradiction of the creation and expansion of Israel – 'our exposed nerve' – and she quickly found that 'something special' connected her to refugees and the camps in which they lived. 'I felt at home there', Hass writes, 'in the temporary permanence, in the longing that clings to every grain of sand, in the rage that thrives in the alleyways. Only gradually, and just to a few friends in Gaza and

Israel, did I begin to explain that it was my heritage, a singular autobiographical blend passed on by my parents, that had paved my way to the Gaza Strip.'

Both Roy and Hass, through their political analysis, also know something else: that Israel as a nation-state has over the decades, and with incredible, one might say brilliant, political, military, economic and technological skill, pursued a policy of occupation and settlement that insures that the cycle of violence and atrocity will continue. Despite intermittent lulls, peace talks, cease-fires and hopeful signs, all of these punctuated by suicide bombers and armed incursions, Israel's full withdrawal and the creation of a viable Palestinian state with Jerusalem as a joint capital of Israel/Palestine that Roy and Hass so desperately hope for is a dream that will likely not be realized in their lifetime.

A cosmetic public-relations Palestinian state is possible, even probable, one that many in the West will accept as just and celebrate as a feat of diplomacy. Of course, the opposite is also possible: under certain circumstances a further diminution of Palestinian sovereignty and even the transfer of hundreds of thousands of Palestinians to territories outside Israel/Palestine may take place. There is historical precedent for this transfer, and if the maps of Israel from 1948 to the present are any indication, this is as likely a future as the one Roy and Hass fervently hope for. *The burden of proof is on those Jews and Palestinians who argue for a full Israeli withdrawal to the 1967 borders of Israel as the way to solve the present impasse, for the establishment of a viable Palestinian state in the next fifty years would be a major reversal of the history of the last fifty years.*

Is this the fate of Jewish dissent? To want so desperately and deeply to assert justice as the center of Jewish life and as a personal and communal response to the violence of the Holocaust, to end that cycle and yet be denied because Israel as a nation-state is no different than other nations, wanting power, expanding its borders and influence, and denigrating those who stand in its way?

Much of Jewish dissent has involved this anguish. Like Roy's mother and aunt, like Hass' parents, many Jews have wanted another way. The anguish has been complicated because of the historical situation of the Jews and the myths of Jews that others hold and which abound to this day. It is almost as if Jews are surrounded, as I have been, by those who think Jews are unforgiving, control the global economy or the U.S. government, the media, and even the Federal Reserve system.

To me, as a Jew who travels around the world, and not only in the sophisticated and affluent circles that exist in the capitals of Asia, Africa and Latin America, the role of Jews in the imagination of the world's population is extreme and perplexing. In such an environment, it is difficult for Jews to speak of the permanent oppression of Palestinians by those who have power in Israel, aided and abetted by Jews who have power in the United States. In short, Jews who understand the maps of Jewish life, including the Holocaust and what Israel has done to Palestinians, find it difficult to deny the fact of Jewish power in the world. We as Jews must admit that we, like others, use our power to pursue injustice in exactly the same way that other peoples and nation-states do.

However, the major factor remains and this is much beyond the anguish and myths surrounding Jews and Jewish life. The emergence of Israel as a nation-state has changed Jewish reality and has impacted the Judaic as it will be lived in the world. From now on the Judaic will be lived as a hope and as a witness within a Constantinian Judaism and a community linked with empire in the U.S. and Israel. Jews of conscience like Roy and Hass, like Irena Klepfisz, Noam Chomsky and Israel Shahak, join Judah Magnes, Martin Buber and Hannah Arendt in a tradition of dissent that remains alive, even grows, but as a remnant increasingly cut off from mainstream Judaism and Jewish life.

This remnant, though seemingly modern and without ties to the religious tradition of Judaism, is paradoxically embodying the most ancient of Jewish traditions, the refusal of idolatry. By protesting against injustice at a personal sacrifice, by witnessing in history to the possibility of reconciliation and forgiveness, by seeking community over against empire, this remnant embodies the ancient prophetic and covenantal tradition without which Judaism and Jewishness is impossible. Without any religious articulation, and even against such, this tradition of dissent opens the possibility for a renewal of religious life *after* the maps of Jewish life – the Holocaust and Israel – are understood and critically evaluated.

It is here that the question of God becomes important again. In this tradition of dissent Magnes and Buber, both religious but in a creative and hardly normative way, are within a community that is essentially non- or even anti-religious. Thus the religious sensibility has a diminished place within a wider framework of practice that can remind Jews of conscience of the broader contours of Jewish history without dominating the discussion or attempting to simply place other Jews in a context that they do not overtly affirm. The point here is less an assertion of God, or Judaism, or Jewishness, or the Judaic. Rather it is the expression of different views and perspectives within an evolving practice that has at its center, conscience and justice.

Here Shahak's debate without end comes into focus as a practice that raises further questions into history and politics and the deeper levels of reflection and humility. Shahak is right when he speaks of those who disguise injustice with religious language as 'patriotic liars', and Buber is insightful when he refers to the hidden history of the prophets as a series of failures that open history to different paths and ground resistance in patterns of life that can nourish and sustain those who resist.

For what Jew who speaks today at the end of Jewish history *as we have known and inherited it* does not need strength and resources from the Jewish tradition and the broader tradition of faith and struggle outside of Judaism? And what Jew who practices conscience and justice has not benefited from the Jewish tradition in making this witness recognizable as distinctly Jewish?

Indeed the very practice of conscience and justice, the ancient refusal of idolatry updated and embodied in the twenty-first century by this community, makes timely another ancient theme of Jewish history, that of exile. Surely those Jews who practice conscience and justice are in exile from the Jewish community and the world. This existence in exile calls for a deepening practice, what might be called practicing exile?[19]

The practice of exile, like the practice that refuses idolatry, is ancient and contemporary and in fact today they are fused together. The refusal of idolatry leads to exile and the exile, for whom there is little possibility of return, over time demands a new way of life. For the refusal of idolatry has many consequences and the living out of that refusal demands that an essential and consequential 'no' become an affirmation. It is this negation and affirmation, lived out in the world, that becomes the practice of exile. Practicing exile is a 'yes' to a future beyond the cycle of violence and atrocity, beyond empire pursued in the name of Jewish history and the Jewish people, beyond the use of suffering to cause another people's suffering, beyond the ultimate trivialization of Jewish *and* Palestinian suffering.

This witness is bound to fail in our time, so it is fidelity to the past and future of conscience and justice embodied in the world that the practice of exile speaks to. The image that speaks of this witness is the slow movement of Jews of conscience carrying the covenant into exile with them. How will these Jews continue on with failure and derision heaped upon them? How will they relate to one another and others they meet on this journey? How will they pass this witness on to their children? How will they speak of their Judaism, their Jewishness, or even the Judaic? One wonders what will happen to Jewish particularity in this exile. On the one hand, it could be that the practice of exile will spell the end of Jewish particularity in any meaningful sense. On the other hand, it might give rise to a renewed Jewish particularity that speaks to Jews and the world.

The answers to these questions lie in the future. For Jews of conscience there is only the practice of exile as a witness in history to the possibility of justice and healing.

A debate without end? Yes, and surely more. The survival of the Judaic? Perhaps.

Epilogue: Out of the Ashes

I have always been averse to the idea of remnant, a small number of Jews of conscience who somehow transcend the ethics and morals of the rest of Jewry. So, too, with the title 'prophet' or 'rabbi', as if somehow I, or someone else, towered over those with less ethical sensibilities or leadership qualities. Rather, I have tried to see my voice as one among others, with a particular point of view to be sure, but one enfolded in the long sweep of Jewish history.

Likewise, there are no communities without tendencies toward uncritical self-assertion, nor are there communities without propensities toward empire. The aspirations toward establishment status are rife with self-delusion. The Jewish establishment in Israel and America is assimilating to power and the state, and in the name of innocence the Jewish left has too often positioned itself to become the next Jewish establishment and in so doing has acted in ways too similar to the establishment they endeavor to succeed.

I cannot argue with complete assurance that Jewish empowerment is unnecessary, especially given the history of the Jews under the aegis of Christian power. There is no people or community on earth that has not empowered itself without violence and conquest. Jews who criticize Israel's method of empowerment should not pretend that they are innocent, in their homes, workplaces or political movements, whether in Israel or America. Judaism and Jewish life were never pure, nor are those who resist Israeli policies themselves pure. It may be that life is a battle until the end, to secure one's own being and community against all comers.

Surely the struggle for dignity, conscience and justice is conducted within limitations, failure and self-centeredness. No person or community is released from either side of the struggle, for the struggle is the essence of life as we know it. In the end, though, we are defined by our participation in that struggle and the sides we choose. As Hannah Arendt understood, new beginnings represent the adventure of the human spirit. What we choose and what we refuse defines our participation in that adventure.

Martin Buber extended Arendt's understanding when he wrote that we are responsible for our beginnings, not the end. For the end of things will not come in our lifetimes, and within our own lives every end is also a beginning. Seen in this light, failure is not failure, at least as the world knows it; if conscience and justice are at the forefront, then what appears to be a failure is in fact a witness. And witness, though at times highlighted and even acknowledged by others, is for the long haul, hidden, flawed, sometimes derided and even misunderstood by those closest to you.

The *tikkun* of ordinary decency is small and insignificant. Elaborate theories are spun and, often as not, violated by the very people who clarify a principle that others may find to be the key to the future. The center of faith and fidelity is less certainty or purity than it is the openness within oneself and to history for the new, unexpected, and perhaps even miraculous beginning. The center of faith and fidelity is simply this: *that history is open; community is possible; empire does not have the final word.*

This is contrary to the more usual understanding of history and of what is commonly considered prudent in the world. It is a patient non-violence that is often violated in thought and action. It is an understanding that is rarely, if ever, timely or efficacious in the world. If fidelity is to take a stand in the world *contra* acceptable wisdom and community opinion, then the history one identifies with is also unrecognizable to the world. Hence exile in a personal and collective sense.

Is it possible to be in exile without God? I remember entering that question in a deep way when confronted with Edward Said's journey, a Palestinian wandering who was, in his own articulation, explicitly godless. In a life lived between commentary as diverse as the dialogue in Ireland where the Catholic sister thought Jews were incapable of forgiveness, and therefore incapable of new beginnings, and the Jewish bully in Christchurch who articulated Jewishness in a language of violence and hate, it is difficult to keep one's bearings. Where are the resources for reflection, for self-correction, for activity in the world that resists injustice and seeks a future beyond it?

In Ireland and New Zealand, two of the most unlikely places for clarification about Jewishness and Jewish history, I once again came face to face with choice and thus with my freedom. I could hate and use the Holocaust as a fist, clenched against the world, and Israel as a weapon that forged Jewish identity beyond the reach of question and accountability. But what would that mean to me as a Jew and as a person? How could I pass on this sensibility to my children as defining of Jewish life?

In the end, after the theology and the maps, the accusations and the questions, I simply could not – and cannot – bequeath to my children an inheritance that places violence and atrocity at the heart of Jewish history; that the essence of the Jewish witness is carried by helicopter gunships; that the Jewish covenant, now and forever, will be infected with dislocation and death.

I often ask myself what I am learning about life during the days of uprising, calls for Jewish unity, organizing to end the occupation, invasions and suicide bombers. Is the lesson that no one, myself included, is innocent? Is the lesson that in the end we are betrayed by all, institutions, nation-states, faith communities?

The tendency toward cynicism is always before us. No victory is permanent or without unintended consequences nor any defeat solely at the hands of the powerful. The end is always near. And in that end is always a beginning.

But that beginning is never a return and the slogans of return are tinged with a justified resentment that often as not leads to violence. We seem constantly to be re-emerging, seeking points of entry, on the periphery, outside looking in, or inside looking out. Where there is no future, there is a future. We may be in between, in a dark place, knowing that there is light somewhere and having difficulty finding it.

Learning is that light, a learning that is personal and communal. Often one is ahead of the other, so that another person or the community is ahead or behind, if indeed learning can be defined as a progression. If learning is a process, then the Jewish people have a learning curve, especially after the Holocaust, that is unparalleled in history. The movement from the death camps with millions helpless before the Nazi onslaught to the Israeli military that can punish anyone who advances against them is only one, albeit significant, Jewish advance.

The United States Holocaust Memorial Museum in Washington, D.C., inaugurated by Elie Wiesel and President Bill Clinton, is another advance, that a survivor of Auschwitz should stand as a free man with the leader of the most powerful country in the world – unimaginable decades earlier. Senator Joseph Lieberman as a Vice-Presidential candidate is another expression of that empowerment, as is his wife, her parents Holocaust survivors.

The story is manifold and the learning continues. For we now know that empowerment, in itself a blessing, can bring us in another way close to the ashes from which we recently emerged. A victim of the cycle of violence and atrocity can throw others into that cycle which is, after all, only one step away from becoming a victim again. Or rather, becoming a victim in another way.

One lesson is that being reduced to ashes does not ennoble a people. Another is that placing others into the ashes does not heal us of the previous trauma. Instead it increases the trauma by emptying us of the very resources that allowed us to survive with our dignity intact in the first place. It may be that survival without dignity is survival without meaning. Later generations find this survival without meaning and begin their own journey toward a critical appraisal of history and a judgement on those who went before.

The sad aspect of life is that retrieval of purpose and meaning often comes too late. The deed accomplished makes the possibility of remedy remote. Native Americans are an obvious example, but so too is the German desire to reconcile with the Jewish people after the Holocaust. That desire is worked out through a distant Jewish population in Israel, fraught with its own cycle of violence and atrocity, and in an artificial way.

The only reconciliation possible is with the Jews of Germany; because of the Nazi 'success', that, of course, is impossible. What is so difficult to accept is the squandering of Jewish and Palestinian reconciliation when it remains a possibility, since the native and warring populations live in the same land in almost equal numbers in an encounter that remains within the living memory of many. History cries out for the reconciliation that today is further beyond reach than it was years ago.

What have Jews learned through the empowerment of Israel? What have Palestinians learned? Can Jews and Palestinians learn together? What is the meaning of that learning when power is unequal and therefore suffering is as well? What is the importance of learning when there is so much suffering, suffering that will continue into the foreseeable future?

Surely Jews and Palestinians are learning the limitations of nationalism, that pretenses to innocence are illusions and that dreams of empowerment often become nightmares in reality. Both Jews and Palestinians see themselves as special, different, with a destiny beyond the ordinary fate of peoples. The last decades have reinforced this sensibility on both sides, but the people themselves cry out for the ordinary trials and tribulations of life. The extraordinary, when hailed in banners and slogans, is one step from the grave, from the ashes. In the ashes, the ordinary is hope, indeed extraordinary. Out of the ashes is the extraordinary re-establishment of the ordinary so foundational to life.

That is why Jerusalem must be shared as the broken middle of Israel/Palestine. Not to vindicate either side in their quest for nationhood and flag or to punish Jews and Palestinians for their hubris, the sharing of Jerusalem instead is the sign that an ordinariness is being forged where difference is honored *and* bridged and where political and religious aspirations are disciplined by an in-between reality of give and take. In the broken middle of Jerusalem the dead are buried and mourned and the ideologies of Israel and Palestine, the destinies of both peoples, take a different turn.

There is no finality here on earth and the sharing of Jerusalem reinforces that limitation. This is another learning and perhaps the most difficult lesson: that the centers of power and identity must always be tempered by the 'other' who, as it turns out, is not other but shares a universal humanity and a particular identity that is always evolving. Is the great fear of Jews and Palestinians in sharing Jerusalem the fear of that evolution, that somehow both Jewish and Palestinian identity will be embraced *and* transcended?

As Jews we come after the Holocaust and after the creation of Israel. The memories of Deir Yassin and now Jenin, the haunting sound of helicopter gunships and Hebrew being spoken to order the demolition of homes and to halt Palestinians burying their dead cannot be ignored or transcended as if nothing has happened to us as a people. There are Jews of conscience who accept this culpability, but they are beginning to understand that this acceptance is not a return to innocence or even a prelude to a new Israel.

The sharing of Jerusalem is farther from sight and is becoming, like the calls to end the occupation and establish a Palestinian state, a slogan that is in essence a lie. I now understand that there will not be an end to the occupation or the establishment of a Palestinian state in my lifetime unless the definitions of those terms are stretched beyond their common meaning as known today. There is a permanence to the occupation that will define a certain Palestinian 'autonomy'. That occupation/autonomy arrived in its broadest contours with Oslo and was hammered home during the last years of uprising and invasion. Is there any doubt of this permanence today after the invasions of Ramallah, Bethlehem and Jenin?

There are some who say that the permanence of occupation and the autonomy found within it are impractical, unsustainable, even suicidal for Israel. Others point out that what seems to be permanent is not – witness the collapse of the Iron Curtain in Europe and apartheid in South Africa. This may be the case in the long run, over the next hundred years or so. I leave that to a future generation to discuss.

I am certain, however, that this discussion will be taken up by generations to come because the hoped-for limitations will not be realized in the short term, as they have not been realized in earlier understandings. Over time, of course, we have witnessed a steady extension of power and control by Israel and a constant diminution of Palestinian land and opportunity. Only the slogan-bearing can see this history and its trajectory as coming closer to a just solution of the Israeli–Palestinian conflict.

Another lesson being learned: rhetoric, narrative and power in history can prepare us for a defeat that seems like victory. The two-state solution with Israel occupying 78 per cent of Palestine and 22 per cent of Palestine becoming the Palestinian state, an almost utopian ideal at this point in history, is itself unjust and a defeat. Barak's 'generous' offer was a further defeat within the overall cataclysm. For the foreseeable future even less will be offered, but that will none the less be seen as the way out of this impasse, an offer that should be grasped rather than spurned.

We should at the same time be alert to the fact that what seems to be bottom is not necessarily so. Where social, political and economic conditions seem not able to get worse, they can and have. It may be that millions of Palestinians cannot live in the conditions that they are living in today and that fact will drive the force of history in their favor. But again the history of this conflict leaves other possibilities open. I do not predict a final expulsion of Palestinians from Jerusalem and the West Bank, but the arguments have been made on the Israeli side and, subject to certain conditions, may be made by Jews living outside of Israel.

For those Jews who have not spoken out yet, is there any event which would bring their voices to the fore? We know as Jenin was being invaded and systematically destroyed the call from the Jewish establishment was for unity. As tanks surrounded Yassir Arafat's compound in Ramallah and the ordinary citizens of that city were under almost complete closure and curfew, the call from the Jewish establishment was for increased support for Israel. The assaults on Bethlehem and Hebron drew similar responses. Would a large-scale expulsion of Palestinians draw the same reaction, satisfaction that the 'terrorist nests' were finally being emptied?

Surely the Constantinian phase of Judaism is now firmly in place. Like the limits of ending the occupation and establishment of Palestinian autonomy, this is part of our future. The bully in Christchurch was extreme in his rhetoric and his honesty; most Jews will cover the brutal reality of Palestinian subjugation with an ethic drawn from the biblical promise and the Holocaust – and now from the need to end terrorism. Judaism and Jewish life cannot be explained without justice and reconciliation at the center, and since the Jewish community is living contrary to that vision, a rhetoric is devised to assert the practice of justice where it is not now found.

In this sense we have learned a lesson from Christianity: speak justice and compassion and do otherwise. Or define injustice and brutality as justice and compassion. The ecumenism of the powerful cites the need for difference and orthodoxy as their practice becomes a form of syncretism. At this point in history there is little difference between mainline Judaism and mainline Christianity. Symbolism aside, they have for all practical purposes become the same religion.

Jews of conscience are on their own, and as amazing as the silence of the Jewish establishment is, their speech in the last years is audacious and plentiful. A further learning: There will always be Jews who speak truth to power. There will always be Jews who say no to injustice. There will always be Jews who refuse silence and accept exile rather than complicity in injustice.

Here Jews are on their own and yet not completely alone. For there are many around the world, from every culture and geography, indeed from every religion, who are also in exile and who in their own way refuse to be silent. As the Jewish community assimilates to power and the state, the prophetic voice is spoken by those who bequeathed it to the world, but also by others who have received this contribution and now participate in its extension. It is in this sense that the Jewish population of the world increases even as most Jews assimilate to other religions.

And here lies the hope for the future. Jews of conscience in concert with others can continue to chart an alternative way of life even in exile. For Jews and Palestinians in Israel/Palestine can begin to act as if the divisions between Israel and Palestine do not exist and as if solidarity with one another is the norm.

Since millions of Jews and Palestinians live in the same land, the challenge is to move toward a life that emphasizes inclusion in the personal, cultural, economic and political spheres. Politics and boundaries will divide and in the years ahead this will be decisive, but the desire for inclusion will also become a political factor. Over time a new narrative of Israel's origins and history will evolve and the foundation of separation will lose its ethical and normative force. Militaries can enforce boundaries, but those boundaries can be crossed by narratives and thus become permeable, perhaps one day only an insignificant formality.

Israel's military victory is now assured. The prophetic voice will remain in the land but also in the diaspora. Decisive work is already being done in the Jewish and Palestinian diasporas, especially in Europe and the United States. Here a solidarity is firmly in place and has been for some time. Jews on the left who have abandoned that course during the recent uprising have only made the bonds between Jews of conscience and Palestinians stronger. There is a sense of a mutual destiny forged in disappointment and sorrow but also holding forth a great hope – a learning, if you will, at the end of Jewish history and the end of Palestine, *at least as we have known and inherited them*.

It is here at the end that we begin again. Out of the ashes arises a learning that is applied to human relations within and across cultures and boundaries. Politically, at least initially, there is a weakness that is a peculiar kind of suffering. Suffering with a hope not of restoration or even justice – for both have been banished – but a willed persistence that community can be created within empire and that somehow over the long haul community will achieve its rightful place. A reversal is not in order, for community will not triumph over empire; it will only survive, or perhaps even flourish, within empire.

Is this not the way of the world? So why should Jews and Palestinians be exempt from this dilemma? For now the empire is Israel and perhaps if Palestine had been victorious it would have chosen empire as well. Jews and Palestinians have little reason to pretend to innocence. After romanticizing Jewish and Palestinian nationalism, both are left disillusioned and abandoned by their own leadership and flags. In the ashes the forces of community must look beyond nationalism, even as parts of each community pursue it with a vengeance.

There *are* reasons to pursue the nation and the state. Yet in the end the elite and well-connected benefit and the majority is left to its own survival. Who should know this better than the Israeli soldiers who have been sacrificed in the war of the settlements? Or even those Jews killed by suicide bombers?

The leaders of Israel know full well the number of Jews that will die in the war to secure an expanded state of Israel. From their perspective the number of Jewish dead is acceptable in light of their understanding of Jewish history and destiny. Is the sacrifice of the young and the innocent worth the dreams of an Israel that stretches from Tel Aviv to the Jordan River? And will there be an end to that sacrifice without the enslavement of the Palestinian people or their expulsion? And what then would be our inheritance? That the soldiers of Israel died in order to make servile or eliminate a native population?

Thus those Jews who seek community must prepare a future worth bequeathing to our children even as the destruction continues. Those who seek to oppose with mobilization and slogan, as if political victory is possible today, should do so. Even those who see a darker vision of the contemporary landscape may participate in this movement. But this participation must be half-hearted and sporadic. The borders are, more or less, sealed for the foreseeable future. A vision beyond such closure must be nurtured.

It is strange that the recent empowerment, affluence and status of the Jewish world has brought a time of darkness. How can the energy and strength of contemporary Jewish life be at the same time a dark age? The synagogues of today are like the cathedrals of Europe, monuments to a power that has lost its way. Will the future of the synagogue lie, like the cathedrals, in tourism, where people travel to see a glory that was undermined by the actions of the faithful?

Here, as in Christianity, we are left with the haunting question: What does it mean to be Jewish? Like any religion, that definition is always contextual and evolving, interpreting and reinterpreting the foundational themes of canonical literature. And history as well. For the journey of a people is a learning, a deep reckoning with revelation and reality. This is the essence of *halakhah*, Jewish law or teaching, navigating the ideal in the world.

The purpose of *halakhah* is less perfection in belief or motivation but the commandment to continue on in actions that help approach a wholeness in a fractured world, the pursuit of the ordinary in the face of displacement and destruction so that the latter will not be the norm nor utopian politics the standard. Instead it is the argument for rationality and humanity in situations that propose injustice and suffering as the norm.

Today Jews of conscience carry *halakhah* in the world; they embody the covenant as they travel into exile. That they travel away from the cathedrals of modern Jewish life – from the synagogues and the Holocaust memorials – is an effort to prevent these institutional representatives of Judaism and Jewish life from claiming the heart of this ancient tradition. In this way, Jews of conscience are like the ancient rabbis of Yavneh, retreating in the face of Roman power to rethink the tradition and its future. Ironically, the rabbis withdrew from Jerusalem as the Romans were conquering her; today Jews of conscience withdraw from the forces that have placed Jerusalem firmly in the hands of Jewish power.

Is this exile a journey into weakness? Is it a refusal to face the responsibilities of power? Does it hand over power to the Jewish establishment in Israel and America without a fight? Is it a refusal to dirty one's hands? By withdrawing, will this understanding of Judaism and Jewish life be unavailable to future generations? Will the children of the exiles remain Jewish and how will they define that Jewishness? Is this the last exile in Jewish history?

As with most questions in life, the answers to these questions are complicated and beyond the scope of one person or even one generation. That which is normative to one generation for the next is grounds for rebellion, and yet such rebellion is often seen as dubious by subsequent ones. The inability to hold fast for all time does not lessen the need for each generation to find its way, to test itself, whether as part of the community or even as an individual.

The prophetic can be communal or individual at different times and sometimes communities break apart and refashion themselves over the questions of commitment and fidelity. Often continuity of tradition is stressed over the discontinuities: viewed from the present, history is polished and the retrospective vision is freed from the bumps and angles of a history that struggled for its voice.

There will always be Jews who speak and live the prophetic in the ashes and beyond. The commanding voices of Sinai and Auschwitz demand no less and can be heard only here: in the visible struggle to end the cycle of violence and atrocity that has engulfed the Jewish people and now ties them irrevocably to the Palestinian people. The desire is less to rescue or even resurrect a Judaism that is disappearing from the earth than it is to rescue from oblivion the lives of the victims of violence, past and present.

That rescue is our task. It is also our failure. There is no choice but to persevere against the odds and against the worldly wisdom that cautions against division and weakness. Worldly wisdom tells us that the alternative to expansion and might are the ashes but, in another way, we are already there, crying out.

Notes

Introduction

1. At the same time, Gush Shalom published a manifesto entitled '80 Theses for a New Peace Camp', their attempt to rethink Israeli understandings of the Palestinians and Israeli history as well. See *Tikkun* 16 (July/August 2001), pp. 17–23. Earlier a petition signed by nearly 350 Israeli academics and concerned citizens called for this international intervention. See ibid., p. 16.
2. The arrival of Hebrew-speaking Gentiles is raised by Akiva Orr, *Israel: Politics, Myths and Identity Crisis* (London: Pluto Press, 1994).
3. Emil Fackenheim is part of a generation of Holocaust theologians about which I write more in the coming pages. Fackenheim's announcement of the 614th Commandment is found in the Charles F. Deems Lectures he delivered at New York University in 1968. They were published under the title *God's Presence in History: Jewish Affirmations and Philosophical Reflections* (New York: New York University Press, 1970).
4. Like Fackenheim but with a deep and abiding popular appeal to Jews and Christians in the West, Wiesel has been *the* major player in the link between Holocaust memory and liberal support for the state of Israel. For an extended critical study of Wiesel see Mark Chmiel, *Elie Wiesel and the Politics of Moral Leadership* (Philadelphia: Temple University Press, 2001).

Chapter 1

1. I have outlined this position in more detail in *O' Jerusalem: The Contested Future of the Jewish Covenant* (Minneapolis: Fortress, 1999). I have recently written about the consequences of the refusal of Jewish academic and institutional leaders to confront these questions. The result is an exile of Jews who cannot live with this question unanswered. My own sense is that these Jews in exile are now in a global and ecumenical diaspora that will be named in this century. The title of this book is *Practicing Exile: The Religious Odyssey of an American Jew* (Minneapolis: Fortress, 2002).
2. The promise of the covenant has been interpreted in many ways, usually encompassing the election of the Jewish people and the Jewish journey through history. The promise of the covenant includes obligations and possibilities referring to justice and the land.
3. Yosef Hayim Yerushalmi, *Zakhor: Jewish History and Jewish Memory* (Seattle: University of Washington Press, 1982).
4. Ibid., pp. 9–10.
5. Ibid., pp. 5, 11.

6. Ibid., pp. 99–101. Yerushalmi writes that some reorientation is required: 'The task can no longer be limited to finding continuities in Jewish life, not even "dialectical" ones. Perhaps the time has come to look more closely at ruptures, breaches, breaks, to identify them more precisely, to see how Jews endured them, to understand that not everything of value that existed before a break was either salvaged or metamorphosed, but was lost, and often some of what fell by the wayside can become, through retrieval, meaningful to us' (p. 101).
7. Ibid., p. 95.
8. Irving Greenberg, *The Jewish Way: Living the Holidays* (New York: Summit, 1988), p. 320.
9. Ibid., p. 321.
10. Ibid.
11. Irving Greenberg, 'The Ethics of Jewish Power', *Perspectives* (New York: National Jewish Center for Learning and Leadership, 1988).
12. David Roskies, *Against the Apocalypse: Responses to Catastrophe in Modern Jewish Culture* (Cambridge, MA: Harvard University Press, 1984), pp. 198, 197.
13. Ibid., p. 35.
14. Ibid., pp. 275, 305.
15. Ibid., p. 262. Roskies suggests that the Hebrew word *Shoah*, meaning calamity, ruin, desolation, and the Yiddish *der driter khurbm*, meaning Third Destruction, have problems of their own when referring to the Holocaust. See his discussion on pp. 261–2.
16. Ibid., pp. 263, 268, 301.
17. Ibid., p. 302.
18. Irena Klepfisz, *Dreams of an Insomniac: Jewish Feminist Essays, Speeches and Diatribes* (Portland, OR: Eighth Mountain, 1990), pp. 124–6. I am indebted to Hilda Silverman for introducing me to the work of Irena Klepfisz.
19. Ibid., pp. 130–1.
20. Ibid., pp. 134–5.
21. For the classic statement of his early position see Emil Fackenheim, *God's Presence in History: Jewish Affirmations and Philosophical Reflections* (New York: New York University Press, 1970).
22. Emil Fackenheim, *To Mend the World: Foundations of Post-Holocaust Jewish Thought* (New York: Shocken, 1982), p. 307.
23. Ibid., p. 312.
24. Baruch Goldstein was a religious Jew who in 1994 entered a mosque in Hebron and murdered scores of Palestinian Muslims at prayer.
25. Cynthia Ozick, 'The Consensus That Plagues Israel', *New York Times*, December 2, 1995; Michael Walzer, 'Reasons to Mourn', *New Yorker*, November 20, 1995.
26. Cynthia Ozick, 'Notes Toward Finding the Right Question', in *On Being a Jewish Feminist*, ed. Susannah Heschel (New York: Shocken, 1983), pp. 120–51.
27. Ibid., pp. 135, 144, 149–50.
28. Ibid., p. 151.
29. Quoted in the *New York Times*, September 14, 1993.

30. James E. Young, *Writing and Rewriting the Holocaust: Narrative and the Consequences of Interpretation* (Bloomington: Indiana University Press, 1988). Also see his subsequent books that include *The Texture of Memory: Holocaust Memorials and Meaning* (New Haven: Yale University Press, 1994) and *Holocaust Memorials in History: The Art of Memory*, ed. James E. Young (New York: Jewish Museum with Prestel-Verlag, 1994).
31. Young, *Writing and Rewriting the Holocaust*, pp. 138–9.
32. Yossi Safid, 'The Night of the Broken Clubs', *Ha'aretz*, May 4, 1989.
33. Gideon Spiro, 'You Will Get Used to Being a Mengele', *Al Hamishar*, September 19, 1988.
34. B'Tselem, 'On Human Rights in the Occupied Territories: Al Aqsa Intifada', *B'Tselem Journal* 7 (June 2001), p. 12.
35. Gush Shalom, '80 Theses for a New Peace Camp', *Tikkun* 16 (July/August 2001), pp. 17–23.
36. The text of the reservists' letter can be found at <www.seruv.org>.
37. See an extended discussion of this refusal in James Bennet, 'Citizen-Soldiers Attack a Policy,' *New York Times*, February 10, 2002.
38. The briefing and the letter from Eyal Rozenberg are printed under the titles 'Fighting the Media War' and 'Just Deserter' in *Harper's*, May 2001, pp. 24–6.
39. David Vital, *The Future of the Jews* (Cambridge, MA: Harvard University Press, 1990).
40. Meron Benvenisti, 'A Footnote for the Future', *Ha'aretz*, December 13, 2001. See also his 'Coexistence Is the Only Choice', *New York Times*, October 27, 2000.
41. Meron Benvenisti, *Sacred Landscape: The Buried History of the Holy Land Since 1948* (Berkeley: University of California Press, 2000), p. 145.
42. Ibid., p. 147.
43. Baruch Kimmerling, 'I Accuse', *Kol Ha'Ir*, February 1, 2002.

Chapter 2

1. For a more detailed analysis of Holocaust theology see Marc H. Ellis, *Beyond Innocence and Redemption: Confronting the Holocaust and Israeli Power* (San Francisco: HarperCollins, 1990), pp. 1–31. Also see Michael L. Morgan, *Beyond Auschwitz: Post-Holocaust Jewish Thought in America* (Oxford: Oxford University Press, 2001).
2. See Irving Greenberg's 'The Ethics of Jewish Power', *Perspectives* (New York: National Jewish Center for Learning and Leadership, 1988).
3. Janet O'Dea Aviad, *Return to Judaism: Religious Renewal in Israel* (Chicago: University of Chicago Press, 1983).
4. Ian Lustick, *For the Land and the Lord: Jewish Fundamentalism in Israel* (New York: Council on Foreign Relations, 1988), p. 98.
5. Michael Lerner, 'Settler Violence and the Rape of Judaism', *Tikkun* 9 (May/June 1994), pp. 27–8.
6. Avishai Margalit, 'Settling Scores', *New York Review of Books* 48 (September 20, 2001), pp. 20–5.

7. Roy's analysis can be found in Sara Roy, 'The Palestinian-Israeli Crisis: An Analysis', presented at the United States in the Middle East: Politics, Religion & Violence Conference, University of Delaware, February 2001, or in Sara Roy, 'Why Peace Failed: An Oslo Autopsy', *Current History* (January 2002), pp. 8–16.
8. James Bennet, 'Hopes Are Modest as Israelis and Palestinians Await the Bush Plan', *New York Times*, October 12, 2001.
9. Ibid.
10. 'Be Heard', *New York Times*, August 29, 2001.
11. Elie Wiesel, transcript of speech, New York Israel Solidarity Rally (New York, October 12, 2000); Internet available from <http://www.aish.com>; accessed March 30, 2002.
12. Amir Chesin, Bill Hutman and Avi Melamed, *Separate and Unequal: The Inside Story of Israeli Rule in East Jerusalem* (Cambridge, MA: Harvard University Press, 1999), p. 10.
13. Ibid., pp. 10–11, 251.
14. Amos Elon's analysis is found in a review essay of Bernard Wasserstein, *Divided Jerusalem: The Struggle for the Holy City*, in *New York Review of Books* 47 (October 18, 2001), pp. 6–11.
15. Elie Wiesel, 'A Common Enemy', *Jewish Week*, September 14, 2001.
16. For the origins of Constantinian Christianity see H.A. Drake, *Constantine and the Bishops: The Politics of Intolerance* (Baltimore: Johns Hopkins University Press, 2000).
17. These thoughts are developed in more detail in Marc H. Ellis, *O' Jerusalem: The Contested Future of the Jewish Covenant* (Minneapolis: Fortress, 1999).
18. An earlier draft of parts of this section was delivered at the 34th World Congress of the International Institute of Sociology, Tel Aviv, Israel/Palestine, July 11–15, 1999.
19. For an understanding of this reality see Anthony Lewis, 'The Irrelevance of a Palestinian State', *New York Times*, June 20, 1999.
20. For an extended discussion of the movement of local religions to world religions and the consequences of that movement with reference to 1492 see Marc H. Ellis, *Ending Auschwitz: The Future of Jewish and Christian Life* (Louisville: Westminster/John Knox, 1994).
21. A provocative understanding of the formation and consequences of monotheism is found in Regina Schwartz, *The Curse of Cain: The Violent Legacy of Monotheism* (Chicago: University of Chicago Press, 1997).
22. The Palestinian writer, Edward Said, has been making this point for years beginning with his first book on the subject, *The Question of Palestine* (New York: Vintage, 1980).
23. The history of the 'unification' of Jerusalem after the Israeli victory in the 1967 Arab–Israeli War as a policy of expulsion and division is analysed in Chesin et al., *Separate and Unequal.*
24. The argument of the preceding and following paragraphs is pursued in more detail in Ellis, *O'Jerusalem.*
25. See Amiel Alcalay, *After Jews and Arabs: Remaking Levantine Culture* (Minneapolis: University of Minnesota Press, 1993).

26. The philosophical understanding of the broken middle is found in Gillian Rose, *The Broken Middle* (Oxford: Oxford University Press, 1992).
27. For a fascinating study of continuity and discontinuity in Jewish history see Efraim Schmueli, *Seven Jewish Cultures: A Reinterpretation of Jewish History and Thought* (Cambridge: Cambridge University Press, 1990).
28. A more recent statement of opposition to the Oslo accords can be found in Edward Said, *Peace and Its Discontents* (New York: Vintage, 1996).
29. Lewis, 'The Irrelevance of a Palestinian State'.
30. Deborah Sontag, 'Ehud Barak: Serving by Waiting Out Opponents', *New York Times*, June 19, 1999.
31. John Broder, 'Clinton Favors Broad Rights in Palestinians' Resettlement', *New York Times*, July 2, 1999. It is unclear whether Clinton understood the implications of his own statement. Barak issued his first sustained communication in reaction to this statement. See Deborah Sontag, 'Next Israeli Leader Steps Out of His Silence', *New York Times*, July 3, 1999.
32. James Bennet, 'Sharon Invokes Munich in Warning U.S. on "Appeasement"', *New York Times*, October 5, 2001.
33. *Dabru Emet* is published in Tikva Frymer-Kensky et al. (eds), *Christianity in Jewish terms* (Boulder, CO: Westview, 2000), pp. xviii–xx.

Chapter 3

1. Emmanuel Levinas, *Difficult Freedom: Essays on Judaism* (Baltimore: Johns Hopkins University Press, 1990), p. 212.
2. Ibid., p. 213.
3. Both Buber and Heschel wrote extensively and creatively about the prophetic. For my understanding of both writers with regard to the prophetic see Marc H. Ellis, *Revolutionary Forgiveness: Essays on Judaism, Christianity and the Future of Religious Life* (Waco, TX: Baylor University Press, 2000), pp. 259–72.
4. See Walter Brueggemann, *The Prophetic Imagination* (Philadelphia: Fortress, 1978) and Gustavo Gutierrez, *A Theology of Liberation: History, Politics and Salvation* (Maryknoll: Orbis, 1973).
5. Richard Rubenstein, *After Auschwitz: Radical Theology and Contemporary Judaism* (Indianapolis: Bobbs-Merril, 1966). It has also been published in a second edition by the Johns Hopkins University Press with a new subtitle, *History, Theology and Contemporary Judaism.*
6. See Richard Rubenstein's *My Brother Paul* (New York: Harper & Row, 1972); *Power Struggle* (Lanham, MD: University Press of America, 1986); *The Cunning of History: Mass Death and the American Future* (New York: Harper & Row, 1975).
7. See William D. Miller's *A Harsh and Dreadful Love: Dorothy Day and the Catholic Worker Movement* (New York: Liveright, 1973); *Dorothy Day: A Biography* (New York: Harper & Row, 1982).
8. I recall these years in more depth in *Revolutionary Forgiveness*, pp. 51–98.
9. The Sh'ma is the biblical verse (Deut. 6:4) which Jews are to recite daily and comes closest to being Judaism's credo.

10. For a fascinating discussion of these themes see Joseph Blenkinsopp, *Prophecy and Canon: A Contribution to the Study of Jewish Origins* (Notre Dame: University of Notre Dame Press, 1977).
11. Borrowing and divisions among and between religions is one way of looking at the development of Judaism, Christianity and Islam. Another way of tracing these is through the concept of invention and reinvention of religions and religious traditions. See Donald Harman Akenson, *Surpassing Wonder: The Invention of the Bible and the Talmuds* (Chicago: University of Chicago Press, 2001).
12. I am suggesting here that history after the closing of the canon be considered part of the canon, yielding new books of the Torah and new gospels in the New Testament. In Judaism we now need to add the Book of Palestine; in Christianity, among others, the Gospel of 1492 and the Gospel of Treblinka.
13. Outside the theological world of contemporary Christian biblical scholars grappling with the prophetic quality of Jesus' life is largely unknown. An example of the recovery of the prophetic Jesus is found in John Dominic Crossan, *The Historical Jesus: The Life of a Mediterranean Jewish Peasant* (San Francisco: Harper San Francisco, 1991).
14. For the thought of Magnes, Buber and Arendt on these themes, see Judah Magnes, *Dissenter in Zion: From the Writings of Judah L. Magnes*, ed. Arthur A. Gordon (Cambridge, MA: Harvard University Press, 1982); *A Land of Two Peoples: Martin Buber on Jews and Arabs*, ed. Paul Mendes-Flohr (Oxford: Oxford University Press, 1983); Hannah Arendt, *The Jew as Pariah: Jewish Identity and Politics in the Modern Age*, ed. Ron H. Feldman (New York: Grove, 1978).

Chapter 4

1. This theme of invention and reinvention of Judaism is carried through by Akenson as alluded to earlier but also by Efraim Schmueli, *Seven Jewish Cultures: A Reinterpretation of Jewish History and Thought* (Cambridge: Cambridge University Press, 1990). Akenson and Schmueli's understandings directly confront Israel Shahak's more limited understanding of the Jewish tradition as we shall see.
2. Shahak's book *Jewish History, Jewish Religion*, was published by Pluto Press in 1994. Chomsky's comments about Shahak's work are worth noting: 'Shahak is an outstanding scholar, with remarkable insight and depth of knowledge. His work is informed and penetrating, a contribution of great value.'
3. Ibid., p. 22.
4. Ibid., p. 29.
5. Emmanuel Levinas, *Difficult Freedom: Essays on Judaism* (Baltimore: Johns Hopkins University Press, 1990), p. 199.
6. *Toward a Jewish Theology of Liberation* (Maryknoll: Orbis, 1987) was followed by two subsequent books that dealt with the unfolding difficulties facing Jewish identity. See *Beyond Innocence and Redemption: Confronting the Holocaust and Israeli Power* (San Francisco: HarperCollins,

1990) and *Ending Auschwitz: The Future of Jewish and Christian Life* (Louisville: Westminster/John Knox, 1994).

7. Carter Heyward and Anne Gilson, *Revolutionary Forgiveness: Feminist Reflections on Nicaragua* (Maryknoll: Orbis, 1987), p. 108.
8. Richard Rubenstein, *After Auschwitz: Radical Theology and Contemporary Judaism* (Indianapolis: Bobbs-Merril, 1966). Also see his second edition with a somewhat changed emphasis; *After Auschwitz: History, Theology and Contemporary Judaism* (Baltimore: Johns Hopkins University Press, 1992).
9. Richard Rubenstein, *The Cunning of History: Mass Death and the American Future* (New York: Harper & Row, 1975). Also see Hannah Arendt, *The Origins of Totalitarianism* (New York: Harcourt Brace, 1951).
10. Hannah Arendt, *The Human Condition: A Study of the Central Dilemmas Facing Modern Man* (Garden City, NY: Doubleday, 1959), pp. 214–15.
11. Ibid., p. 218.
12. Ibid., pp. 220, 216.
13. Adi Ophir, 'Between Eichmann and Kant: Thinking on Evil after Arendt', *History and Memory: Studies in Representation of the Past* 8 (Fall 1996), pp. 96, 93.
14. Ibid., p. 99.
15. Ibid., pp. 126–7.
16. Johannes Baptist Metz, *The Emergent Church: The Future of Christianity in a Post-Bourgeois World* (New York: Crossroad, 1981), p. 19.
17. Amira Hass, 'Separate and Unequal on the West Bank', *New York Times*, September 2, 2001.
18. Ibid., *Drinking the Sea at Gaza: Days and Nights In a Land Under Siege* (New York: Henry Holt, 1996), pp. 6–7.
19. I discuss this theme extensively in my *Practicing Exile: The Religious Odyssey of an American Jew* (Minneapolis: Fortress, 2002).

Index

Compiled by Sue Carlton